ADVANCED ACCOUNTING

ADVANCED ACCOUNTING

[For B.B.A. 5th Semester Students of Bangalore City University, and also useful for allied courses of other universities]

Revised and Updated Strictly according to Provisions of the Companies Act (as Amended upto date)

S.P. JAIN
Ex-Associate Professor in Commerce
Shaheed Bhagat Singh College
(University of Delhi)
Sheikh Sarai, Phase II, **New Delhi**

K.L. NARANG
Formerly Head
Department of Commerce
Government College, Chandigarh and
Principal, Government College
Kapurthala (Punjab)

SIMMI AGRAWAL
Ph.D. FCA, ACMA
Director, Institute of Financial Education & Learning
Ghaziabad (U.P.)

MONIKA SEHGAL
Associate Professor
Post-Graduate Govt. College for Girls
Sector 42, **Chandigarh** (U.T.)

KALYANI PUBLISHERS

LUDHIANA • NEW DELHI • NOIDA (U.P.) • HYDERABAD • CHENNAI
KOLKATA • CUTTACK • GUWAHATI • KOCHI • BENGALURU

KALYANI PUBLISHERS

Head Office

B-3251/B, Street No. 5, Backside Sandhu Tower, Gurdev Nagar, **Ludhiana**-141 001 • Ph : 0161-2760031
E-mail : kalyanibooks@yahoo.co.in **Website :** www.kalyanipublishers.co.in

Administration Office

4779/23, Ansari Road, Daryaganj, **New Delhi**-110 002 • Ph : 011-23271469, 23274393
E-mail : kalyani_delhi@kalyanipublishers.in

Works

B-16, Sector-8, **NOIDA** (U.P.)

Branches

1, Mahalakshmi Street, T. Nagar, **Chennai**-600 017 • Ph : 044-24344684
Gopabandhu Lane, Behind Govt. Bus Stand, Badambadi, **Cuttack**-753 012 (Odisha) • Ph : 0671-2311391
4-3-65/2/A, Behind HVS Public School, Raghunath Bagh
Sultan Bazar, **Hyderabad**-500 095 • Ph : 040-24750368
10/2B, Ramanath Mazumdar Street, **Kolkata**-700 009 • Ph : 033-22416024
Arunalaya, 1st Floor, Saraswati Road, Pan Bazar, **Guwahati**-781 001 • Ph : 0361-2731274
Koratti Parambil House, Convent Road, **Kochi**-682 035 • Ph : 0484-2367189
No. 24 & 25, 1st Floor, Hameed Shah Complex, Cubbonpet Main Road, **Bengaluru**-560 002

T 39701 05 10 + 274 = 284 Pages 20" x 30" 35.5 Forms

Typesetting at
Times Printographic

PRINTED IN INDIA
At B.B. Press, A-37, Sector-67, Noida-201301

Preface

We are happy to present the first edition of Advanced Accounting for B.B.A. 5th Semester students of Bangalore City University. This edition has been prepared in accordance with the latest syllabus of Bangalore City University.

The book contains fresh illustrations and questions which are according to the latest syllabus and current pattern of the examination.

We are sure that this book will meet the requirements of students and expectation of teachers.

We are grateful to M/s Kalyani Publishers and Times Printographic for bringing out the book in a nice get up.

At last we would like to add that in a book on a technical subject, such as the present one, it is futile to expect that printer's devil has not crept in. We shall be grateful if the mistakes and deficiencies are pointed out to us by the readers.

2024

S.P. Jain
K.L. Narang
Simmi Agrawal
Monika Sehgal

Bangalore City University

Name of the Program : Bachelor of Commerce (B.Com.)

Course Code : COM A1

Name of the Course : Advanced Accounting

Course Credits	No. of Hours per Week	Total No. of Teaching Hours
3 Credits	4 Hrs.	56 Hrs.

Pedagogy: Classroom Lectures, Case Studies, Tutorial Classes, Group Discussion, Seminar and Field Work, etc.

Course Outcomes: On successful completion of the course, the students will be able to :

(*a*) Understand the key principles and theories of Advanced Accounting.

(*b*) Learn various valuation methods and techniques used in practice.

(*c*) Develop skills in Advanced Accounting.

(*d*) Explore the challenges and considerations involved in preparation of financial statements of Banking and Insurance companies.

(*e*) Gain knowledge of Advanced Accounting and their impact on business.

Syllabus — Hours

Module 1 : Buy Back of Shares — 06

Introduction and Meaning—Objectives and Benefits of Buy-back—Provisions Regarding By-back of Shares under the Companies Act, 2013—SEBI Regulations regarding Buy-back of Shares. Methods of Buy-back through Tender Offer to Existing Shareholders—Through Open Market and through Book-building—Accounting Entries for Buy-back of Shares—Problems.

Module 2 : Investment Accounts — 14

Meaning of Investments—Types or Classification of Investments—Valuation of Investments—Cost of Investments—Accounting Treatment for Re-classification of Investments—Disposal of Investments and Income from Investments—Problems.

Module 3 : Financial Statements of Banking Companies 14

Introduction—Functions of a Bank—Important Provisions of the Banking Regulation Act, 1949 with regard to Minimum Capital and Reserves—Statutory Reserve—Cash Reserve—Statutory Liquidity Ratio etc.—Special Features of Bank Accounting. Final Accounts of Banking Companies—Components and Formats—Accounting Treatment for Rebate on Bills Discounted—Acceptance —Endorsement and Other Obligations—Problems on Preparation of Bank Final Accounts.

Module 4 : Financial Statements of Life Insurance Companies 14

Introduction—Classification of Insurance Business—Life Insurance and General Insurance Components of Financial Statements of Life Insurance Business—Revenue Account—Profit and Loss Account—Balance Sheet and Schedules. Problems.

Module 5 : Financial Statements of General Insurance Companies 08

Components of Financial Statements of General Insurance Business—Revenue Account—Profit and Loss Account—Balance Sheet and Schedules—Accounting Principles for Preparation of Financial Statements of Insurance Companies—Problems on Revenue Accounts of Fire and Marine Business only

Skill Development Activities

1. List any six companies which have exercised buy back along with the terms of Buy back.
2. Prepare an Investment Account with imaginary figures.
3. Prepare a table of rebate on bills discounted with imaginary figures.
4. Prepare a schedule of premiums with imaginary figures in respect of Life Insurance Company.
5. Prepare a statement of claims with imaginary figures of General Insurance Company.

Contents

Buyback of Shares

Buyback of shares and securities is popular in United States of America. Till October, 1998, the scheme of buyback of shares and securities was not known to the Indian companies. Mr. Atal Bihari Vajpayee, then the Prime Minister of India, unveiled an economic package to reverse the sagging capital market on 24th October, 1998 at the 71st annual session of the Federation of Indian Chambers of Commerce and Industry (FICCI). One of the items of the economic package was the introduction of the scheme of buyback of shares and securities. Within a week followed by this announcement by the Prime Minister, the Government of India issued an ordinance on October 31, 1998 for buyback of shares, amending the Companies Act, 1956. Prior to the amendment of the Companies Act, 1956, the buyback of shares in India was prohibited.

Meaning of Buyback of Shares

When a company wants to buy its own stock from the shareholders, it is known as buy-back of shares. Buyback is a method of cancellation of share capital. It leads to a reduction in the share capital of a company as opposed to issue of shares which results in an increase in the share capital.

Objectives of Buyback of Shares

The objectives of buy-back are to :

(*i*) Increase the EPS (*i.e.* Earning per Share) of the shares bought back. The EPS of the company will go up assuming no reduction in the earnings of the company.

(*ii*) Increase in the promoters' holding in the company.

(*iii*) Increase the market price of the share as the buy-back price is higher than the market price.

(*iv*) Send a signal among the investors about company's financial strength and prospects.

(*v*) Help the company to distribute its surplus cash among the investors.

(*vi*) Alter the capital structure.

Criteria of Buyback of Shares

In order to make buyback beneficial, the company may undertake buyback after meeting the following criteria :

(*i*) The company has exhausted all avenues of fresh investments/outlay in the near future.

(*ii*) Buyback can be undertaken without jeopardising the lender's risk.

(*iii*) The company enjoys a return on capital employed which is significantly higher than the normal cost of borrowing.

(*iv*) The market price of the company's share is far lower than its intrinsic value.

Reasons for Buyback

The main impact of reacquiring shares is that the supply of stock in the open market reduces, which acts as a support for the price. It is a sign that the company is confident about its prospects. For example, Reliance Infrastructure Ltd.'s Board on 14 February approved a proposal to buy back shares of up to ₹ 1,000 crore. A company statement said it is doing so to "reduce short-term volatility" in share prices and "reiterate the confidence of management in future prospectus."

Sometimes companies buy back shares to ward off hostile takeovers. Fewer shares floating in the market would make it difficult to buy enough shares to launch a takeover bid. Companies also buy back shares if they have surplus cash that is not needed for business and want to reward their shareholders. They make an offer to buy back shares at a considerably higher price than the existing market price.

Following are the main reasons due to which a company must go for buyback of its shares :

(*i*) To shrink equity base thereby injecting much needed flexibility.

(*ii*) To prevent hostile take-over bids.

(*iii*) To return surplus cash to shareholders.

(*iv*) In increasing the underlying share value.

(*v*) To support the share price during periods of temporary weakness.

(*vi*) To achieve or maintain a target capital structure.

Regulations of Buyback of Shares in Indian Scenario

According to Section 68 of the Companies Act, 2013, a company may purchase its own shares or other specified securities out of :

(*i*) its free reserves (*i.e.* reserves which are free for distribution as dividend); or

(*ii*) the securities premium account ; or

(*iii*) the proceeds of the issue of any shares or other specified securities.

Note. No buyback of any kind of shares or other specific securities shall be made out of the proceeds of an earlier issue of the same kind of shares or same kind of other specified securities.

Specified securities include employees' stock option or other securities as may be notified by the Central Government from time to time. It is not compulsory for the investor to accept the offer. Investor should consider the factors such as the number of outstanding shares of the company, the future prospectus, the reason for such a buy-back, percentage of shares he offers that would be accepted by the company before taking the decision. **Buyback of shares of any kind is not allowed out of fresh issue of shares of the same kind. In other words, if equity shares are to be bought back, preference shares or debentures may be issued for buyback of equity shares.**

Companies are allowed to buyback their own shares if they fulfill certain conditions as given in the Companies Act.

No company shall purchase its own shares or other specified securities unless :

(*a*) the buyback is authorised by its articles ;

(*b*) a special resolution has been passed at a general meeting of the company authorising the buyback ;

Provided that nothing contained in this clause shall apply to a case where—

(*i*) the buy-back is 10% or less of the total paid-up equity capital and free reserves of the company; and

(*ii*) such buy-back has been authorised by the Board by means of a resolution passed at its meeting ;

(*c*) the buyback is twenty-five per cent or less of the total paid up capital and free reserves of the company:

Provided that the buyback of equity shares in any financial year shall not exceed twenty-five percentage of its total paid up equity capital in that financial year;

(*d*) **the ratio of the debt owed by the company is not more than twice the capital and its free reserves after such buyback ;**

(*e*) **all the shares or other specified securities for buyback are fully paid up ;**

(*f*) the buyback of the shares or other specified securities listed on any recognised stock exchange is in accordance with the regulations made by the Securities and Exchange Board of India in this behalf ;

(*g*) the buyback in respect of shares or other specified securities other than those specified in clause (*f*) is in accordance with the guidelines as may be prescribed.

(*h*) The buy back is made out of free reserves (which includes securities premium) or out of the proceeds of a fresh issue of any shares or other specified securities.

(*i*) The buy back is completed within 12 months of the passing of the special resolution or resolution passed by the Board.

(*j*) Before making such buy back, a listed company has to file with the Registrar of the Companies and SEBI a declaration of solvency in the prescribed form.

Provided that no offer of buy-back shall be made within a period of one year reckoned from the date of the closure of the preceding offer of buyback, if any.

According to Section 68 (5), the buyback may be made :

(*a*) from the existing shareholders or security-holders on a proportionate basis; or

(*b*) from the open market; or

(*c*) by purchasing the securities issued to employees of the company pursuant to a scheme of stock option or sweat equity.

According to Section 68(6), where a company has passed a special resolution to buyback its own shares or other securities, it shall, before making such buyback, file with the Registrar and the Securities Exchange Board of India a declaration of solvency in the form as may be prescribed and verified by an affidavit to the effect that the Board has made a full enquiry into the affairs of the company as a result of which they have formed an opinion that it is capable of meeting its liabilities and will not be rendered insolvent within a period of one year of the date of declaration adopted by the Board, and signed by at least two directors of the company, one of whom shall be the managing director, if any.

As per Section 68(6) no declaration of solvency shall be filed with the Securities and Exchange Board of India by a company whose shares are not listed on any recognised stock exchange.

According to Section 68(7), where a company buys-back its own securities, it has to extinguish and physically destroy the securities so bought-back within seven days of the last date of completion of buyback.

Section 68(8) states that where a company completes buyback of its shares or other specified securities, it cannot make further issue of the same kind of shares or specified securities within a period of six months, except by way of bonus issue or in the discharge of subsisting obligations such as conversion of warrants, stock option schemes, sweat equity or conversion of preference shares or debentures into equity shares.

As per Section 68(9), where a company buys back its shares or other specified securities, it shall maintain a register of the shares or securities so bought, the consideration paid for the shares or securities bought back, the date of cancellation of shares or securities, the date of extinguishing and physically destroying the shares or securities and such other particulars as may be prescribed.

As per Section 68(10), a company shall after the completion of buyback file with the Registrar and Exchange Board a return containing such particulars relating to the buyback within 30 days of such completion, as may be prescribed. Provided that no return shall be filed with the Securities and Exchange Board by a company whose shares are not listed on any recognised stock exchange.

As per Section 68(11), if a company makes any default in complying with the provisions of this section or any regulation made by the SEBI, for buy-back of shares or securities, the company shall be punishable with fine which shall not be less than one lakh rupees but which may extend to three lakh rupees and every officer of the company who is in default shall be punishable with fine which shall not be less than one lakh rupees but which may extend to three lakh rupees.

Section 70 states that no company shall purchase its shares or other specified securities :

(*i*) through any subsidiary company including its own subsidiary companies; or

(*ii*) through any investment company or group of investment companies ; or

(*iii*) if a default, by the company, in repayment of deposit or interest payable thereon, redemption of debentures or preference shares or payment of dividend to any shareholder or repayment of any term loan or interest payable thereon to any financial institution or bank, is subsisting.

As per Section 69, where a company purchases its own shares out of free reserves or Securities Premium Account then a company is required to transfer a sum equal to the nominal value of the shares so bought back to Capital Redemption Reserve Account.

After the completion of buy-back, return containing the particulars relating to the buy-back as prescribed, may be field with the Registrar of Companies and SEBI within thirty days of such completion.

Free Reserves. It means those reserves which are as per last audited Balance Sheet of the company are free for distribution as dividend. It will include :

(*i*) Balance to the credit of securities premium account.

(*ii*) Realised capital profits arising out of sale of fixed assets/investments.

(*iii*) Balance in general reserve and surplus account.

(*iv*) Dividend equalisation or fluctuation reserve.

(*v*) Capital redemption reserve created under Section 55 of the Companies Act.

As far as possible, the entire free reserve should not be utilised for the purpose of buy-back. The net amount of free reserves which can be utilised for the purpose of buy-back is to be calculated after making the adjustment of the following items :

(*i*) Unamortised deferred revenue expenditure

(*ii*) Unamortised miscellaneous expenditure

(*iii*) Contingent liabilities likely to mature and not provided for

(*iv*) Purchased goodwill

(*v*) Any diminution of long term investments not provided for

(*vi*) Any impairment in the value of tangible assets not provided for.

SEBI Guidelines for Buyback of Shares

The SEBI (Buyback of Securities) Regulations, 1998 were formulated to ensure greater transparency in the buyback procedure for listed shares and securities.

1. Notice of special resolution is to be passed by the members of the company and it should contain explanatory statement giving details of the buyback deal as prescribed in Schedule I of SEBI Regulations.
2. If buying back of shares is from members through tender offer, the maximum price at which the company intends to buyback the shares should be indicated in the notice of the general meeting of shareholders.
3. The company which intends to make buyback of shares should make a public announcement in at least one English National Daily, one Hindi National Daily and one regional newspaper all with wide circulation giving details prescribed in Schedule II of SEBI Regulations.
4. Public announcement will mention the specified date for the purpose of determining the names of shareholders to whom letter of offer shall be sent. Draft of offer letter giving prescribed details should be submitted to SEBI along with prescribed fees at least 21 days before despatch of letter of offer to shareholders.
5. If buyback of shares is through stock exchange, special resolution of members should prescribe maximum price at which shares can be bought and the buyback shall not be made from promoters or persons having control of the company.
6. The company should appoint a merchant banker and it has to certify that letter of offer is in compliance with the Regulations.
7. Bonus shares will not be announced when the buyback offer is open.
8. Buyback offers will not be withdrawn after public pronouncement.

Recent Additional Guidelines for Buyback of Shares

Following are the recent additional guidelines of SEBI for buyback of shares :

1. Companies should utilise at least 75% of the amount earmarked for buyback of shares as specified in the resolution of Board of Directors or shareholders.
2. Companies should undertake at least 40% of the amount earmarked for buyback within half of the duration of buyback period of shares by a company.
3. Differ will be open for a period of 5 workings days instead of 7 days.

Proportionate Buy-back

In case the number of securities tendered for buy-back are more than the number of securities to be bought back, the number of securities to be bought back from each member shall be determined by the following formula :

$$\text{Acceptance tendered by a member} \times \frac{\text{Number of securities to be bought back}}{\text{Total acceptances tendered}}$$

Escrow Account

Escrow, in ordinary language, means a contract or bond deposited with a third person, by whom it is to be delivered to the guarantee on the fulfillment of some condition. Under the scheme of buy-back of shares, the company in order to perform its obligations, is required to open an Escrow Account consisting of—

(*a*) cash deposited with a commercial bank; or

(*b*) bank guarantee in favour of a merchant banker; or

(*c*) deposit of acceptable securities with appropriate margin; or

(*d*) combination of (*a*), (*b*) and (*c*) with the merchant banker with an amount equal to 25% of the consideration payable if consideration is not more than 100 crores plus 10% of the consideration exceeding ₹ 100 crores. This amount is held till the consideration of buy-back of shares is paid to the shareholders. It will be returned back to the company after completion of all obligations. If the company fails to meet its obligations, the balance standing in the Escrow Account will be forfeited by SEBI.

Advantages of Buyback of Shares

Following are the main advantages of buyback of shares :

1. Companies having large amount of free reserves are *free to use funds* to acquire shares and other specified securities under the buyback process.
2. Buyback of shares is helpful to a company *to reduce its share capital* which is bloated (*i.e.* excessive wealth) unnecessarily for the time being. Unused and excessive share capital is reduced to give more benefits to the shareholders by trimming the capital structure.
3. Buyback of shares *results in* lower capital base, enhances post-buyback earning per share and appreciates considerably the price-earning ratio.
4. After buyback of shares the company will have the advantage of servicing a *reduced capital base with higher dividend yield*.
5. Buyback of shares is allowed under Section 68 if the liquid position of the company is good. Companies which have defaulted in repayment of deposits, redemption of debentures or

preference shares or repayment of term loans or interest payable thereon from banks and financial institutions are not allowed to buyback shares. It is a good *check on the companies.*

6. Buyback provides capital appreciation to investors which may otherwise be not available.
7. Buyback gives a signal to the market that shares are undervalued.
8. Buyback of shares helps the promoters to formulate an *effective defense strategy* against hostile take over bids.

Disadvantages of Buyback of Shares

Following are the main disadvantages of buyback of shares :

(*i*) The buybacks *imply under valuation of companies stock.* The companies plough back some of the outstanding shares thereby creating a shortage of shares in the market.

(*ii*) Companies go for announcing buybacks when they can not find anything better to do with their cash and hence there exists *less or no scope for further expansion.*

(*iii*) Well timed buyback of shares is a *clever way for managers to invest cheaply* in a company they know (their own) rather than expensively (through a merger at a premium) in a company they do not know.

(*iv*) Theoretically buyback of shares should make no difference to the shareholders, whether the company returns cash in the form of increased dividends or by way of repurchase. However, buybacks have an *impact on the underlying forces on which investor behaviour is based.* For example, when a company increases its dividends, it has to keep rising it in future to keep up with the expectations of stockholders, however, buyback does not have such implications.

Misuse of Buyback by Corporate Entities at the Cost of Innocent Investors

The buyback of shares may be misused by the corporate entities at the cost of innocent investors because of the following reasons :

(*a*) It will provide an ample *opportunity for inside trading*. The promoters, before the buyback, may understate the earnings by manipulating accounting policies in respect of depreciation, valuation of inventories, etc. and highlight other unfavourable factors affecting the earnings. This would lead to a fall in the quoted prices of shares and the promoters would buy them at low quotations. In this manner the insiders would make extra money when the company buybacks these shares at a lower price.

(*b*) Buyback may lead to *artificial manipulations of stock prices.*

(*c*) *The position of the minority shareholders is weakened* as buyback enables the management to increase their control over the company.

Accounting Entries on Buyback of Shares

Following entries may be required to record buyback of shares :

(*a*) *When investments are sold for buyback of own shares*

Bank A/c Dr.
Surplus A/c Dr. (for loss on sale of investments)
  To Investment A/c
  To Capital Reserve A/c (for profit on sale of non-trade investments)
  To Surplus A/c (for profit on sale of trade investments)

(*b*) For issue of debentures or other specified securities (excluding shares of the kind to be bought back) for buyback purpose :

Bank A/c Dr.

To Debentures/Other Specified Security A/c

To Securities Premium A/c (if any)

(*c*) For cancellation of shares bought back :

Equity Share Capital A/c Dr.

(with nominal value of shares bought back)

Free Reserves/Securities Premium A/c Dr.

(with premium payable on buyback of shares)

To Shareholders A/c

(with actual cost of buyback shares)

(*d*) For making the payment on buyback of shares

Shareholders A/c Dr.

To Bank A/c

Alternative to (c) and (d) entries

(*c*) *For cancellation of shares bought back*

(*i*) Equity Share Capital A/c Dr.

Buyback Premium A/c Dr.

To Shares Buy-back A/c

(*ii*) *For adjustment of buyback premium*

Securities Premium A/c Dr.

General Reserve A/c Dr.

To Buy-back Premium A/c

(*iii*) *For making payment of buyback of shares*

Shares Buy-back A/c Dr.

To Bank A/c

(*e*) For transfer of nominal value of shares bought back out of free reserves or Securities Premium Account

Free Reserves/Securities Premium A/c Dr.

To Capital Redemption Reserve A/c

(*f*) *For expenses incurred in buyback of shares*

Buyback Expenses A/c Dr. (with the amount)

To Bank A/c

(*g*) *For transfer of expenses of buyback of shares*

Surplus A/c Dr.

To Buyback Expenses A/c

ILLUSTRATION 1. Bharat Ltd. decides to buyback 10% of ₹ 100 crores paid up equity capital. The face value per equity share is ₹ 10 but the market price per share is ₹ 15. Bharat Ltd. takes the following steps for buyback of its shares :

1. To issue 14% debentures of ₹ 100 each at par for face value of ₹ 10 crores. 2. To utilise general reserve. 3. To sell investments of ₹ 7 crores for ₹ 8 crores. 4. To buyback the shares at the market price. 5. To immediately cancel the shares bought back.

Journalise the above transactions.

SOLUTION

Bharat Ltd.

JOURNAL ENTRIES

(In crores)

				₹	₹
	Bank A/c	Dr.		10	
	To 14% Debentures A/c				10
	(Being issue of 14% debentures at par for buy-back of shares)				
	Bank A/c	Dr.		8	
	To Investments A/c				7
	To Surplus A/c				1
	(Being sale of investments and profit on sale transferred to Surplus A/c)				
	Equity Share Capital A/c	Dr.		10	
	General Reserve A/c	Dr.		5	
	To Shareholders A/c				15
	(Being cancellation of bought back shares of nominal value of ₹ 10 crores and general reserve utilised for premium of ₹ 5 per share payable on 1 crore shares of ₹ 10 each bought back @ ₹ 15 per share)				
	Shareholders A/c	Dr.		15	
	To Bank A/c				15
	(Being amount payable on buyback of shares paid to shareholders)				

ILLUSTRATION 2. Following figures have been extracted from the books of ABC Ltd. as on 31-3-2023.

	₹
Authorised Capital :	
50,00,000 Equity Shares of ₹ 10 each	5,00,00,000
Issued and Subscribed Capital :	
50,00,000 Equity Shares of ₹ 10 each, fully paid-up	5,00,00,000

Reserves & Surplus :

General Reserve ₹ 80,00,000 ; Surplus A/c ₹ 20,00,000 ; Capital Reserve ₹ 30,00,000 ; Securities Premium A/c ₹ 15,00,000 ; 14% Debentures ₹ 50,00,000 ; Cash and Bank Balance ₹ 1,00,00,000.

The company decided to buyback 25% of the paid up equity share capital at face value. It was also decided to issue further 14% debentures of ₹ 50,00,000 at par for the purpose of buyback. Pass necessary Journal Entries.

SOLUTION

ABC Ltd.

JOURNAL ENTRIES

				Dr. ₹	Cr. ₹
	Bank A/c	Dr.		50,00,000	
	To 14% Debentures A/c				(1) 50,00,000
	(Being issue of debentures of ₹ 50,00,000 at par for the purpose of buyback of shares)				

Equity Share Capital A/c Dr. To Shareholders A/c (Being cancellation of 25% of paid up capital on account of 25% shares bought back)		1,25,00,000	1,25,00,000
General Reserve Dr. To Capital Redemption Reserve A/c (Being transfer of general reserve to Capital Redemption Reserve A/c to meet the requirement of law for buyback of shares : Total shares bought back ₹ 1,25,00,000 – ₹ 50,00,000 issue of debentures)		(1) 75,00,000	75,00,000
Shareholders A/c Dr. To Bank A/c (Being payment made for shares bought back)		1,25,00,000	1,25,00,000

Working Note (1) : Total nominal value of shares bought back 1,25,00,000

Less : Issue of 14% Debentures 50,00,000

Amount to be transferred to C.R.R. 75,00,000

ILLUSTRATION 3. Supreme Ltd. had authorised capital of ₹ 20 crores of ₹ 100 each equity shares and an Issued and Subscribed Capital of ₹ 10 crores. The company decided to buy-back 25% of its share capital direct from its shareholders at ₹ 75 per share. The company had issued ₹ 2 crores, 10% preference shares two months back for the purpose of buy-back, the balances in the following accounts were :

Securities Premium Account	**₹ 10,00,000**
General Reserve Account	**₹ 80,00,000**

Record the transactions in the books of the company in accordance with the provisions of the Act.

SOLUTION

JOURNAL

			₹	₹
(*i*)	Securities Premium A/c Dr. General Reserve A/c Dr. To Capital Redemption Reserve A/c (Being transfer of ₹ 10,00,000 from Securities Premium Account and ₹ 40,00,000 from General Reserve to Capital Redemption Reserve Account)		10,00,000 40,00,000	(1) 50,00,000
(*ii*)	Equity Share Capital A/c Dr. To Capital Reserve A/c To Equity Shareholders A/c (Being amount payable to the Equity Shareholders on buy-back of 2,50,000 equity shares of ₹ 100 each at ₹ 75 per share)		2,50,00,000	62,50,000 1,87,50,000
(*iii*)	Equity Shareholders A/c Dr. To Bank A/c (Being payment made to equity shareholders for buy-back of shares)		1,87,50,000	1,87,50,000

Working Note (1) :

	₹
Total nominal value of shares bought back	2,50,00,000
Less : Issue of 10% Preference Shares	2,00,00,000
Amount to be transferred to Capital Redemption Reserve A/c	50,00,000

ILLUSTRATION 4. Equity, Liabilities and Assets of Zee Ltd. as at 31.3.2023 are given below:

	₹
I. Equity and Liabilities	
(1) *Shareholders' Funds*	
(*a*) Share Capital :	
20,00,000 Equity Shares of ₹ 10 each	2,00,00,000
(*b*) Reserves and Surplus :	
(*i*) Securities Premium Account	20,00,000
(*ii*) General Reserve	1,80,00,000
(2) *Non-current Liabilities*	
14% Redeemable Debentures	1,00,00,000
(3) *Current Liabilities*	1,00,00,000
Total	6,00,00,000
	₹
II. Assets	
(1) *Non-current Assets*	
Property, Plant and Equipment : Freehold Property	2,00,00,000
(2) *Current Assets*	
(*a*) Stock-in-Trade	1,20,00,000
(*b*) Sundry Debtors	1,00,00,000
(*c*) Cash and Bank Balance	1,80,00,000
Total	6,00,00,000

It was resolved at the meeting of shareholders :

(*i*) to buyback 20% of equity shares @ ₹ 12 per share ;

(*ii*) to utilise general reserve for buyback of shares ;

(*iii*) to utilise securities premium for premium on buyback of shares ;

(*iv*) to immediately cancel the shares bought back.

Pass necessary Journal entries and draw up the Balance Sheet after the above transactions have been given effect to .

SOLUTION

Zee Ltd.

JOURNAL ENTRIES

				Dr.	Cr.
				₹	₹
2023 March 31	General Reserve	Dr.		40,00,000	
	To Capital Redemption Reserve A/c				40,00,000
	(Being shares of nominal value of ₹ 40,00,000 bought back out of general reserve; amount provided thus to the extent of nominal value of shares transferred to Capital Redemption Reserve A/c as per provision of Section 69 of the Companies Act, 2013).				
	Equity Share Capital A/c	Dr.		40,00,000	
	Securities Premium A/c	Dr.		8,00,000	
	To Shareholders A/c				48,00,000
	(Being amount due on buyback of 4,00,000 shares of ₹ 10 each at a premium of ₹ 2 per share)				

	Shareholders A/c Dr. To Bank A/c (Being amount paid for buyback of 4,00,000 shares of ₹ 10 each @ ₹ 12 per share)		48,00,000	48,00,000

BALANCE SHEET OF ZEE LTD.
as at 31st March, 2023

	Note No.	₹
I. Equity and Liabilities		
(1) *Shareholders' Funds* :		
(*a*) Share Capital	1	1,60,00,000
(*b*) *Reserves and Surplus*	2	1,92,00,000
Shareholders' Funds		3,52,00,000
(2) *Non-current Liabilities* :		
14% Debentures		1,00,00,000
(3) Current Liabilities		1,00,00,000
Total Equity and Liabilities (1) + (2) + (3)		5,52,00,000
II. Assets		₹
(1) *Non-current Assets* :		
Property, Plant and Equipment : Freehold Property		2,00,00,000
(2) *Current Assets*		
Inventory (Stock in Trade)		1,20,00,000
Trade Receivables (Debtors)		1,00,00,000
Cash and Cash Equivalents		1,32,00,000
		3,52,00,000
Total Assets (1) + (2)		5,52,00,000

Notes to Accounts

	₹
1. Share Capital	
Paid up Share Capital	
16,00,000 Equity Shares of ₹ 10 each fully paid up	1,60,00,000
2. Reserves and Surplus	₹
Capital Redemption Reserve	40,00,000
Securities Premium A/c	12,00,000
General Reserve	1,40,00,000
	1,92,00,000

ILLUSTRATION 5. On 31st March, 2023, following was the information taken from the books of New Era Ltd. :

	₹ in lakhs
I. Equity and Liabilities	
(1) *Shareholders' Funds*	
(*a*) Share Capital :	
Equity fully paid-up shares of ₹ 10 each	2,400
(*b*) Reserves and Surplus :	
(*i*) Securities Premium Account	350
(*ii*) General Reserve	930
(*iii*) Surplus Account	340

(2) *Non-current Liabilities*		
12% Debentures		1,500
(3) *Current Liabilities*		
(*a*) Sundry Creditors		750
(*b*) Sundry Provisions		390
	Total	6,660
		₹ in lakhs
II. Assets		
(1) *Non-current Assets*		
(*a*) Property, Plant and Equipment :		
(*i*) Machinery		3,600
(*ii*) Furniture		452
(*b*) Investments		148
(2) *Current Assets*		
(*a*) Stock		1,200
(*b*) Debtors		520
(*c*) Cash at Bank		740
	Total	6,660

On 1st April, 2023, the company announced the buyback of 25% of its equity shares @ ₹ 15 per share. For the purpose, it sold all of its investments for ₹ 150 lakh and issued 2,00,000 14% preference shares of ₹ 100 each at par, the entire amount being payable with application.

The issue was fully subscribed. The company achieved the target of the buyback.

Later, the company issued one fully paid up equity share of ₹ 10 by way of bonus share for every four equity shares held by the equity shareholders.

Show Journal Entries for all the transactions including cash transactions.

SOLUTION

In the Book of New Era Ltd.

JOURNAL ENTRIES

(₹ in lakhs)

	Bank A/c Dr. To Investment A/c To Surplus A/c (Being investments sold at a profit of ₹ 2 lakhs)		150	 148 2
	Bank A/c Dr. To 14% Pref. Share App. & Allotment A/c (Being receipt of application money on 2 lakhs 14% preference share of ₹ 100 each)		200	 200
	14% Pref. Share App. & Allotment A/c Dr. To 14% Pref. Share Capital A/c (Being transfer of app. and allotment money to Pref. Share Capital Account)		200	 200
	General Reserve A/c Dr. To Capital Redemption Reserve A/c (Being balance of amount not covered by fresh issue of shares for redemption of preference shares credited to Capital Redemption Reserve A/c)		400	 400

Particulars		Dr.	Cr.
Equity Share Capital A/c	Dr.	600	
Securities Premium A/c	Dr.	300	
To Sundry Equity Shareholders A/c			900
(Being amount payable to equity shareholders on buyback of equity shares)			
Sundry Equity Shareholders A/c	Dr.	900	
To Bank A/c			900
(Being payment to equity shareholders to buy back shares)			
Capital Redemption Reserve A/c	Dr.	400	
Securities Premium A/c	Dr.	50	
To Bonus to Equity Shareholders A/c (See note)			450
(For issue of one bonus share for every four shares held ; Capital Redem. Reserve & Securities Premium A/c utilised)			
Bonus to Equity Shareholders A/c	Dr.	450	
To Equity Share Capital A/c			450
(Being issue of 45,00,000 bonus shares of ₹ 10 each @ one bonus share for every four equity shares held)			

Working Note :

	₹ in lakhs
Equity Share Capital	2,400
Less : Buyback of 25% shares	600
Equity share capital after buyback.	1,800

∴ Bonus Shares issued = 25% of ₹ 1,800 lakhs = ₹ **450 lakhs**

ILLUSTRATION 6. Data taken from the books of Modern Marbles Ltd. as at 31st March, 2023 is as follows :

	₹
I. Equity and Liabilities	
(1) *Shareholders' Funds*	
(*a*) Share Capital :	
Equity Shares of ₹ 10 each	50,00,000
(*b*) Reserves and Surplus :	
(*i*) Securities Premium Account	5,40,000
(*ii*) General Reserve	6,50,000
(*iii*) Surplus Account	3,75,000
(2) *Non-current Liabilities*	
12% Debentures	38,25,000
(3) *Current Liabilities*	8,67,000
Total	**1,12,57,000**

	₹
II. Assets	
(1) *Non-current Assets*	
(*a*) Property, Plant and Equipment	66,00,000
(*b*) Investments	18,00,000
(2) *Current Assets*	
(*a*) Stock	11,87,000
(*b*) Sundry Debtors	9,60,000
(*c*) Cash and Bank Balance	7,10,000
Total	**1,12,57,000**

The shareholders adopted the resolution on the date of the above mentioned Balance Sheet to :

(*a*) buyback 20% of the paid up capital @ ₹ 15 each.

(*b*) issue 13% debentures of ₹ 5,00,000 at a premium of 10% to finance the buyback of shares.

(*c*) maintain a balance of ₹ 3,00,000 in General Reserve Account and

(*d*) sell investments worth ₹ 8,00,000 for ₹ 6,50,000.

You are required to pass the necessary Journal Entries to record the above transactions and prepare Balance Sheet immediately after the buyback.

SOLUTION

In the Books of Modern Marbles Ltd.

JOURNAL ENTRIES

			₹	₹
Bank A/c	Dr.		6,50,000	
Surplus A/c	Dr.		1,50,000	
To Investments A/c				8,00,000
(Being sale of investments at loss)				
Bank A/c	Dr.		5,50,000	
To 13% Debentures A/c				5,00,000
To Securities Premium A/c				50,000
(Being issue of debentures at premium of 10%)				
Equity Share Capital A/c	Dr.		10,00,000	
Securities Premium A/c	Dr.		5,00,000	
To Shareholders A/c				15,00,000
(Being cancellation of 1,00,000 equity-shares of ₹ 10 each on buyback and adjustment of Securities Premium Account for premium of ₹ 5 per share)				
General Reserve A/c	Dr.		3,50,000	
Surplus A/c	Dr.		1,50,000	
To Capital Redemption Reserve A/c				5,00,000
(Being the amount transferred from reserves and surplus to meet buyback requirement as per Section 69 of the Companies Act, 2013)				
Shareholders A/c	Dr.		15,00,000	
To Bank A/c				15,00,000
(Being buyback of 1,00,000 equity shares @ ₹ 15 each)				

BALANCE SHEET OF MODERN MARKETS LTD.

as at ...... (after buyback)

	Note No.	₹
I. Equity and Liabilities		
(1) *Shareholders' Fund*		
(*a*) Share Capital	1	40,00,000
(*b*) *Reserves and Surplus*	2	9,65,000
Shareholders' Funds		49,65,000
(2) *Non-current Liabilities*		
Secured Loans : 12% Debentures		38,25,000
13% Debentures		5,00,000
		43,25,000

		₹
(3) *Current Liabilities*		
Current Liabilities		8,67,000
Total Equity and Liabilities (1) + (2) + (3)		1,01,57,000
II. Assets		₹
(1) Non-current Assets : Property, Plant and Equipment		66,00,000
Investments (Assumed to be non-current)		10,00,000
Total		76,00,000
(2) *Current Assets*		
Stock		11,87,000
Trade Receivables (Debtors)		9,60,000
Cash and Cash Equivalents : Cash & Bank (1)		4,10,000
Total		25,57,000
Total Assets (1) + (2)		1,01,57,000

Notes to Accounts

	₹
1. Share Capital	
4,00,000 Equity Shares of ₹ 10 each fully paid up	40,00,000
(1,00,000 Equity Shares of ₹ 10 each bought back @ ₹ 15)	
2. Reserves and Surplus	
Capital Redemption Reserve	5,00,000
Securities Premium A/c	90,000
General Reserve	3,00,000
Surplus Account	75,000
	9,65,000

Working Note :

(1) CASH AND BANK ACCOUNT

	₹		₹
To Balance b/d	7,10,000	By Shareholders A/c	15,00,000
To Investments A/c	6,50,000	By Balance c/d	4,10,000
To 13% Debentures A/c	5,00,000		
To Securities Premium A/c	50,000		
	19,10,000		19,10,000

(2) It is assumed that Securities Premium Account has been utilised exclusively for the payment of premium on buyback of shares. Hence, as a matter of prudence, for the transfer of nominal value of shares bought back to Capital Redemption Reserve, the available balance in General Reserve and Surplus Account is taken into account.

ILLUSTRATION 7. (*Typical*) **Sources and uses of funds of AB Ltd. as at 31st March, 2023 were as follows :**

Sources of Funds	₹	*Employment of Funds*	₹
8,000 'A' Class Equity Shares of		Property, Plant and Equipment	
₹ 100 each fully paid	8,00,000	Net of Depreciation	28,00,000
2,000 'B' Class Equity Shares of		Working Capital	7,00,000
₹ 100 each fully paid	2,00,000		

Security Premium Account	1,00,000	
General Reserve	4,00,000	
10% Debentures of ₹ 100 each	14,00,000	
Secured Loans	6,00,000	
	35,00,000	35,00,000

You are given the following information :

(*a*) 'B' Class Equity Shares are with differential rights as to dividends, voting or otherwise.

(*b*) On 1st April 2023 company in terms of its articles and through its special resolution decided to buy-back the 'B' Class equity shares at a premium of ₹ 50 per share. Necessary approvals were obtained in due course and the buy-back arrangement was completed by 30th June, 2023.

(*c*) On 30th September 2023 company declared the issue of fully paid bonus shares ('A' Class) to 'A' Class equity shareholders in the ratio of one share for every four shares held and the issue was successfully completed by 31st December, 2023.

Journalise the transactions in the books of AB Ltd.

SOLUTION

JOURNAL

Date	Particulars		Dr. ₹	Cr. ₹
2023				
June 30	2,000 'B' Class Equity Share Capital A/c	Dr.	2,00,000	
	Securities Premium A/c	Dr.	1,00,000	
	To 'B' Class Equity Shareholders A/c			3,00,000
	(Being the transfer of 'B' Class equity share capital and the premium payable to 'B' Class Shareholders Account on Buy-back arrangement.)			
June 30	General Reserve A/c	Dr.	2,00,000	
	To Capital Redemption Reserve A/c			2,00,000
	(Being the amount set aside from General Reserve equal to the face value of 'B' Class share capital to Capital Redemption Reserve A/c pursuant to buy-back arrangement.)			
"	'B' Class Equity Shareholders A/c	Dr.	3,00,000	
	To Bank A/c			3,00,000
	(Being the payment of 'B' class equity shareholders for the shares bought-back.)			
Sept. 30	General Reserve A/c	Dr.	2,00,000	
	To Bonus to 'A' Class Equity Shareholders A/c			2,00,000
	(Being the amount set aside from general reserve towards bonus issue to 'A' class shares as per company's resolution in the ratio of 1 share for every 4 shares held.)			
"	Bonus to 'A' Class Equity Shareholders A/c	Dr.	2,00,000	
	To 'A' Class Equity Share Capital A/c			2,00,000
	(Being issue of bonus shares to 'A' class equity shareholders)			

ILLUSTRATION 8. **The summarised Balance Sheet of SM Limited as on 31st March, 2023 was as follows :**

Particulars	₹	*Amount* (₹)
1. Equity and Liabilities		
(*a*) *Shareholders' Fund*		
Share Capital		
(60,000 Equity Shares of ₹ 10 each)		6,00,000
Reserves and Surplus		
Securities Premium	70,000	
General Reserve	63,000	
Surplus	1,40,000	2,73,000
(*b*) *Non-current Liability*		
9% Debentures (Secured)		3,00,000
(*c*) *Current Liabilities*		
Term Loan		40,000
Creditors		65,000
Provision for Taxation		15,000
		12,93,000
		₹
2. Assets		
(1) *Non-current Assets*		
(*a*) Property, Plant and Equipment		6,00,000
(*b*) *Non-current Investment*		1,50,000
(2) *Current Assets*		
Stock	2,00,000	
Debtors	2,60,000	
Bank	83,000	5,43,000
		12,93,000

The shareholders adopted the resolution on 31st March, 2023 to :

(*i*) **Buyback 25% of the paid up capital @ ₹ 15 each.**

(*ii*) **Issue 10% debentures of ₹ 60,000 at a premium of 10% to finance the buyback of shares.**

(*iii*) **Maintain a balance of ₹ 20,000 in General Reserve.**

(*iv*) **Sell investments worth ₹ 1,00,000 for ₹ 80,000.**

(*v*) **Buyback expenses were ₹ 2,000.**

You are required to pass necessary journal entries to record the above transactions and prepare Ledger of Bank Account.

SOLUTION

In the Books of SM Ltd.
JOURNAL ENTRIES

	Particulars			Debit (₹)	Credit (₹)
	Equity Share Capital A/c	Dr.		1,50,000	
	Premium on Buyback of Shares A/c	Dr.		75,000	
	To Equity Shareholders A/c				2,25,000
	(Being the amount due to equity shareholders on buyback of 15,000 equity shares of ₹ 10 each at a premium of ₹ 5 per share)				
	Bank A/c	Dr.		66,000	
	To 10% Debentures A/c				60,000
	To Securities Premium A/c				6,000
	(Being issue of 10% debentures at a premium of 10% to finance the buyback of equity shares)				
	Bank A/c	Dr.		80,000	
	Surplus A/c	Dr.		20,000	
	To Investments				1,00,000
	(Being sale of investments at loss)				
	Buyback Expenses A/c	Dr.		2,000	
	To Bank A/c				2,000
	(Being payment of buyback expenses)				
	Securities Premium A/c	Dr.		75,000	
	Surplus A/c	Dr.		2,000	
	To Premium on Buyback of Shares A/c				75,000
	To Buyback Expenses A/c				2,000
	(Being premium on buyback of shares and buyback expenses charged to Securities Premium A/c and Profit & Loss A/c)				
	General Reserve (₹ 63,000 – ₹ 20,000 to be kept)	Dr.		43,000	
	Surplus A/c	Dr.		1,07,000	
	To Capital Redemption Reserve A/c				1,50,000
	(Being amount equal to nominal value of shares bought back transferred to Capital Redemption Reserve A/c as required by Section 69 of the Companies Act, 2013)				
	Equity Shareholders A/c	Dr.		2,25,000	
	To Bank A/c				2,25,000
	(Being payment made to equity shareholders for buyback to shares)				

BANK ACCOUNT

		₹			₹
	To Balance b/d	83,000		By Equity Shareholders A/c	2,25,000
	To 10% Debentures	60,000		By Balance c/d	4,000
	To Securities Premium A/c	6,000			
	To Investments A/c	80,000			
		2,29,000			2,29,000

ILLUSTRATION 9. Balance Sheet of Premier Ltd. as at 31-3-2023 is given below :

	₹
I. Equity and Liabilities	
(1) *Shareholders' Funds*	
(*a*) Share Capital :	
1,20,000 Equity Shares of ₹ 10 each	**12,00,000**
(*b*) Reserves and Surplus :	
(*i*) Securities Premium Account	**6,00,000**
(*ii*) Free Reserves	**18,00,000**
(2) *Non-current Liabilities*	
Debentures	**25,00,000**
(3) *Current Liabilities*	
Creditors	**11,00,000**
Total	**72,00,000**
II. Assets	₹
(1) *Non-current Assets*	
Property, Plant and Equipment	**36,00,000**
(2) *Current Assets*	
Stock	**10,00,000**
Debtors	**8,00,000**
Cash and Bank Balance	**18,00,000**
Total	**72,00,000**

On the above date shares are bought back by the company to the extent possible, at a premium of ₹ 40 per share. Journalise and give the Balance Sheet after buyback of shares.

SOLUTION

The amount of buyback of shares will be the least of the following three amounts:	₹
Paid up Capital before buyback of shares	12,00,000
Free Reserves	24,00,000
Total of Paid up Capital, Free Reserves and Securities Premium A/c	36,00,000
(1) 25% of Free Reserves, Securities Premium A/c and paid up Capital	9,00,000

(2) Buy-back of equity shares in any financial year shall not exceed 25% of equity capital in that financial year. Equity capital is ₹ 12,00,000, so permissible limit of buy-back is 25% of ₹ 12,00,000 = ₹ 3,00,000.

(3) Amount of Equity Capital available after satisfying minimum post buyback Debt Equity Ratio is calculated as follows :

$$\text{Debt Equity Ratio} = \frac{\text{Debt (after buyback)}}{\text{Equity (after buyback)}}$$

$$\text{2 (Permissible Limit)} = \frac{\text{₹ 25,00,000 (Debentures)} + \text{₹ 11,00,000 (Creditors)}}{\text{Equity (after buyback)}}$$

$$\text{Equity after buyback} = \frac{\text{₹ 36,00,000}}{2} = \text{₹ 18,00,000.}$$

Amount of Equity Available for Buyback

= Equity before Buyback – Equity Required after buyback

= ₹ 36,00,000 – ₹ 18,00,000 = ₹ 18,00,000

(Equity before Buyback = Equity Capital + Free Reserves + Securities Premium A/c
= ₹ 12,00,000 + ₹ 18,00,000 + ₹ 6,00,000 = ₹ 36,00,000)

Amount of buyback permissible is ₹ 3,00,000 (*i.e.* lower of the three amounts ₹ 9,00,000; ₹ 3,00,000 and ₹ 18,00,000).

JOURNAL ENTRIES

				Dr.	Cr.
				₹	₹
2023	Equity Share Capital A/c	Dr.		3,00,000	
Mar. 31	Securities Premium A/c	Dr.		6,00,000	
	To Equity Shareholders A/c				9,00,000
	(Being cancellation of 30,000 equity shares bought back and Securities Premium Account utilised for premium payable on buyback of 30,000 shares @ ₹ 20 per share)				
	Free Reserves A/c	Dr.		3,00,000	
	To Capital Redemption Reserve A/c				3,00,000
	(Being transfer of free reserves to Capital Redemption Reserve A/c to the extent of nominal value of 30,000 shares bought back)				
	Equity Shareholders A/c	Dr.		9,00,000	
	To Bank A/c				9,00,000
	(Being payment made for 30,000 shares bought back @ ₹ 30 per share)				

BALANCE SHEET OF PREMIER LTD.

as on 31-3-2023

	₹
I. Equity and Liabilities	
(1) *Shareholders' Funds*	
(*a*) *Share Capital* :	
90,000 Equity Shares of ₹ 10 each fully paid up	9,00,000
(*b*) *Reserves and Surplus*	
Capital Redemption Reserve	3,00,000
Free Reserves	15,00,000
Total Shareholders' Funds	27,00,000
(2) *Non-Current Liabilities*	
Long-term Borrowings :	
Secured Loan : Debentures	25,00,000
(3) *Current Liabilities* :	
Creditors	11,00,000
Total Equity and Liabilities (1) + (2) + (3)	63,00,000
II. Assets	₹
(1) *Non-Current Assets*	
Property, Plant and Equipment	36,00,000
(2) *Current Assets*	
Stock	10,00,000
Debtors	8,00,000
Cash and Bank Balance	9,00,000
Total Assets (1) + (2)	63,00,000

ILLUSTRATION 10. SMM Ltd. has the following capital structure as on 31st March 2023:

₹ In Crores

Particulars	*Situation I*	*Situation II*
(*i*) Equity Share Capital (shares of ₹ 10 each)	**1,200**	**1,200**
(*ii*) Reserves:		
General Reserve	**1,080**	**1,080**
Securities Premium	**400**	**400**
Surplus	**200**	**200**
Infrastructure Development Reserve (Statutory Reserve)	**320**	**320**
(*iii*) Loan Funds	**3,200**	**6,000**

The company has offered a buy-back price of ₹ 30 per equity share. You are required to calculate maximum permissible number of equity shares that can be bought back in both situations and also required to pass necessary Journal Entries.

SOLUTION

The amount of buy-back of shares will be the least of the following three amounts :	₹ In crores
Paid-up capital before buy-back of shares	1,200
Add : Free Reserves :	
General Reserves	1,080
Securities Premium	400
Surplus	200
Total of Paid-up Capital and Free Reserves	2,880

(1) 25% of Paid-up Capital and Free Reserves — 720

(2) 25% of Equity Capital $\left(i.e. \frac{25}{100} \times ₹\ 1{,}200 \text{ crores}\right)$ — 300

(3) The ratio of the debt (secured and unsecured) owed by the company is not more than twice the capital and its free reserves after such buy-back.

$$\text{Debt Equity Ratio (Permissible Limit 2)} = \frac{\text{Debt after Buy-back}}{\text{Equity Capital and Free Reserves after Buy-back}}$$

Situation I

$$2 = \frac{₹\ 3{,}200 \text{ crores}}{\text{Equity Capital and Free Reserves}}$$

$$\text{Equity Capital and Free Reserves after Buy-back} = \frac{₹\ 3{,}200 \text{ Crores}}{2} = ₹\ 1{,}600 \text{ crores}$$

Calculation of Amount of Equity Capital available for buy-back :	₹ in crores
Amount of Equity Capital and Free Reserves (before buy-back of shares)	2,880
Less : Equity Capital and Free Reserves required for buy-back	1,600
Amount of Equity Capital available for buy-back	1,280
Least of the three amounts ₹ 720 crores, ₹ 300 crores and ₹ 1,280 crores available for buyback of shares in Situation I	300

Situation II

Amounts in first two alternatives will be same as figures are same in two situations.

***Alternative III* :**

$$\text{Debt Equity Ratio} = \frac{\text{Debt after buy-back}}{\text{Equity Capital and Free Reserves}}$$

$$2 = \frac{₹\ 6{,}000 \text{ Crores}}{\text{Equity Capital and Free Reserves after buy-back}}$$

$$\text{Equity Capital and Free Reserves (after buy-back)} = \frac{₹\ 6{,}000 \text{ crores}}{2} = ₹\ 3{,}000 \text{ crores}$$

Amount of Equity Capital available for buy-back :	₹ in crores
Amount of Equity Capital and Free Reserves before buy-back of Shares	2,880 (Same as in Situation I because figures of capital and reserves are same)
Less : Equity Capital and Free Reserves required after buy-back	3,000
	(–) 120
Since figure is negative, amount of Equity Capital available for buy-back	Nil

Therefore in Situation II buy-back of shares is not possible because least figure is nil.

JOURNAL ENTRIES UNDER SITUATION I

				In ₹ Crores	In ₹ Crores
1.	Equity Share Capital A/c	Dr.		300	
	Premium on Buy-back A/c	Dr.		600	
	To Equity Shareholders A/c				900
	(Being 30 crores equity shares of ₹ 10 each bought back at a premium of ₹ 20 per share and cancelled as per Board's Resolution No..........dated)				
	Securities Premium A/c	Dr.		400	
	General Reserve	Dr.		200	
	To Premium on Buy-back A/c				600
	(Being premium on buy-back of shares provided out of Securities Premium A/c and balance from General Reserve)				
	General Reserve A/c	Dr.		300	
	To Capital Redemption Reserve A/c				300
	(Being transfer of General Reserve to Capital Redemption Reserve A/c to the extent of nominal value of ₹ 300 crores bought back)				
	Equity Shareholders A/c	Dr.		900	
	To Bank A/c				900
	(Being Payment of 30 crores shares bought back @ ₹ 30 per Share)				

QUESTIONS

SHORT ANSWER TYPE

1. What do you understand by Buyback of Shares ?
2. Mention the sources where from buyback of shares can be made.
3. State the conditions which are required to be satisfied by a company to buy its equity shares ?

4. How buyback of shares can be made ?
5. What are the institutions through which a company can purchase its own shares ?
6. Write a note on Free Reserves.
7. Explain the advantages and disadvantages of buyback of shares.
8. What are the various Journal Entries which are passed in the books of company for buyback of shares ?
9. What is Escrow Account ?
10. X Co. Ltd. decided to buyback 10,000 equity shares of ₹ 10 each. It sold investments (Face value) ₹ 70,000 for ₹ 95,000. It bought 10,000 equity shares in the open market for ₹ 90,000 out of free reserves. The Shares bought back were cancelled. The expenses of buyback were ₹ 1,000.

    Pass necessary Journal Entries in the books of X Co. Ltd. to record the above transactions.

LONG ANSWER TYPE

1. What do you mean by buyback of shares ? State the conditions to be fulfilled for buyback of shares.
2. What are the legal requirements for buyback of shares ? Also give advantages and disadvantages of buyback of shares.
3. Give the journal entries that are to be passed to record buyback of shares in the books of company.
4. Briefly give guidelines and regulations made by SEBI relating to buyback of shares.

PRACTICAL PROBLEMS

1. XYZ Ltd. decides to buyback 25% of its ₹ 4 crores paid up equity capital. The face value per equity share is ₹ 10 whereas the market price is ₹ 25. XYZ Ltd. takes the following steps for buyback of its shares :

    (*a*) To issue 14% debentures of ₹ 100 each at par for face value of ₹ 1 crore at par.

    (*b*) To utilise general reserve to the extent required.

    (*c*) To sell investments of ₹ 50,00,000 for ₹ 52,00,000.

    (*d*) To buyback the shares at the market price.

    Journalise the above transactions.

2. Following figures have been extracted from the books of Metals Product Ltd. as on 31-3-2023.

    Paid up Capital 9,00,000 Equity Shares of ₹ 10 each ₹ 90,00,000 ; General Reserve ₹ 15,00,000 ; Surplus A/c ₹ 5,00,000 ; Securities Premium A/c ₹ 3,00,000 ; 14% Debentures ₹ 10,00,000 ; Bank Balance ₹ 20,00,000.

    The company decided to buyback 25% of the paid up equity share capital at face value. It was also decided to issue further 14% debentures of ₹ 10,00,000 at par for the purpose of buyback of shares. Journalise the above transactions relating to buyback of shares.

3. Data taken from the books of ABC Ltd. as at 31-3-2023 is given below :

	₹
I. Equity and Liabilities	
(1) *Shareholders' Funds*	
(*a*) Share Capital :	
8,00,000 Equity Shares of ₹ 10 each	80,00,000

	₹
(b) Reserves and Surplus :	
(i) Securities Premium Account	8,00,000
(ii) General Reserve	72,00,000
(2) *Non-current Liabilities*	
Secured Loan : 13% Debentures	40,00,000
(3) *Current Liabilities*	40,00,000
Total	2,40,00,000
II. Assets	₹
(1) *Non-current Assets*	
(a) Property, Plant and Equipment	80,00,000
(2) *Current Assets*	
(a) Stock in Trade	48,00,000
(b) Sundry Debtors	40,00,000
(c) Bank Balance	72,00,000
Total	2,40,00,000

It was decided at the meeting of shareholders :

(i) to buyback 20% of equity shares @ ₹ 12 per share ;

(ii) to utilise general reserve for buyback of shares ;

(iii) to utilise securities premium for premium payable on buyback of shares.

Pass necessary Journal Entries and draw up the Balance Sheet after the above transactions have been given effect to.

Ans. [B/S Total ₹ 2,20,80,000]

4. Siddhant Limited had issued capital of ₹ 1,00,00,000 of ₹ 10 equity shares. The balance in the Securities Premium Account was ₹ 1,00,000 and general reserves ₹ 15,00,000. The company decided to buy-back 20% of its share capital direct from its shareholders at ₹ 8 per share. The company had issued ₹ 5,00,000, 10% preference shares two months back for the purpose of buy-back. Record the transactions relating to buy-back in the books of the company in accordance wit the provisions of the Companies Act, 2013.

Ans. [Transfer to Capital Redemption Reserve A/c ₹ 15,00,000]

5. Ledger balances of Prakash Ltd. as at 31-3-2023 are given below :

Cr. Balances	₹	*Dr. Balances*	₹
Paid-up Capital		Property, Plant and Equipment	9,00,000
30,000 Equity Shares of ₹ 10 each	3,00,000	Stock	2,00,000
Free Reserves	4,50,000	Debtors	1,50,000
Securities Premium Account	1,50,000	Bank Balance	5,50,000
Debentures	6,25,000		
Creditors	2,75,000		
	18,00,000		18,00,000

On the above date shares are bought back by the company to the extent possible, at a premium of ₹ 40 per share. Pass Journal Entries and show the Balance Sheet after buyback of shares.

Ans. [Number of shares to be bought back = 3,750; B/S Total ₹ 16,12,500].

6. Equity, liabilities and assets of Surya Electricals Ltd. as on 31-3-2023 stood as under :

	₹
I. Equity and Liabilities	
(1) *Shareholders' Funds*	
(*a*) Share Capital :	
20,00,000 Equity Shares of ₹ 10 each fully paid	2,00,00,000
(*b*) Reserves and Surplus :	
(*i*) Securities Premium Account	22,00,000
(*ii*) General Reserve	25,00,000
(*iii*) Surplus Account	15,00,000
(2) *Non-current Liabilities*	
(*a*) 9% Debentures	75,00,000
(*b*) Term Loans	80,00,000
(3) *Current Liabilities*	
(*a*) Creditors	29,00,000
(*b*) Provision for Tax	6,00,000
Total	4,52,00,000
II. Assets	₹
(1) *Non-current Assets*	
(*a*) Property, Plant and Equipment	2,73,60,000
(*b*) Investments	75,00,000
(2) *Current Assets*	
(*a*) Stock	47,80,000
(*b*) Debtors	40,20,000
(*c*) Cash and Bank Balance	15,40,000
Total	4,52,00,000

At a meeting of the shareholders held on the date of the above stated Balance Sheet, the following decisions were taken :

(*i*) 15% of the paid up shares would be bought back @ ₹ 16 each.

(*ii*) 10% of debentures of ₹ 20,00,000 at a premium of 15% would be issued to finance buyback.

(*iii*) General Reserve would be used leaving a balance of ₹ 10,00,000.

(*iv*) Investments worth ₹ 20,00,000 could be sold out for ₹ 28,00,000.

You are required to pass the necessary Journal Entries to give effect to the above transactions and also to present the Balance Sheet after buyback.

Ans. [Balance Sheet Total ₹ 435 lakhs].

7. Following are the equity, liabilities and assets of D Ltd. as on 31st March, 2023

	₹ in '000
I. Equity and Liabilities	
(1) *Shareholders' Funds*	
(*a*) Share Capital :	
3,00,000 Equity Shares of ₹ 10 each	3,000
(*b*) Reserves and Surplus :	
(*i*) Securities Premium Account	5
(*ii*) General Reserve	100

(2) *Non-current Liabilities*	
14% Debentures	1,400
(3) *Current Liabilities*	
Sundry Creditors	1,560
Total	6,065
II. Assets	₹ in '000
(1) *Non-current Assets*	
(*a*) Property, Plant and Equipment	
(*i*) Land & Building	630
(*ii*) Plant & Machinery	2,350
(*iii*) Furniture & Fittings	350
(*b*) Investments	370
(2) *Current Assets*	
(*a*) Stock	1,200
(*b*) Sundry Debtors	590
(*c*) Cash and Bank Balance	575
Total	6,065

On 1st April, 2023 the shareholders of the company have approved the scheme of buy-back of equity shares as under :

(*i*) 15% of the equity shares would be bought back at ₹ 9.

(*ii*) General Reserve and Securities Premium Account balance may be utilised to be fullest extent for this purpose.

(*iii*) Issue 12% Redeemable Preference Shares of ₹ 10 each as per requirements.

Pass the Journal Entries to record the above transactions and prepare Balance Sheet of the company immediately after the buyback of shares.

Ans. [Balance Sheet Total ₹ 6,005 thousands].

8. Following are the ledger balances of Excel Engineering Ltd. as on 31st March, 2023:

(₹ *in '000*)

Cr. Balances	₹	*Dr. Balances*	₹
Issued and Paid-up Capital		Land & Building	1,900
10,00,000 Equity Shares of		Plant & Machinery	7,080
₹ 10 each	10,000	Furniture & Fittings	1,000
General Reserve	1,100	Investments	1,160
Securities Premium Account	1,515	Stock	3,600
15% Debentures	4,200	Sundry Debtors	1,800
Sundry Creditors	1,380	Cash and Bank	1,655
	18,195		18,195

At a meeting held on 1st April, 2023, the shareholders of the company approved the scheme of buy-back of equity shares as under :

(*i*) 10% of the equity shares would be bought back at ₹ 20.

(ii) If deemed necessary, General Reserve balance may be utilised for this purpose.

(iii) Premium paid on buy-back of shares is to be met from the balance in Securities Premium Account.

(iv) Investments would be sold out for ₹ 12,00,000.

You are required to pass Journal Entries to give effect to the above transactions and prepare the Balance Sheet of the company after the buy-back.

Ans. **[₹ 16,235 thousands]**

9. On 31st March, 2023 following was the data taken from the books of Green India Ltd.

(*₹ in lakh*)

Cr. Balances	*Amount*	*Dr. Balances*	*Amount*
	₹		₹
Equity Share Capital (fully paid-up shares of ₹ 10 each)	2,400	Machinery	3,000
		Furniture	312
		Investments	148
Securities Premium Account	350	Stock	1,200
General Reserve	930	Debtors	520
Surplus A/c	340	Cash at Bank	740
Sundry Creditors	1,900		
	5,920		5,920

On 1st April, 2023, the company announced the **buy-back** of 25% of its equity shares @ ₹ 15 per share. For this purpose, it sold all its investments for ₹ 150 lakh and issued 2,00,000 12% preference shares of ₹ 100 each at par with the entire amount being payable on application.

The issue was fully subscribed. The company achieved the target of the buy-back. Show Journal Entries for all the transactions.

10. M Ltd. furnishes the following equity, liabilities and assets as at 31st March, 2023 :

	₹ in '000	₹ in '000
Equity & Liabilities		
Share Capital :		
Authorised Capital		5,000
Issued and Subscribed Capital :		
3,00,000 Equity Shares of ₹ 10 each fully paid up	3,000	
20,000 9% Preference Shares of 100 each (issued two months back for the purpose of buy back)	2,000	5,000
Reserves and Surplus :		
Capital Reserve	10	
Revenue Reserve	4,000	
Securities Premium Account	500	
Surplus A/c	1,800	
		6,310
Non-current Liabilities :		
10% Debentures		400
Current Liabilities and Provisions		40
		11,750

Assets	₹ in '000	₹ in '000
(1) *Non-Current Assets*		
(a) Property, Plant and Equipment :		
Cost	3,000	
Less : Provision for Depreciation	250	
		2,750
(b) Non-current Investments at Cost		5,000
(2) Current Assets, Loan and Advances (Including cash and bank balances)		4,000
		11,750

1. The company passed a resolution to **buy back** 20% of its equity capital @ ₹ 15 per share. For this purpose, it sold its investments of ₹ 30 lakhs for ₹ 25 lakhs.
2. The company redeemed the preference shares at a premium of 10% on 1st April, 2023.
3. Included in its investments were investments in own debentures costing ₹ 3 lakhs (face value ₹ 3.30 lakhs). These debentures were cancelled on 1st April, 2023.

You are required to pass necessary Journal entries and prepare the Balance Sheet on 1-4-2023.

Ans. [Balance Sheet Total ₹ 7,850 thousands]

11. KG Limited furnishes the following information as at 31st March, 2023.

Liabilities	*₹ in lakhs*	*Assets*	*(₹ in lakhs)*
Equity Share Capital	1,200	Machinery	1,800
(fully paid up shares of ₹ 10 each)		Furniture	226
Securities Premium Account	175	Investment	74
General Reserve	265	Stock	600
Capital Redemption Reserve	200	Debtors	260
Surplus A/c	170	Cash at Bank	740
12% Debentures	750		
Sundry Creditors	745		
Other Current Liabilities	195		
	3,700		3,700

On 1st April, 2023, the company announced the buy back of 25% of its equity shares @ ₹ 15 per share. For this purpose, it sold all of its investments for ₹ 75 lakhs.

On 30th April, 2023, the company achieved the target of buyback. On 30th April, 2023 the company issued one fully paid up equity share of ₹ 10 by way of bonus for every four equity shares held by the equity shareholders.

You are required to :

Pass necessary Journal Entries for the above transactions.

12. The following were the ledger balances taken from the books of Wonder World Ltd. as at 31-3-2023 :

(₹ in lakhs)

Cr. Balances	₹	*Dr. Balances*	₹
1 lakh Equity Shares of ₹ 10		Plant and Machinery	13.50
each fully paid	10.00	Furniture	2.40

Securities Premium Account	3.50	Investments	1.80
General Reserve	3.10	Stock	7.20
Surplus A/c	1.10	Sundry Debtors	2.30
14% Debentures	7.50	Bank	3.00
Sundry Creditors	5.00		
	30.20		30.20

On 1-4-2023, the company decided to buy-back 20% of its equity shares at a premium of ₹ 10 per share. For this purpose, the company sold its entire investments for ₹ 2.30 lakhs and issued 1,500, 12% Preference shares of ₹ 100 each at par. The amount payable was ₹ 60 on application and ₹ 40 on allotment. The issue was fully subscribed. Thereafter the company issued bonus shares of ₹ 10 at the rate of one bonus share for every five equity shares held by the equity shareholders.

Show Journal entries and Balance Sheet after the above transactions were completed.

Ans. [Balance Sheet Total ₹ 28.20 lakhs]

Investment Accounts

Meaning of Investment

The term 'Investment' refers to funds invested in various securities consisting of government and semi-government loans, debentures of local authorities such as port trusts, municipal corporations and the like and debentures and shares of companies. Investments can be defined as, **"Investments are assets held by an enterprise for earning income by way of dividends, interests and rentals, for capital appreciation, or for other benefits to the investing enterprise. Assets held as stock-in-trade are non-investments"**. Securities may be fixed interest securities and variable yield securities. *Fixed interest securities* are those securities which carry a fixed rate of interest while the securities (such as shares of companies) on which dividend may fluctuate from year to year are called *variable yield securities*.

Investments are freely bought and sold in the stock exchange **through banks and brokers, who charge a small commission for their services. The contracts for the purchase and sale of securities require the prescribed stamp duty. On purchase of a security, Bank's commission or brokerage and stamp duty become the part of the cost of purchase while on the sale of securities such charges are deducted from the sale proceeds realised.**

Market price of a security is not the same as its face value and may be governed by many factors such as prevailing rate of interest, yield obtainable from the security, political situation existing at any particular time, safety of money invested, the chance of appreciation or depreciation, the volume of speculation in the market etc. If the price of a security is the same as the face value, it is said to be *at par* ; if it is lower than the face value it is said to be at *a discount* and if it exceeds the face value, it is said to be *at a premium*.

Investments may be fixed assets or current assets. If the investments are held permanently for a long period of more than one year for the purpose of earning continuing income and/or to control the affairs of another enterprise, they will be regarded as *fixed assets*, such as investments held by banks, insurance companies, investments trust companies and industrial companies, etc. Such investments are known as **trade investments.** But where the object of the business is to buy and sell securities or these are held as a temporary investment of surplus liquid resources for not more than one year, then they will be regarded as **current assets or marketable securities.** Such types of investments are expected to be converted into cash within a short period of time. These are short term investments made to earn some income on idle cash with the firm. In this chapter, we are concerned with marketable securities.

ILLUSTRATION 1. How will you deal with following in the financial statement of the Paridhi Electronics Ltd. as on 31-3-2023 ?

(*i*) Paridhi Electronics Ltd. invested in the shares of another unlised company on 1st May 2019 at a cost of ₹ 3,00,000 with the intention of holding for more than a year. The published accounts of unlisted company received in January, 2023 reveals that the company has incurred cash losses with decline market share and investment of Paridhi Electronics Ltd. may not fetch more than ₹ 45,000.

(*ii*) Also Paridhi Electronics Ltd. has current investment (X Ltd.'s shares) purchased for ₹ 5 lakhs, which the company wants to reclassify as long term investment. The market value of these investments as on date of Balance Sheet was ₹ 2.5 lakhs.

SOLUTION

(*i*) Investments classified as long term investments should be carried in the financial statements at cost. However, provision for diminution shall be made to recognise a decline, other than temporary, in the value of the investments, such reduction being determined and made for each investment individually. It is further stated that indicators of the value of an investment are obtained by reference to its market value, the investee's assets and results and the expected cash flows from the investment.

On this basis, the facts of the given case clearly suggest that the provision for diminution should be made to reduce the carrying amount of shares to ₹ 45,000 in the financial statements for the year ended 31st March, 2023 and charge the difference of loss of ₹ 2,55,000 to Profit and Loss Account.

(*ii*) Where investments are reclassified from current to long-term, transfers are made at the lower of cost of fair value at the date of transfer.

In the given case, the market value of the investment (X Ltd. shares) is ₹ 2.50 lakhs, which is lower than its cost *i.e.*, ₹ 5 lakhs. Therefore, the transfer to long term investments should be made at cost *i.e.*, ₹ 2.50 lakhs. The loss of ₹ 2.50 lakhs should be charged to Profit and Loss Account.

Investment Accounts

The accounts of investments are kept in the same way as the accounts of any other asset. A separate investment account should be opened for each kind of security and on the head of the account particulars regarding the nature of the security, dates when interest or dividend is due, the date of redemption etc. should be stated. When the number of investments carried is large, a separate Investment Ledger is kept for recording all investment accounts.

Purposes of maintaining an investment ledger are as follows :

1. It helps in *keeping a record* of each security separately.
2. It helps to *ascertain the value* of securities at the end of the accounting period.
3. It is helpful in *collection of interest and dividend* as and when they become due.
4. It is helpful in *ascertaining the amount of accrued income* at the end of the accounting period.
5. It is helpful in *ascertaining the total income* on various investments for a particular year.
6. It facilitates the *determination of the profit or loss on sale* of any security.

On the purchase of an investment, Investment Account will be debited and Cash Account credited with the cost thereof *i.e.*, the purchase price plus the bank's or broker's commission and on the sale of investment, Cash Account will be debited and Investment Account credited with the net proceeds realised.

Interest or Dividend Account. In addition to the accounts of investments it will be necessary to maintain an Interest or Dividend Account for recording the income derived from various investments. It means that there will be many investment accounts for different kinds of securities held ; but there will be only one Interest or Dividend Account for recording the income derived from all of them.

Investment Transactions

In writing up investment accounts special attention should be given to the purchase and sale of securities-cum-dividend or ex-dividend.

Cum-Dividend (or Cum-Interest) Quotations

On fixed investments interest goes on accruing day by day but it is paid periodically on fixed dates. The transactions of investments do not necessarily take place on those dates and so at the time of the sale of investment, it has to be settled as to who will get the next instalment which in the absence of an agreement goes to the purchaser. A company pays dividend on a share to the person whose name appears on the date of the payment of dividend in the books of the company as its holder. Even if a person has held a share for as long a period of eleven months but has sold it to another shortly before the payment of dividend, the company would pay dividend to the new purchaser and not to the former holder. Naturally, therefore, the seller charges the purchaser a price which, in his opinion, includes dividend accrued on the share upto the date of sale. The share is then said to have been sold "cum-dividend" or together with dividend, the right of receiving dividend being passed on to the purchaser. It should, therefore, be noted that **when an investment is purchased cum-dividend or cum-interest the purchaser pays for it a higher price than the normal price, the difference representing the dividend or interest accrued on the investment upto the date of purchase. Therefore, while debiting Investment Account with the purchase price, the same should be split up into the normal price and the dividend/interest accrued, the normal price being debited to Investment Account and the dividend or interest accrued debited to the Dividend or the Interest Account.**

Similarly, when an investment is sold cum-dividend or cum-interest, the price received includes dividend or interest accrued on the investment upto the date of sale. Therefore, it should be split into the normal price and the dividend or interest accrued, the normal price being credited to the particular Investment Account and the dividend or interest accrued credited to the Dividend or the Interest Account. In respect of *Government securities price quoted is ex-interest* unless otherwise stated whereas in respect of Non-Government securities, it is cum-interest unless otherwise stated.

ACCOUNTING ENTRIES

In the Books of Buyer

(*i*) *On an investment being purchased cum-dividend (or* ***cum Interest****)*

Shares in—Co. Ltd. or Investment A/c	Dr.	(Capital Cost)
Dividend or Interest A/c (on Investment A/c)	Dr.	(Dividend or Interest)
To Bank A/c		(Capital Cost & Dividend or Interest)

(Actual Purchase Price or Capital Cost of Investment = Purchase Price + Purchase Expenses – Interest for the period from the last interest payable to the date of transaction)

(ii) *On receipt of dividend or interest*

Bank A/c	Dr.	With the amount of Dividend or Interest received
To Dividend or Interest A/c (on Investment A/c)		

(iii) *For Accrued Interest*

Accrued Interest A/c	Dr.
To Interest A/c	

Note : At the close of the accounting period, the balance of Interest or Dividend Account will be transferred to P & L. A/c.

In the Books of Seller

(1) *On an investment being sold cum-dividend (or* ***cum Interest****)*

Bank A/c	Dr.	(Amount received)
To Shares in — Co. Ltd. or Investment A/c		(Actual sale price)
To Dividend or Interest (on Investment A/c)		(Dividend or Interest)

(Actual Sale Price of Investment = Sale Price – Sale Expenses – Accrued interest for the period from the last interest payable date to the date of sale).

(2) *On receipt of dividend or interest*

Bank A/c	Dr.	For amount of Dividend or Interest
To Dividend or Interest A/c		

ILLUSTRATION 2. On 31st January, 2023, X purchased for cash from Y four 6% ₹ 100 Debentures of the Mehta Ltd. at 110$\frac{1}{2}$% cum-interest ; interest being payable on 1st June and 1st December each year.

How will you record the transaction in the books of X and Y if each party had to pay bank commission of 25 paise per cent on face value ?

SOLUTION

IN THE BOOKS OF X

	₹
Purchase Price of 4 Debentures @ ₹ 110.50 each cum-interest	442
Add : Bank Commission @ 25 paise per cent on ₹ 400 face value	1
Total Cost	443
Less : Accrued interest for the past 2 months from Dec. 1, 2022 to Jan. 31, 2023 @ 6% p.a. on ₹ 400	4
Value of Investment	439

JOURNAL

			₹	₹
Investment A/c	Dr.		439	
Interest A/c	Dr.		4	
To Cash A/c				443
(Being purchase of investment of ₹ 400 nominal value at 110$\frac{1}{2}$% cum-interest plus commission paid)				

Note. On June 1, total interest for 6 months shall be credited in the books. Commission paid on purchase is capitalised.

IN THE BOOKS OF Y

	₹
Cum-interest price of security	442
Less : Bank commission paid	1
Total Cost	441
Less : Accrued interest	4
Capitalised Cost of Investment	437

JOURNAL

			₹	₹
Cash A/c	Dr.		441	
To Investment A/c				437
To Interest A/c				4
(Being sale of investment of ₹ 400 nominal value at $110\frac{1}{2}$% cum-interest less commission paid)				

IMPORTANT NOTE. *Interest* is always calculated with reference to the face value of bonds and *brokerage* is calculated on cum-interest or ex-interest price.

Ex-Dividend (or Ex-Interest) Quotations

When an investment is purchased "Ex-Dividend or Ex-Interest" the price paid is below the normal price, *i.e.*, it is arrived at after deducting from the normal price dividend or interest receivable on the investment from the date of interest or dividend payment to the date of purchase. Therefore, *when an investment is purchased Ex-Dividend or Ex-Interest, the purchaser has to pay to the seller the accrued interest upto the date of purchase in addition to the price paid for the investment.*

Important Note. *Unless otherwise stated, the price quotation will be cum-interest quotation.*

ILLUSTRATION 3. Work out the problem given in Illustration 1 if the quotation is ex-interest.

SOLUTION

IN THE BOOKS OF X

	₹
Purchase price of 4 debentures @ ₹ 110.50 ex-interest	442
Add : Bank Commission @ 25 paise per cent on ₹ 400, the face value of 4 debentures @ ₹ 100	1
Total Cost of Investment	443

JOURNAL ENTRIES

			₹	₹
Investment Account	Dr.		443	
Interest Account	Dr.		4	
To Cash Account				447
(Being purchase of 4 debentures @ ₹ 110.50 ex-interest plus commission ₹ 1 and interest paid for 2 months from Dec. 1 to Jan. 31 @ 6% p.a. on ₹ 400 f ace value of debentures)				

IN THE BOOKS OF Y

	₹
Selling price of 4 debentures @ 110.50 ex-interest	442
Less : Bank Commission paid @ 25 paise per cent on ₹ 400	1
Net amount realised on account of sale of investment	441

JOURNAL ENTRIES

			₹	₹
Cash Account	Dr.		445	
To Investment Account				441
To Interest Account				4
(Being sale of 4 debentures @ ₹ 110.50 ex-interest minus commission ₹ 1 and interest received for 2 months @ 6% p.a. on ₹ 400, the face value of 4 debentures)				

Difference Between Cum-Interest and Ex-Interest

Following are the main differences between Cum-Interest and Ex-Interest :

1. In case of cum-interest *purchase price* includes the interest accrued upto the date of purchase whereas this is not included in case of ex-interest.

2. In case of cum-interest nothing is payable for *interest accrued* whereas it is payable in case of ex-interest.

3. In case of cum-interest, *purchase price is less than the real price* of the security but purchase price is the real price in case of ex-interest.

Balancing the Investment Account

When the whole of an investment has been sold, the difference between the two sides of an Investment Account will be profit or loss on the sale.

Where only part of an investment has been sold during the year, **the cost of the remaining investment will be brought down as a balance** in the Investment Account and the difference between its two sides will be profit or loss on the investments sold.

When the investment is a fixed asset, any profit or loss made on the sale thereof will be of a capital nature and should be treated accordingly.

ILLUSTRATION 4. On 1st June, 2023 Mr. Arthur purchased ₹ 9,000 5% debentures of ₹ 100 each in the Patel Engineering Works Ltd. at ₹ 105 cum-interest, interest being payable on 31st March and 30th September each year. Expenses on stamps amounted to ₹ 80. On 1st November, 2023 he sold ₹ 3,000 debentures at ₹ 107 cum-interest.

Brokerage is payable on each transaction @$\frac{1}{8}$% on nominal value. Make entries in Arthur's books and show Investment Account and Interest Account as on 31st December, 2023.

SOLUTION

JOURNAL ENTRIES

Date	Particulars		L.F.	Dr. ₹	Cr. ₹
2023 June 1	Investment A/c (1)	Dr.		9,466.25	
	Interest A/c	Dr.		75.00	
	To Bank A/c				9,541.25
	(Being investment made in ₹ 9,000 5% debentures of ₹ 100 each at ₹ 105 cum-interest; 5% p.a. interest for 2 months of April and May included in the purchase price deducted from the purchase price and debited to Interest A/c ; brokerage @ $\frac{1}{8}$ % on ₹ 9,000 nominal value and stamp fee ₹ 80 added to the purchase price of the investment)				
Sept. 30	Bank A/c	Dr.		225.00	
	To Interest A/c				225.00
	(Being interest received on ₹ 9,000 nominal value of debentures @ 5% p.a. for 6 months)				
Nov. 1	Bank A/c	Dr.		3,206.25	
	To Investment A/c				(2) 3,193.75
	To Interest A/c				12.50
	(Being investment of nominal value of ₹ 3,000 sold at ₹ 107 cum-interest; interest for October month @ 5% p.a. deducted from sale value and brokerage ₹ 3.75 paid @ $\frac{1}{8}$% on ₹ 3,000 nominal value also deducted from the selling price of the investment)				
Nov. 1	Investment A/c	Dr. (3)		38.33	
	To Profit & Loss A/c				38.33
	(Profit on sale of investment transferred to Profit & Loss A/c)				
Dec. 31	Accrued Interest A/c	Dr.		75	
	To Interest A/c				75
	(Being accrued interest on ₹ 6,000 nominal value @ 5% p.a. for 3 months from October 1 to Dec. 31)				
Dec. 31	Interest A/c	Dr.		237.50	
	To Profit and Loss A/c				237.50
	(Being interest on investment earned during the year transferred to Profit & Loss A/c)				

INVESTMENT ACCOUNT

(5% Debentures of Patel Engineering Works Ltd.)

(Interest Payable on 31st March and 30th September)

Date	Particulars	Nominal Value	Amount	Date	Particulars	Nominal Value	Amount
2023		₹	₹	2023		₹	₹
June 1	To Bank A/c (1)	9,000	9,466.25	Nov. 1	By Bank A/c (2)	3,000	3,193.75
Nov. 1	To Profit & Loss A/c		(3) 38.33	Dec. 31	By Balance c/d	6,000	6,310.83
		9,000	9,504.58			9,000	9,504.58
2024							
Jan. 1	To Balance b/d	6,000	6,310.83				

INTEREST ACCOUNT

2023		₹	2023		₹
June. 1	To Bank A/c (1)	75.00	Sept. 30	By Bank A/c	225.00
Dec. 31	To Profit & Loss A/c	237.50	Nov. 1	By Bank A/c (2)	12.50
			Dec. 31	By Accrued Interest A/c (4)	75.00
		312.50			312.50

Working Notes :

(1) ***Purchase price of ₹ 9,000 debentures on June 1, 2023*** ₹

	₹
Amount paid ₹ 9,000 × $\frac{105}{100}$	9,450.00
Add: Brokerage $\frac{1}{8} \times \frac{1}{100}$ × ₹ 9,000	11.25
Stamp fee	80.00
Total amount paid	9,541.25
Less : Interest for 2 months (April & May) ₹ 9,000 × $\frac{2}{12} \times \frac{5}{100}$	75.00
Amount to be Debited to Investment A/c	9,466.25

(2) ***Sale value of Investment on November 1, 2023*** ₹

		₹
Gross sale proceed : ₹ 3,000 × $\frac{107}{100}$		3,210.00
Less : Amount paid for brokerage $\frac{1}{8} \times \frac{1}{100}$ × ₹ 3,000	₹ 3.75	
Interest included in gross sale proceed for month of October ₹ 3,000 × $\frac{5}{100} \times \frac{1}{12}$	₹ 12.50	
		16.25
Amount to be Credited to Investment A/c		3,193.75

(3) ***Profit on Sale of Investment*** ₹

	₹
Purchase price of ₹ 9,000 debentures	9,466.25
Therefore, purchase price of ₹ 3,000 debentures $\left(\frac{₹ 9,466.25}{₹ 9,000} \times ₹ 3,000\right)$	3,155.42
Selling Price of Investment	3,193.75
Less: Purchase Price of investment	3,155.42
Profit on Sale of Investment	38.33

(4) ***Accrued Interest on ₹ 6,000 for 3 months @ 5% p.a.*** ₹ 75

Columnar Investment Accounts

Concerns holding a large number of investments may find it more convenient to use a separate ledger called an *Investment Ledger*, for keeping the accounts of all their investments. Such a ledger is kept on the columnar system and is ruled differently from an ordinary ledger. As the issuing authority of a security pays interest to the holder at a certain rate calculated on its face value, it is desirable that the face value (also known as the nominal value) as well as the interest or dividend received should appear side by side with the capital invested in it. Therefore, the Investment Ledger is provided with *three columns on either side* headed 'Nominal Value', 'Interest or Dividend' and

'Capital or Principal'. The name of each investment is written at the top of the account followed by the rate of interest or dividend and the dates on when it is payable ; when an investment is *purchased* "cum-dividend", "ex-dividend" its cost is analysed into the nominal price and the dividend or interest accrued and an entry is made on the credit side of the Cash Book, from where it is posted to the respective columns on the debit side of the particular Investment Account in the Investment Ledger. When the whole or part of the investment is *sold*, the price received, similarly split up into the nominal price and the dividend or interest accrued, is entered on the debit side of the Cash Book, from where it is posted to the respective columns on the credit side of the particular Investment Account in the Investment Ledger. Expenses by way of brokerage, stamps etc., will be debited to the capital account. When dividend or interest accrued on an investment is received, it is first entered on the debit side of the Cash Book and then posted to the credit side of the particular Investment Account in the 'Dividend or Interest' column in the Investment Ledger. *At the close of the financial year*, the dividend or interest accrued on different investments, but not received, is brought into account by crediting the 'Dividend or Interest' columns of the different investment accounts in the Investment Ledger and bringing down such balances as an asset after the accounts have been balanced.

The *first column* is of Nominal Value and in it on the credit side is entered the nominal value of investments on hand and the totals on both sides will then agree.

The *second column* is of Interest or Dividend and it will always show a credit balance representing interest or dividend on investments for the period and it will be carried to Profit and Loss Account.

The *third column* is for Capital or Principal. In this column against the closing balance will be entered the value of securities is hand and the difference of the two sides will show profit or loss on the sale of investments during the period. Value of securities in hand is the lower of cost and fair value.

The carrying amount for *current investments* is the lower of cost and fair value. In respect of investments for which an active market exists, market value generally provides the best evidence of fair value. The valuation of current investments at lower of cost and fair value provides a prudent method of determining the carrying amount to be stated in the balance sheet.

***Long-term investments* should be carried at cost. However, in case of such investments, it is necessary to create a provision for diminution to recognise a permanent decline in the value, if any.**

ILLUSTRATION 5. MY Ltd. has acquired 200 equity shares of YZ Ltd. at ₹ 105 per share on 1-1-2023 and paid ₹ 200 towards brokerage, and stamp duty. On 31st March, 2023, shares of YZ Ltd., were traded at ₹ 110 per share. At what value investment is to be shown in the Balance Sheet of MY Ltd. as at 31st March, 2023.

SOLUTION

	₹
Purchase price of Equity Shares of YZ Ltd. (200 shares × ₹ 105 per share)	21,000
Add : Brokerage and stamp duty	200
Cost of Investment	21,200

If the investment is a *long term investment*, then it will be shown at cost. Therefore, value of investment will be ₹ 21,200. However, if the investment is a *current investment*, then it will be shown at lower of cost (*i.e.* ₹ 21,200) or net realizable value (*i.e.* ₹ 200 × 110 = ₹ 22,000). Therefore, value of investment will be ₹ 21,200.

ILLUSTRATION 6. Kolkata Investments hold 400, 12 per cent Debentures of ₹ 100 each in Acme Ltd. as on 1st April, 2022 at a cost of ₹ 50,000. Interest is payable on 30th June and 31st

December each year. On 1st June, 2022, 200 debentures are purchased cum-interest at ₹ 21,400. On 1st November, 2022, 300 debentures are sold ex-interest at ₹ 28,650. On 30th November, 2022, 200 debentures are purchased ex-interest for ₹ 19,200. On 31st December, 2022, 300 debentures are sold cum-interest for ₹ 32,250.

Prepare Investment Account valuing closing stocks as on 31st March, 2023, at cost (applying FIFO method) or market price, whichever is lower. The debentures were quoted at par on 31st March, 2023.

(For Solution please see page II/1·11)

ILLUSTRATION 7. During the year ended 31st December 2023, Ivory Investments Ltd. purchased and sold investments as per details below :

31st March—Purchased 10,000, 5 per cent Debentures of ₹ 100 each of Asbestoes Ltd. at ₹ 97, brokerage and stamp duty amounting to ₹ 25,600. Interest is payable on the debentures on 1st July and 1st January.

1st May—Purchased 10,000, 6 per cent Cumulative Preference Shares of ₹ 100 each of Andhra Cements Ltd. at ₹ 95, brokerage and stamp duty being ₹ 24,200. Dividends are payable on 30th June and 31st December.

1st July—Sold ₹ 6,00,000 Debentures of Asbestoes Ltd. at ₹ 99 per hundred, less brokerage, etc. ₹ 3,600.

1st October—Purchased a further 4,000, 6 per cent, Cumulative Preference Shares of ₹ 100 of Andhra Cements Ltd. at ₹ 90, brokerage and stamp duty being ₹ 8,600.

Write up Ledger Accounts of the two investments for the year 2023.

(For Solution see pages II/1·12 & II/1·13)

ILLUSTRATION 8. On 1st July, 2022, Sen Investment Ltd. held ₹ 1,00,000, 6 per cent Debentures of X Ltd, in the books at ₹ 95,600. Interest is payable on 31st July and 31st January. On 1st September, 2022, a further ₹ 50,000 of the debentures in X Ltd. were bought at ₹ 98 cum-interest and on 1st January, 2023 a further ₹ 40,000 debentures were bought at ₹ 97 ex-interest.

On 31st March, 2023, ₹ 80,000 Debentures were sold at ₹ 101 cum-interest and on 15th June ₹ 60,000 debentures were sold at ₹ 102 ex-interest.

Show the Investment Account for the period ending 30th June, 2023 valuing balance of Investment Account at the end of the year at average cost of the year.

(For Solution see page II/1·14)

[(1) Note. The amount to credit of Interest Account, ₹ 8,350 to be made as follows :

		₹
₹ 1,00,000—July 1 to Sept. 1, 2 months at 6%	=	1,000
₹ 1,50,000 — Sept 1 to Jan. 1, 4 months at 6%	=	3,000
₹ 1,90,000 — Jan. 1 to March 31, 3 months at 6%	=	2,850
₹ 1,10,000 — April 1 to June 15, $2\frac{1}{2}$ months at 6%	=	1,375
₹ 50,000 — June 15 to June 30, $\frac{1}{2}$ month at 6%	=	125
		8,350

SOLUTION (*ILLUSTRATION 6*)

12% DEBENTURES IN ACME LTD.

(Interest payable on 30th June and 31st December)

Date	Particulars	Nominal	Interest	Principal	Date	Particulars	Nominal	Interest	Principal
		₹	₹	₹			₹	₹	₹
2022 April 1	To Balance b/d $\left(₹ 40,000 \times \frac{12}{100} \times \frac{3}{12}\right)$	40,000	1,200	50,000	2022 June 30	By Bank A/c $\left(₹ 60,000 \times \frac{12}{100} \times \frac{6}{12}\right)$	—	3,600	—
June 1	" Bank A/c $\left(₹ 20,000 \times \frac{5}{12} \times \frac{12}{100}\right)$	20,000	1,000	20,400	Nov. 1	" Bank A/c $\left(₹ 30,000 \times \frac{12}{100} \times \frac{4}{12}\right)$	30,000	1,200	28,650
Nov. 30	" Bank A/c	20,000	1,000	19,200	" 1	" P. & L. A/c (Loss on Sale) (₹ 37,500 – ₹ 28,650)			8,850
2023 Mar. 31	" Profit & Loss A/c	—	5,200		Dec. 31	" Bank A/c $\left(₹ 30,000 \times \frac{12}{100} \times \frac{6}{12}\right)$	30,000	1,800	30,450
					" 31	" Profit & Loss (Loss on Sale) (₹ 32,900 – ₹ 30,450)			2,450
					" "	" Bank A/c (Interest) $\left(₹ 20,000 \times \frac{12}{100} \times \frac{6}{12}\right)$		1,200	
					2023 Mar. 31	" Balance c/d $\left(₹ 20,000 \times \frac{12}{100} \times \frac{3}{12}\right)$	20,000	600	19,200
		80,000	8,400	89,600			80,000	8,400	89,600

SOLUTION (*ILLUSTRATION 7*)

INVESTMENT ACCOUNT
(5% DEBENTURES OF ASBESTOES LIMITED)

Dr. | **Cr.**

Date	Particulars	Face Value ₹	Interest ₹	Principal ₹	Date	Particulars	Face Value ₹	Interest ₹	Principal ₹
31-3-2023	To Cash Account 9,70,000 *Add*: Brokerage 25,600 = 9,95,600	10,00,000	12,500	9,83,100 (9,95,600 – 12,500 Interest)	1-7-2023	By Cash Account (Interest)	—	25,000	—
					" "	" Cash Sold @ 99% — ₹ 5,94,000 $\left(6,00,000 \times \frac{99}{100}\right)$ *Less*: Expenses 3,600 = 5,90,400	6,00,000	—	5,90,400
1-7-2023	" Profit & Loss Account (1)	—	—	540					
31-12-2023	" Profit & Loss Account		22,500		31-12-2023	" Accrued Interest Account $\left(₹ 4,00,000 \times \frac{5}{100} \times \frac{6}{12}\right)$	—	10,000	—
					"	" Balance c/d (at cost)	4,00,000	—	3,93,240
		10,00,000	35,000	9,83,640			10,00,000	35,000	9,83,640

(1) Calculation of Profit on Sale of Debentures on 1-7-2023

Amount realised on sale of debentures (nominal value ₹ 6,00,000)	₹ 5,90,400
Less: Purchase price of ₹ 6,00,000 Debentures $\left(\frac{₹ 9,83,100}{₹ 10,00,000} \times ₹ 6,00,000\right)$	₹ 5,89,860
Profit on Sale of Debentures	₹ 540

INVESTMENT ACCOUNT
(6% CUM. PREF. SHARES IN ANDHRA CEMENTS LIMITED)

Dr. *Cr.*

Date	Particulars	Face value	Income	Investment	Date	Particulars	Face value	Income	Investment
	₹	₹	₹	₹			₹	₹	₹
1-5-2023	To Cash Account 9,50,000 *Add* : Brokerage 24,200 9,74,200	10,00,000	(1) 20,000	9,54,200 (9,74,200 – 20,000 Dividend)	30-6-2023	By Cash Account (Dividend) $\left(₹\ 10,00,000 \times \frac{6}{100} \times \frac{6}{12}\right)$	—	30,000	—
1-10-2023	To Cash Account 3,60,000 *Add* : Brokerage 8,600 3,68,600	4,00,000	(2) 6,000	3,62,600	31-12-2023	" Cash Account (Dividend)	—	42,000	—
					" "	" Balance (at cost) c/d	14,00,000	—	13,16,800
31-12-2023	To Profit & Loss Account	—	46,000	—					
		14,00,000	72,000	13,16,800			14,00,000	72,000	13,16,800

(1) Dividend on ₹ 10,00,000 Preference Shares @ 6% p.a. for 4 months from 1-1-2023 to 30-4-2023

$$\left(₹\ 10,00,000 \times \frac{6}{100} \times \frac{4}{12}\right) = ₹\ 20,000$$

(2) Dividend on ₹ 4,00,000 Preference Shares @ 6% p.a. for 3 months from 1-7-2023 to 30-9-2023

$$\left(₹\ 4,00,000 \times \frac{6}{100} \times \frac{3}{12}\right) = ₹\ 6,000.$$

Note. Price for purchase of preference shares is cum-dividend.

SOLUTION (*ILLUSTRATION 8*)

SEN INVESTMENT LTD.'S BOOKS
INVESTMENT ACCOUNT (6% DEBENTURES)
(Interest payable on 31st July and 31st January)

Date	Particulars	Nominal	Income	Capital	Date	Particulars	Nominal	Income	Capital
2022		₹	₹	₹	2022		₹	₹	₹
July 1	To Balance b/d	1,00,000		95,600	July 31	By Bank (Interest on ₹ 1,00,000 at 6% p.a. for half year)		3,000	
" 1	" Balance accruing interest for 5 months		2,500		2023 Jan. 31	" Bank (Interest on ₹ 1,90,000 at 6% p.a. for half year)		5,700	
Sept. 1	" Bank : Purchase at ₹ 98 cum-interest	50,000	250	48,750	March 31	" Bank : Sale at ₹ 101 cum interest, ₹ 80,000	80,000	800	80,000
2023 Jan. 1	" Bank : Purchase at ₹ 97 Ex-interest : ₹ 40,000	40,000	1,000	38,800	June 15	" Bank : Sale at ₹ 102 ex-interest ₹ 60,000	60,000	1,350	61,200
June 30	" Interest Account (1)		8,350		June 30	" Accrued Interest		1,250	
June 30	" Profit & Loss A/c (Bal. Fig. : Profit on sales)			6,247		Balance c/d $\frac{₹\,50,000}{₹\,1,90,000} \times ₹\,1,83,150$	50,000		48,197
		1,90,000	12,100	1,89,397			1,90,000	12,100	1,89,397
July 1	To Balance b/d	50,000	1,250	48,197					

ILLUSTRATION 9. On 1st March, 2023 XY Corporation Ltd. purchased ₹ 30,000, 5% Government stock at ₹ 95 cum-interest. On 1st May, 2023 the company sold ₹ 10,000 of stock at ₹ 97 cum-interest. On 15th December, 2023, another ₹ 10,000 stock was sold at ₹ 93 ex-interest. On 31st December, 2023, the closing date of the financial year, the market price of the stock was ₹ 92. Half-yearly interest is received every year as on 30th June and 31st December.

Prepare a ledger account in the investment ledger. Ignore income tax and brokerage.

(For Solution see page II/1·16)

ILLUSTRATION 10. Naresh held on 1-1-2023, ₹ 3,00,000 of 12% Government Securities (tax free) of ₹ 100 each at ₹ 2,82,500. On 1-6-2023 Naresh purchased a further ₹ 2,00,000 of the security at $96\frac{1}{2}$ cum-interest, brokerage being $\frac{1}{2}$% on face value.

On 31-7-2023, ₹ 2,50,000 of the security was sold at $94\frac{1}{2}$ ex-interest, brokerage being $\frac{1}{2}$% on face value. On 1-12-2023, ₹ 1,00,000 of the security was again sold at ₹ 96 cum-interest.

Interest on the security was paid each year on 31st March and 30th September and was credited by the bank on 3rd April and 4th October respectively. The price of the security on 31-12-2023 was ₹ 94. Naresh closes its books on 31st December each year.

Draw up the Investment Account in the books of Naresh.

(For Solution see page II/1·17)

ILLUSTRATION 11. Bonanzaa Limited held on 1st April, 2022 ₹ 2,00,000 of 9% Government Loan (2024) at ₹ 1,90,000. (Face Value of Loan ₹ 100 each). Three months' interest had accrued on the above date. On 31st May, 2022 the company purchased the same Government Loan of the face value of ₹ 80,000 at ₹ 95 (net) cum-interest. On 1st June, 2022, ₹ 60,000 face value of the loan was sold at ₹ 94 (net) ex-interest. Interest on the loan was paid each year on 30th June and 31st December and was credited by the bank on the same date. On 30th November, 2022 ₹ 40,000 face value of the Loan was sold at ₹ 97 (net) cum-interest. On 1st December, 2022 the company purchased the same loan ₹ 10,000 at par ex-interest. On 1st March, 2023 the company sold ₹ 10,000 face value of the loan at ₹ 95 ex-interest. The market price of the loan on 31st March, 2023 was ₹ 96. Draw up the 9% Government Loan (2024) Account in the books of Bonanzaa Limited. *First in first out method shall be followed* and the balance of the loan held by the company shall be valued at total *average cost or market price, whichever is lower.* Calculations shall be made to the nearest rupee or multiple thereof.

(For Solution see page II/1·18)

SOLUTION (*ILLUSTRATION 9*)

In the Books of XY Corporation Ltd.
5% GOVERNMENT STOCK ACCOUNT
[Interest Payable : 30th June & 31st December]

Dr. **Cr.**

Date	Particulars	Nominal Value	Interest (₹)	Cost (₹)	Date	Particulars	Nominal Value	Interest (₹)	Cost (₹)
1-3-2023	To Bank A/c (1)	30,000	250	28,250	1-5-2023	By Bank A/c (2)	10,000	167	9,533
31-12-2023	To Profit & Loss A/c (Bal. Fig.)	—	896	—	30-6-2023	By Bank A/c (Interest)	—	500	—
					15-12-2023	By Bank A/c (3)	10,000	229	9,300
					31-12-2023	By Bank A/c (Interest)	—	250	—
					31-12-2023	By Profit & Loss A/c (Bal. Fig.)	—	—	217
					31-12-2023	By Balance c/d (4)	10,000	—	9,200
		30,000	1,146	28,250			30,000	1,146	28,250

Working Notes :

(1) Purchase of 5% Stock (cum-interest) on 1-3-2023

	₹
Nominal Value	30,000
Total Amount Paid $\left(300 \times ₹\ 95 \text{ or } ₹\ 30{,}000 \times \frac{95}{100}\right)$	28,500
Less : Accrued Interest for 2 months (₹ 30,000 × 5/100 × 2/12)	250
	28,250

(2) Sale of Stock (cum-interest) on 1-5-2023

	₹
Nominal Value	10,000
Sales Proceeds $\left(₹\ 10{,}000 \times \frac{97}{100}\right)$	9,700
Less : Accrued Interest for 4 months (₹ 10,000 × 5/100 × 4/12)	167
	9,533

(3) Sale of Stock (ex-interest) on 15-12-2023

	₹
Nominal Value	10,000
Sale Proceeds $\left(100 \times ₹\ 93 \text{ or } ₹\ 10{,}000 \times \frac{93}{100}\right)$	9,300
Accrued Interest for $5^1/_2$ months (₹ 10,000 × 5/100 × 11/24)	229

(4) Cost of Stock on 31-12-2023

	₹
(*i*) Cost Price (28,250/30,000 × ₹ 10,000)	9,417
(*ii*) Market Price $\left(100 \times ₹\ 92 \text{ or } ₹\ 10{,}000 \times \frac{92}{100}\right)$	9,200
Value of Stock will be ₹ 9,200 (being lower than cost price)	

SOLUTION (*ILLUSTRATION 10*)

In the Books of Naresh
INVESTMENT ACCOUNT
(12% Govt. Security - Tax Free)

Date	Particulars	Nominal	Interest	Principal	Date	Particulars	Nominal	Interest	Principal
2023		₹	₹	₹	2023		₹	₹	₹
Jan. 1	To Balance b/d	3,00,000	9,000	2,82,500	April 3	By Bank (Interest on ₹ 3,00,000 for 6 months @ 12% p.a.)		18,000	
June 1	To Bank (Purchased at $96\frac{1}{2}$% cum-interest + Brokerage $\frac{1}{2}$ % on 2,00,000)	2,00,000	4,000	1,90,000	July 31	By Bank (Sale at $94\frac{1}{2}$ % – Brokerage $\frac{1}{2}$ %)	2,50,000	10,000	2,35,000
Dec. 31	To Profit & Loss A/c (Interest Transferred)		(2) 36,500		Oct. 4	By Bank (Int. on ₹ 2,50,000 for 6 months @ 12% p.a.)		15,000	
					Dec. 1	By Bank—Sale at 96% cum-interest	1,00,000	2,000	94,000
					" 31	By Profit & Loss A/c (Bal. Figure: Loss on Sale)			2,500
					" 31	By Balance c/d	1,50,000	4,500	(1) 1,41,000
		5,00,000	49,500	4,72,500			5,00,000	49,500	4,72,500

Notes : (1) Stock of investment on 31-12-2023 having nominal value of ₹ 1,50,000 has been valued at 94% at market value being lower than cost of 95% purchased on June 1.

(2) Loss on Sale of investment during the year is ₹ 2,500 which is the balancing figure of Investment A/c

SOLUTION (*ILLUSTRATION 11*)

IN THE BOOKS OF BONANZAA LTD.

9%GOVERNMENT LOAN (2024) ACCOUNT

(Interest payable on 30th June and 31st December)

Dr. Cr.

Date	Particulars	Nominal Value	Income	Capital	Date	Particulars	Nominal Value	Income	Capital
		₹	₹	₹			₹	₹	₹
2022					2022				
April 1	To Balance b/d (1)	2,00,000	4,500	1,90,000	June 1	By Bank A/c	60,000	2,250	56,400
May 31	" Bank A/c	80,000	3,000	73,000	" 30	" Bank A/c (Interest for 6 months)	—	9,900	—
Dec. 1	" Bank A/c	10,000	375	10,000	Nov. 30	" Bank A/c	40,000	1,500	37,300
					Dec. 31	" Bank A/c (Interest for 6 months)	—	8,550	—
2023					2023				
March 31	" Profit & Loss A/c	—	18,525		March 1	" Bank A/c	10,000	150	9,500
					" 31	" Profit & Loss A/c (Loss on sale) (2)	—	—	1,300
					" "	" Balance c/d (3)	1,80,000	4,050	1,68,500
		2,90,000	26,400	2,73,000			2,90,000	26,400	2,73,000

Working Notes :

(1) ***Interest accrued on balance of Govt. Loan as on 1-4-2022*** :

Interest on ₹ 2,00,000 @ 9% for 3 months = ₹ 2,00,000 × 9/100 × 1/4 = ₹ 4,500.

(2) ***Loss on sale of 9% Govt. Loan:*** Since FIFO basis is to be followed, the sales have been made out of the balance of 9% Govt. Loan in hand as on 1-4-2022.

(A) Cost of ₹ 1,10,000 9% Govt. Loan sold during 2022-23
= ₹ 1,90,000 × 1,10,000/2,00,000 = ₹ 1,04,500

(B) Sale proceeds of ₹ 1,10,000 9% Govt. Loan = ₹ 1,03,200
Loss on sale of 9% Govt. Loan (A-B) ₹ 1,300

(3) ***Cost of closing balance of 9% Govt. Loan on FIFO basis*** : The face value of balance of 9% Govt. Loan as on 31-3-2023 is ₹ 1,80,000. The cost of 9% Govt. Loan as on 31-3-2023 is arrived at as per FIFO basis as below :

	Nominal Value	***Actual Cost***
	₹	₹
Balance out of opening stock of 9% Govt. Loan	90,000	85,500
Balance out of May, 2022 purchase	80,000	73,000
Balance out of December, 2022 purchase	10,000	10,000
	1,80,000	1,68,500

Average cost of 9% Govt. Loan per unit = ₹ 1,68,500/1,800 = ₹ 93.61
Market price of 9% Govt. Loan per unit = ₹ 96.00

Average cost being lower, the closing balance of 9% Govt. Loan is valued at average cost.

Interest accrued on ₹ 1,80,000 @ 9% for 3 months = ₹ 1,80,000 × 9/100 × 1/4 = ₹ 4,050.

ILLUSTRATION 12. Unique Investment Corporation has done the following transactions in 6% State Government Stock between 1st September 2021 and 1st July 2023 and all these transactions are Cum-interest excepting those marked Ex-interest. Interest is payable half-yearly on 1st February and 1st August. The accounting period ends on 30th June every year.

1st September 2021	**—Purchased ₹ 10,000 stock @ 101.50.**
1st October 2021	**—Purchased ₹ 25,000 stock @ 101.**
1st November 2021	**—Sold ₹ 15,000 stock @ 103.25.**
1st November 2021	**—Purchased ₹ 5,000 stock @ 103.**
15th January 2022	**—Sold ₹ 10,000 stock @ 105.25 Ex-Interest.**
1st March 2022	**—Sold ₹ 4,000 stock @ 102.50.**
15th July 2022	**—Purchased ₹ 5,000 stock @ 101.25 Ex-Interest.**
1st November 2022	**—Purchased ₹ 5,000 stock @ 102.**
15th January 2023	**—Sold ₹ 15,000 stock @103.**
1st July 2023	**—Purchased ₹ 2,000 stock @ 102.**

Write up Investment Account in the books of the Corporation, showing the profits and losses on the transactions using the *average cost method* and also showing the amount of interest for each accounting period duly realised.

SOLUTION

6% STATE GOVERNMENT STOCK
(Interest payable half-yearly on 1st February & 1st August)

Date	Particulars	Nominal	Income	Capital	Date	Particulars	Nominal	Income	Capital
2021		₹	₹	₹	2021		₹	₹	₹
Sept. 1	To Cash A/c : Purchase at ₹ 101.50	10,000	50	10,100	Nov. 1	By Cash A/c : Sale at ₹ 103.25	15,000	225	15,262.50
Oct. 1	" Cash A/c : Purchase at ₹ 101	25,000	250	25,000	2022 Jan. 15	" Cash A/c : Sale at ₹ 105.25 ex-interest	10,000	275	10,525.00
Nov. 1	" Cash A/c : Purchase at ₹ 103	5,000	75	5,075	Feb. 1	" Interest on ₹ 15,000 at 6% p.a. for half year		450	
2022 June 30	" Profit & Loss A/c : Profit on transaction			750.50	Mar. 1	" Cash A/c : Sale at ₹ 102.50	4,000	20	4,080.00
	Interest for the period		870		June 30	" Balance c/d Stock at average cost	11,000		11,058.00
						Accruing interest thereon (for 5 months		275	
		40,000	1,245	40,925.50			40,000	1,245	40,925.50
2022 July 1	To Balance b/d	11,000	275	11,058	2022 Aug. 1	" Interest on ₹ 16,000 at 6% p.a. for half year		480.00	
July 15	" Cash A/c : Purchase at 101.25 ex-interest	5,000	137.50	5,062.50	2023 Jan. 15	" Cash A/c : Sale at ₹ 103	15,000	412.50	15,037.50
Nov. 1	" Cash A/c: Purchase at ₹ 102	5,000	75	5,025.00	Feb. 1	" Bank (Interest on ₹ 6,000 for $\frac{1}{2}$ year)		180.00	
2023 June 30	" Profit & Loss A/c				June 30	" Profit & Loss A/c (Loss on transaction)			66.00
	Interest for the period		735		June 30	By Balance c/d Stock at average cost	6,000		6,042.00
						Accruing interest for 5 months		150	
		21,000	1,222.50	21,145.50			21,000	1,222.50	21,145.50
July 1	" Balance b/d	6,000	150	6,042					
" 1	" Cash A/c : Purchase at ₹ 102.	2,000	50	1,990					

SCHEDULE OF PROFIT OR LOSS ON SALES
(*Average cost method*)

		Nominal	Cost	Realised	Profit	Loss
2021		₹	₹	₹	₹	₹
Sept. 1	Purchase	10,000	10,100			
Oct. 1	Purchase	25,000	25,000			
		35,000	35,100			
Nov. 1	Sale	15,000	15,043[1]	15,262.50	219.50	
		20,000	20,057			
Nov. 1	Purchase	5,000	5,075			
		25,000	25,132			
2022						
Jan. 15	Sale	10,000	10,053[2]	10,525	472.00	
		15,000	15,079			
Mar. 1	Sale	4,000	4,021[3]	4,080	59.00	
		11,000	11,058		750.50	
July 15	Purchase	5,000	5,063			
		16,000	16,121			
Nov. 1	Purchase	5,000	5,025			
		21,000	21,146			
2023						
Jan. 15	Sale	15,000	15,104[4]	15,037.50		66.50
		6,000	6,042			

Notes. 1. $\frac{15}{35}$ × ₹ 35,100 = ₹ 15,043 (approx) ; 2. $\frac{10}{25}$ × ₹ 25,132 = ₹ 10,053 (approx) ;

3. $\frac{4}{15}$ × ₹ 15,079 = ₹ 4,021 (approx) ; 4. $\frac{15}{21}$ × ₹ 21,146 = ₹ 15,104 (approx) ;

Equity Shares Accounts

Equity shares are known as variable income bearing securities because income on investment in shares depends on the rate of dividend declared by a company. Following are the *peculiar features* in case the investment accounts are prepared regarding equity shares :

(*i*) Purchase of Equity Shares. If shares are purchased with the intention to hold for short-term period, then these will be shown at the realisable value. However, if equity shares are acquired with an intention to hold for long-term then these will be shown at cost in the Balance Sheet of the Company. However, provision for diminution shall be made to recognise a decline, if other than temporary, in the value of shares. Investment in shares, gold and silver acquired for long-term period should be shown at cost though their realisable value have been increased.

ILLUSTRATION 13. M/s Innovative Garments Manufacturing Company Limited invested in the shares of another company on 1st October, 2022 at a cost of ₹ 2,50,000. It also earlier purchased Gold of ₹ 4,00,000 and Silver of ₹ 2,00,000 on 1st March, 2021. Market value as on 31st March, 2023 of above investments are as follows :

Shares ₹ 2,25,000; Gold ₹ 6,00,000; Silver ₹ 3,50,000.

How above investments will be shown in the books of accounts of M/s Innovative Garments Manufacturing Company Limited for the year ending 31st March, 2023.

SOLUTION

If shares are purchased with an intention to hold for short-term period, then these will be shown at the realisable value of ₹ 2,25,000 as on 31st March, 2023.

However, if *equity shares are acquired with an intention to hold for long-term period, then these will be shown at cost* of ₹ 2,50,000 in the Balance Sheet of the company. However, provision for diminution shall be made to recognise a decline, if other than temporary, in the value of shares.

Investment acquired for long-term period shall be shown at cost. Gold and silver are generally purchased with an intention to hold it for long-term period until and unless given otherwise. Hence, the investment in Gold and Silver (purchased on 1st March, 2021) shall continue to be shown at cost as on 31st Mach, 2023 *i.e.*, ₹ 4,00,000 and ₹ 200,000 respectively, though their realizable values have been increased.

***(ii)* Bonus Shares.** When successful companies issue bonus shares to capitalise their reserves, the shareholders are not required to pay any amount for such shares. The number of shares will be entered in the number column and nothing will be added in the amount of principal or capital column. When bonus shares are sold, the profit on such shares is calculated by deducting average cost of shares sold from sale price of bonus shares. Valuation of investment in shares should be made at market value or average cost price of shares, whichever is lower.

ILLUSTRATION 14. On 1-4-2022, Mr. T. Shekharan purchased 5,000 equity shares of ₹ 100 each in V Ltd. @ ₹ 120 each from a broker, who charged 2% brokerage. He incurred 50 paise per ₹ 100 as cost of shares transfer stamps. On 31-1-2023 bonus was declared in the ratio of 1 : 2. Before and after the record date of bonus shares, the shares are quoted at ₹ 175 per share and ₹ 90 per share respectively. On 31-3-2023, Mr. T. Shekharan sold bonus shares to a broker, who charged 2% brokerage.

Show the Investment Account in the books of T. Shekharan, who held the shares as Current Asset and closing value of investments shall be made at cost or market value, whichever is lower.

SOLUTION

In the Books of T. Shekharan

INVESTMENT ACCOUNT IN EQUITY SHARES OF V LTD.

for the year ended 31st March, 2023

Date	*Particulars*	*Nominal Value* (₹	*Cost* (₹)	*Date*	*Particulars*	*Nominal Value* (₹)	*Cost* (₹)
1-4-22	To Bank A/c (1)	5,00,000	6,15,000	31-3-23	By Bank A/c	2,50,000	2,20,500
31-3-23	To Bonus Shares	2,50,000	—	31-3-23	By Balance c/d	5,00,000	(4) 4,10,000
31-3-23	To Profit & Loss A/c		(3) 15,500				
		7,50,000	6,30,500			7,50,000	6,30,500

Working Notes :

(1) *Cost of equity shares purchased on 1st April, 2022*
= Cost + Brokerage + Cost of transfer stamps
= 5,000 × ₹ 120 + 2% of ₹ 6,00,000 + 1/2% of ₹ 6,00,000 = ₹ 6,15,000

(2) *Sale proceeds of equity shares sold on 31st March, 2023*

= Sale Price – Brokerage

= 2,500 × ₹ 90 – 2% of ₹ 2,25,000 = ₹ 2,20,500

(3) *Profit on sale of bonus shares on 31st March, 2023*

= Sales Proceeds – Average Cost

Sales Proceeds = ₹ 2,20,500

Average Cost = ₹ [6,15,000 × 2,50,000/7,50,000]

= ₹ 2,05,000

Profit = ₹ 2,20,500 – ₹ 2,05,000 = ₹ 15,500.

(4) *Valuation of equity shares on 31st March, 2023*

Cost = ₹ [6,15,000 × 5,00,000/7,50,000] = ₹ 4,10,000 *i.e.* ₹ 82 per share

Market Value = 5,000 shares × ₹ 90 = ₹ 4,50,000

Closing stock of equity shares has been valued at ₹ 4,10,000 *i.e.* cost being lower than the market value.

***(iii)* Rights Shares.** If shares are first offered to the existing shareholders as a matter of their right, such shares are called right shares. Such shares may be purchased by the shareholder or the right may be renunciated in favour of a third party for a consideration. *If the shares are purchased,* the number of shares and amount paid will be entered in the number and principal columns respectively. *If the rights are not subscribed* for but are sold in the market, the amount received will be entered only in the Profit & Loss Account.

When right shares offered are subscribed for, the cost of the right shares is added to the carrying amount of the original holding. If rights are not subscribed for but are sold in the market, the sale proceeds are taken to the profit and loss statement. However, where the investments are acquired on cum-right basis and the market value of investments immediately after their becoming ex-right is lower than the cost for which they were acquired, it may be appropriate to apply the sale proceeds of rights to reduce the carrying amount of such investments to the market value.

(iv) If shares are purchased as cum-dividend, it is not possible to calculate the amount of dividend until it is declared. Then the total price paid is entered in the principal column and as and when dividend is received, it is entered in the capital column on the credit side.

These points will become clear from the following Illustrations :

ILLUSTRATION 15. Tandon carried out the following transactions in the shares of Bright Ltd. :

(*a*) On 1st April, 2022 he *purchased* 20,000 equity shares of ₹ 1 each fully paid for ₹ 30,000 on cum-right basis.

(*b*) On 15th May, 2022, Tandon *sold* 4,000 shares for ₹ 7,600.

(*c*) At a meeting on 15th June 2022, the company decided :

(*i*) to make a *bonus* issue of one fully paid share for every four shares held on 1st June 2022, and

(*ii*) to give its members the *right* to apply for one share for every five shares held on 1st June, 2022 at a price of ₹ 1.50 per share of which 75 paise is payable on or before 15th July, 2022, and the balance, 75 paise per share, on or before 15th September, 2022.

The shares issued under (*i*) and (*ii*) were not to rank for dividend for the year ending 31st March, 2022.

(*d*) Tandon received his bonus shares and took up 2,000 shares under the rights issue, paying the sums thereon when due and selling the rights to the remaining shares at 40 paise per share ; the proceeds were received on 30th September, 2022.

(*e*) On 15th March, 2023, he received a dividend from Bright Ltd. of 15 per cent in respect of the year ended 31st March, 2022.

(*f*) On 30th March, he received ₹ 14,000 for the *sale* of 10,000 shares.

You are required to record these transactions in Investment Account in Tandon's books for the year ended 31st March 2023, transferring any profits or losses on these transactions. Apply *Average basis*. Expenses and tax to be ignored.

(*For Solution see page II/1·25*)

ILLUSTRATION 16. **On 1-4-2023 Sundar had 25,000 equity shares of 'X' Ltd. at a book value of ₹ 15 per share (face value ₹ 10). On 20-6-2023, he purchased another 5,000 shares of the company at ₹ 16 per share. The directors of 'X' Ltd. announced a *bonus and rights* issue. No dividend was payable on these issues. The terms of the issue are as follows :**

Bonus basis 1 : 6 (Date 16-8-2023). Rights basis 3 : 7 (Date 31-8-2023) Price ₹ 15 per share. Due date for payment 30-9-2023.

Shareholders can transfer their rights in full or in part. Accordingly Sundar sold $33\frac{1}{3}\%$ of his entitlement to Sekhar for a consideration of ₹ 2 per share.

Dividends for the year ended 31-3-2023 at the rate of 20% were declared by X Ltd. and received by Sundar on 31-10-2023. Dividends for shares acquired by him on 20-6-2023 are to be adjusted against the cost of purchase.

On 15-11-2023, Sundar *sold* 25,000 equity shares at a premium of ₹ 5 per share.

You are required to prepare in the books of Sundar :

(1) Investment Account (2) Profit & Loss Account.

For your exercise, assume that the books are closed on 31-12-2023 and shares are valued at *average cost*.

(*For Solution of Investment A/c and P. & L. A/c see page II/1·26*)

SOLUTION (*ILLUSTRATION 15*)

IN THE BOOKS OF MR. TANDON
INVESTMENT ACCOUNT (SHARES IN BRIGHT LIMITED)

Dr. Cr.

Date	Particulars	No.	Income	Principal Amount	Date	Particulars	No.	Income	Principal Amount
			₹	₹				₹	₹
2022 April 1	To Bank A/c (Purchase)	20,000	—	30,000	2022 May 15	By Bank A/c (Sale)	4,000	—	7,600
May 15	" Profit & Loss A/c (1)	—	—	1,600	Sept. 30	" Bank A/c (Sale of Right) (1,200 @ 40 paise)	—	—	480
June 15	" Bonus Issue	4,000	—	—	2023 Mar. 15	" Bank A/c (Dividend) (15% on ₹ 16,000)		2,400	—
July 15	" Bank A/c @ 75 p. paid on 2,000 shares)	2,000	—	1,500	" 30	" Bank A/c (Sale)	10,000	—	14,000
Sept. 15	" Bank A/c @ 75 p. paid on 2,000 shares)	—	—	1,500	" 31	" Balance c/d $\left(\frac{12,000}{22,000} \times 26,520\right)$	12,000	—	14,465
2023 Mar. 30	" Profit & Loss A/c (2)	—	—	1,945					
" 31	" Profit & Loss A/c (transferred)	—	2,400	—					
		26,000	2,400	36,545			26,000	2,400	36,545

Working Notes :

(1) Sale on 15-5-2022 :

Cost of 4,000 shares @ ₹ 1.50	₹ 6,000	
Sale Price	₹ 7,600	
Profit		₹ 1,600

(2) Cost of 10,000 shares sold :

Cost of 22,000 shares (₹ 24,000 + ₹ 3,000)	₹ 27,000	
Less : Amount received from rights	₹ 480	
Cost of 22,000 shares		₹ 26,520
∴ Cost of 10,000 shares $\left(\frac{₹\ 26,520}{22,000} \times 10,000\right)$		₹ 12,055
Profit on 10,000 shares (₹ 14,000 – ₹ 12,055)		₹ 1,945

SOLUTION (*ILLUSTRATION 16*)

INVESTMENT ACCOUNT
(*Equity Shares in 'X' Ltd.*)

Date	Particulars	No.	Nominal Value	Amount	Date	Particulars	No.	Nominal Value	Amount
			₹	₹				₹	₹
1-4-2023	To Balance b/d	25,000	2,50,000	3,75,000	30-9-2023	By Bank (Sale of Rights)			10,000
20-6-2023	To Bank	5,000	50,000	80,000	31-10-2023	By Bank (20% dividend			
16-8-2023	To Bonus Issue (1)	5,000	50,000			on 5,000 shares			
30-9-2023	To Bank	10,000	1,00,000	1,50,000		acquired on 20-6-2023)			10,000
	(Rights shares)				15-11-2023	By Bank (Sale of shares)	25,000	2,50,000	3,75,000
15-11-2023	To Profit & Loss A/c (4)			50,000	31-12-2023	By Balance c/d (3)	20,000	2,00,000	2,60,000
		45,000	4,50,000	6,55,000			45,000	4,50,000	6,55,000
1-1-2021	To Balance b/d	20,000	2,00,000	2,60,000					

PROFIT AND LOSS ACCOUNT
for the year ending 31st December, 2023

	₹		₹
		By Investment A/c	50,000
		By Dividend (on 25,000 shares of ₹ 10 each @ 20%)	50,000

Working Notes :

(1) Number of Bonus Shares $= \frac{25,000 + 5,000}{6} = 5,000$

(2) Entitlement of Rights Shares $= \frac{25,000 + 5,000 + 5,000}{7} \times 3 = 15,000$ shares

(3) Cost of 20,000 shares on 31-12-2023 on average cost basis :

$$\frac{₹3,75,000 + ₹80,000 + ₹1,50,000 - ₹10,000 - ₹10,000}{25,000 + 5,000 + 5,000 + 10,000 \text{ shares}} \times 20,000 \text{ shares}$$

$$= \frac{₹\ 5,85,000}{45,000 \text{ shares}} \times 20,000 \text{ shares} = ₹\ 13 \times 20,000 = ₹\ 2,60,000$$

(4) Profit on sale of 25,000 shares @ ₹ 2 = ₹ 50,000

ILLUSTRATION 17. Following transactions of Investor Ltd. took place during the year ended 31st March, 2023 :

2022	
1st April	**Purchased ₹ 12,00,000 8% bonds at ₹ 80·5 cum-interest. Interest is payable on 1st November and 1st May.**
12th April	**Purchased 1,00,000 equity shares of ₹ 10 each in X Ltd. for ₹ 40,00,000.**
1st May	**Received half year's interest on 8% bonds**
15th May	**X Ltd. made a *bonus* issue of three equity shares for every two held. Investor Ltd. *sold* 1,25,000 bonus shares for ₹ 20 each.**
1st July	***Purchased* 50,000 equity shares of ₹ 10 each in C Ltd. at ₹ 7·75 each**
1st October	***Sold* ₹ 3,00,000 8% bonds at ₹ 81 ex-interest.**
1st November	**Received half year's interest on 8% bonds.**
1st December	**Received 18% dividend on all equity shares in X Ltd.**
2023	
1st January	**C Ltd. made a *rights* issue of one equity share for every two held at ₹ 5 per share. Rights sold in the market at ₹ 2·25 per share.**
1st March	**Received 12·5% dividend on all equity shares in C Ltd.**

Prepare relevant Investment Accounts in the books of investor Ltd. for the year ended 31st March, 2023.

(For Solution see pages II/1·28 & II/1·29)

ILLUSTRATION 18. On 1-4-2022, Mr. Krishna Murty purchased 1,000 equity shares of ₹ 100 each in TELCO Ltd. @ ₹ 120 each from a Broker, who charged 2% brokerage. He incurred 50 paise per ₹ 100 as cost of shares transfer stamps. On 31-1-2023 Bonus was declared in the ratio of 1 : 2. Before and after the record date of bonus shares, the shares were quoted at ₹ 175 per share and ₹ 90 per share respectively. On 31-3-2023 Mr. Krishna Murty sold bonus shares to a Broker, who charged 2% brokerage.

Show the Investment Account in the books of Mr. Krishna Murty, who held the shares as current asset and closing value of investments shall be made at Cost or Market value, whichever is lower.

(For Solution see page II/1·30)

SOLUTION (*ILLUSTRATION 17*)

In the Books of Investor Ltd.
8% BONDS ACCOUNT
(Interest payable half-yearly on 1st May & 1st November)

Date	Particulars	Nominal	Interest	Principal Amount	Date	Particulars	Nominal	Interest	Principal Amount
2022		₹	₹	₹	2022		₹	₹	₹
April 1	To Bank	12,00,000	40,000	9,26,000	May 1	By Bank (Int.)		48,000	
2023					Oct. 1	By Bank	3,00,000	10,000	2,43,000
Mar. 31	To Profit & Loss A/c (Int. Income)		84,000		Nov. 1	By Bank (Interest)		36,000	
					2023				
" 31	To Profit & Loss A/c (Profit on Sale)			(1) 11,500	Mar. 31	By Balance c/d	9,00,000	30,000	6,94,500
		12,00,000	1,24,000	9,37,500			12,00,000	1,24,000	9,37,500

EQUITY SHARES IN X LTD.

Date	Particulars	Nominal	Income	Amount	Date	Particulars	Nominal	Income	Amount
2022		₹	₹	₹	2022		₹	₹	₹
April 12	To Bank A/c	10,00,000		40,00,000	May 15	By Bank A/c	12,50,000		25,00,000
May 15	To Bonus Issue	15,00,000			Dec. 1	By Bank (Dividend) A/c		2,25,000	
2023					2023				
Mar. 31	To Profit & Loss A/c (Dividend Transferred)		2,25,000		Mar. 31	By Balance c/d	12,50,000		20,00,000
Mar. 31	To Profit & Loss A/c (Profit on Sale)			5,00,000					
		25,00,000	2,25,000	45,00,000			25,00,000	2,25,000	45,00,000

EQUITY SHARES IN C LTD.

Date	Particulars	Nominal	Income	Amount	Date	Particulars	Nomical	Income	Amount
2022		₹	₹	₹	2023		₹	₹	₹
July 1	To Bank A/c	5,00,000		3,87,500	Jan. 1	By Bank A/c (Sale of Right 25,000 Shares @ ₹ 2·25 per Share)			56,250
2023 Mar. 31	To Profit & Loss A/c (Transfer of Dividend Income)		62,500		Mar. 1	By Bank A/c (Dividend @ 12·5% on ₹ 5,00,000)		62,500	
					Mar. 31	By Balance c/d	5,00,000		3,31,250
		5,00,000	62,500	3,87,500			5,00,000	62,500	3,87,500

Working Note :

(1) ***Profit on Sale of Bonds***

	₹
Amount realised on sale of ₹ 3,00,000 bonds	2,43,000
Less: Purchase Price : $\frac{₹\ 9,26,000}{₹\ 12,00,000} \times ₹\ 3,00,000$	2,31,500
Profit on Sale of Bonds	11,500

SOLUTION (ILLUSTRATION 18)

Some Basic Calculations

(1) *Cost of equity shares purchased on 1-4-2022*

	₹
Purchase price of 1,000 shares @ ₹ 120	1,20,000
Add : Brokerage @ 2% on ₹ 1,20,000	2,400
Cost of share transfer stamps @ 50 paise per ₹ 100 *i.e.* $\frac{1}{2}$% of ₹ 1,20,000 purchase price $\left(₹\,1{,}20{,}000 \times \frac{1}{2 \times 100}\right)$	600
	1,23,000

(2) No. of bonus shares received @ 1 share for every two shares held = $\frac{1}{2}$ × 1,000 shares = 500

(3) Sale proceeds of 500 shares sold on 31-3-2023

	₹
500 shares @ ₹ 90	45,000
Less : Brokerage @ 2%	900
	44,100

INVESTMENT ACCOUNT

(Equity Shares in TELCO Ltd.)

Date	*Particulars*	*Nominal Value*	*Amount*	*Date*	*Particulars*	*Nominal Value*	*Amount*
2022		₹	₹	2023		₹	₹
April 1	To Bank	1,00,000	1,23,000	March 31	By Bank	50,000	44,100
2023				March 31	By Balance c/d	1,00,000	(2) 82,000
Jan. 31	To Bonus Shares (500 × ₹ 100)	50,000					
March 31	To Profit & Loss A/c (1)		3,100				
		1,50,000	1,26,100			1,50,000	1,26,100
April 1	To Balance b/d	1,00,000	82,000				

Working Notes

(1) ***Calculation of Profit on Sale of Bonus Shares on 31-3-2023***

	₹
Sales proceeds of 500 shares	44,100
Less : Average Cost of 500 shares $\left(₹\,1{,}23{,}000 \times \frac{500}{1{,}500}\right)$	41,000
Profit on sale of 500 shares	3,100

(2) ***Calculation of Value of Equity Shares on 31-3-2023***

	₹
Cost of ₹ 1,50,000 nominal value (including bonus shares) shares	1,23,000
∴ Cost of ₹ 1,00,000 nominal value of shares $\left(₹\,1{,}23{,}000 \times \frac{₹\,1{,}00{,}000}{₹\,1{,}50{,}000}\right)$	82,000

Market value of 1,000 shares @ ₹ 90 = 90,000

Closing balance has been valued at ₹ 82,000 cost being lower than market value.

ILLUSTRATION 19. During the year ended 31st March, 2023, Purple Ltd. entered into the following transactions :

1st April, 2022	**Purchased ₹ 4,00,000, 10% Govt. loan (interest payable on 30th April and 31st October) at ₹ 70 cum interest.**
1st April, 2022	**Purchased 6,000 Equity shares of ₹ 5 each in XY Ltd. for ₹ 1,26,000.**
1st October, 2022	**Sold ₹ 80,000, 10% Govt. loan at ₹ 75 ex-interest.**
15th January, 2023	**XY Ltd. made a bonus issue of four equity shares for every three shares held. Purple Ltd. sold all of the bonus shares for ₹ 10 each.**
1st March, 2023	**Received dividend @ 22% on shares in XY Ltd. for the year ended 31st December, 2022.**

Prepare Investment accounts in the books of Purple Ltd.

(For Solution see pages II/1·32)

Working Notes :

1. **Cost of Investment Purchased on 1st April, 2022**

   4,000, 10% Govt. Loan was purchased @ ₹ 70 cum-interest. Total amount paid 4,000 bonds × ₹ 70 = 2,80,000 which includes accrued interest for 5 months, *i.e.*, 1st November, 2022 to 31st March, 2023. Accrued interest will be ₹ 4,00,000 × 10% × 5/12 = ₹ 16,667. Therefore, cost of investment purchased = ₹ 2,80,000 – ₹ 16,667 = ₹ 2,63,333.

2. **Sale of 10% Govt. Loan on 1st October, 2022**

   800, 10% Govt. loan was sold @ ₹ 75 ex-interest, *i.e.*, Total amount received = 800 × 75 + accrued interest for 5 months = ₹ 60,000 + ₹ 3,333.

3. **Cost of 10% Govt. Loan on 31-3-2023**

   Cost of 10% Govt. loan on 31-3-2023 will be $\frac{₹ 2,63,333}{₹ 4,00,000}$ × ₹ 3,20,000 = ₹ 2,10,666.

   Interest accrued on 10% Government Loan on 31-3-2023 = ₹ 3,20,000 × 10% × 5/12 = ₹ 13,333.

4. **Profit on Sale of Bonus Shares**

   Cost per share after bonus issue = ₹ 1,26,000/14,000 = ₹ 9 (average cost method being followed)

   Profit per share sold (₹ 10 – ₹ 9) = ₹ 1.

   Therefore, total profit on sale of 8,000 shares = 8,000 × ₹ 1 = ₹ 8,000.

5. **Profit on Sale of 10% Govt. Loan**

		₹
Sale Price	=	60,000
Cost of ₹ 80,000 10% Government Loan = $\frac{₹ 2,63,333}{₹ 4,00,000}$ × ₹ 80,000	=	52,667
Profit on Sale of 10% Govt. Loan	=	7,333

6. Dividend on equity shares = 6,000 × ₹ 5 × 22% = ₹ 6,600 out of which ₹ 1,650 will be treated as capital receipt as it has been received for the period of 3 months during which shares were not held.

Note: Dividend received is for the period of 12 months ended 31st Dec., 2022, strictly based on the information, given in the question. Hence, dividend received for the period of 3 months (1st January, 2022 to 31st March, 2022 has been treated as pre-acquisition and is, therefore, included in cost column.

SOLUTION (*ILLUSTRATION 19*)

In the Books of Purple Ltd.
10% GOVT. LOAN
(Interest Payable on 30th April and 31st October)

Date	Particulars	Nominal Value (₹)	Interest (₹)	Cost (₹)	Date	Particulars	Nominal Value (₹)	Interest (₹)	Cost (₹)
1-4-22	To Bank A/c (W.N. 1)	4,00,000	16,667	2,63,333	30-4-22	By Bank A/c	—	20,000	—
1-10-22	To Profit & Loss A/c (W.N. 5)			7,333		(4,00,000 × 10% × 6/12)			
31-3-23	To Profit & Loss A/c		35,999		1-10-22	By Bank A/c (W.N. 2)	80,000	3,333	60,000
					31-10-22	By Bank A/c	—	16,000	—
					31-3-23	By Balance c/d (W.N. 3)	3,20,000	13,333	2,10,666
		4,00,000	52,666	2,70,666			4,00,000	52,666	2,70,666

INVESTMENT IN EQUITY SHARES OF ₹ 5 EACH OF XY LTD. ACCOUNT

Date	Particulars	No.	Dividend (₹)	Cost (₹)	Date	Particulars	No.	Dividend (₹)	Cost (₹)
1-4-22	To Bank A/c	6,000		1,26,000	15-1-23	By Bank A/c	8,000		80,000
15-1-23	To Bonus Issue	8,000			1-3-23	By Bank A/c (W.N. 6)		4,950	1,650
15-1-23	To Profit & Loss A/c (W.N. 4)			8,000	31-3-23	By Balance c/d	6,000		52,350
31-3-23	To Profit & Loss A/c		4,950						
		14,000	4,950	1,34,000			14,000	4,950	1,34,000

ILLUSTRATION 20. Raghav Rathore carried out the following transactions in connection with his investments during the year ended 31st March 2023 :

2022

April 15	*Purchased* ₹ 4,00,000 12% convertible debentures in Salora Ltd. at 125.5 Interest is payable on 15 September and 15 March. The debentures are convertible into equity shares of ₹ 10 each at the rate of ₹ 20 for each equity shares.
June 1	*Purchased* ₹ 10,00,000 12% debentures in Sumana Ltd. for ₹ 11,00,000. Interest is due for payment on 1 October and 1 April.
June 15	Converted the debentures in Salora Ltd. into equity shares of ₹ 10 each. On this date, the market price of the shares was ₹ 20. The accrued interest to date was paid.
August 25	Received 20% dividend on the equity shares in Salora Ltd.
December 15	Salora Ltd. made a *rights* issued of one equity share for every 20 shares held at ₹ 16 per share. The market value of shares was ₹ 20.
2023	
January 10	Rathore *sold* the right for ₹ 3 per share.
March 15	*Sold* 4,000 equity shares in Salora Ltd. at ₹ 25 per share.

You are required to record the above transactions in the ledger of Rathore. Maintain separate account for each category of investment. Ignore tax and brokerage charges. Rathore's accounting year ends on 31 March.

(For Solution see pages II/1.34 & II/1·35)

ILLUSTRATION 21. Mr. Brown has made following transactions during the financial year 2022-23 :

Date	*Particulars*
1-5-2022	Purchased 24,000 12% Bonds of ₹ 100 each at ₹ 84 cum-interest. Interest is payable on 30th September and 31st March every year.
15-6-2022	Purchased ₹ 1,50,000 equity shares of ₹ 10 each in Alpha Limited for ₹ 25 each through a broker, who charged brokerage @ 2%.
10-7-2022	Purchased 60,000 equity shares of ₹ 10 each in Beeta Limited for ₹ 44 each through a broker, who charged brokerage @ 2%.
14-10-2022	Alpha Limited made a bonus issue of two shares for every three shares held.
31-10-2022	Sold 80000 shares in Alpha Limited for ₹ 22 each.
1-1-2023	Received 15% interim dividend on equity shares of Alpha Limited.
15-1-2023	Beeta Limited made a right issue of one equity share for every four shares held at ₹ 5 per share. Mr. Brown exercised his option for 40% of his entitlements and sold the balance rights in the market at ₹ 2.25 per share.
1-3-2023	Sold 15,000 12% Bonds at ₹ 90 ex-interest.
15-3-2023	Received 18% interim dividend on equity shares of Beeta Limited. Interest on 12% Bonds was duly received on due dates.

Prepare separate Investment Account for 12% Bonds, Equity Shares of Alpha Limited and Equity Shares of Beeta Limited in the books of Mr. Brown for the year ended on 31st March, 2023.

(For Solution see pages II/1.36)

SOLUTION (*ILLUSTRATION 20*)

In the Books of Raghav Rathore

INVESTMENT IN SALORA LTD. 12% CONVERTIBLE DEBENTURES ACCOUNT

Date	Particulars	Nominal Value	Interest	Principal	Date	Particulars	Nominal Value	Interest	Principal
		₹	₹	₹			₹	₹	₹
2022 April 15	To Bank	4,00,000	4,000	4,98,000	2022 June 15	By Investment in Salora Ltd.'s Equity Shares	4,00,000	12,000	4,98,000
2023 March 31	To Profit & Loss A/c		8,000						
		4,00,000	12,000	4,98,000			4,00,000	12,000	4,98,000

INVESTMENT IN SALORA LTD. EQUITY SHARES ACCOUNT

Date	Particulars	Nominal Value	Dividend	Amount	Date	Particulars	Nominal Value	Dividend	Amount
		₹	₹	₹			₹	₹	₹
2022 June 15	To Investment in Salora Ltd. 12% Convertible Debentures A/c (1)	2,00,000		4,98,000	2022 June 25	By Bank (20% on ₹ 2,00,000)		40,000	
2023 Jan. 15	To Profit & Loss A/c (1)			1,000	2023 June 10	By Bank (Sale of Rights for 1,000 shares @ ₹ 3)			3,000
March 31	To Profit & Loss A/c		40,000		Jan. 15	By Bank (Sale of 4,000 shares @ ₹ 25)	40,000		1,00,000
					March 31	By Balance c/d	1,60,000		3,96,000
		2,00,000	40,000	4,99,000			2,00,000	40,000	4,99,000
April 1	To Balance b/d	1,60,000		3,96,000					

	₹
(1) Purchase price of ₹ 2,00,000 nominal value or 20,000 shares is	4,98,000
Less : Amount realised on sale of right of rights issue	3,000
	4,95,000
∴ Purchase price of ₹ 40,000 nominal value or 4,000 shares $\left(\frac{₹\ 4{,}95{,}000}{20{,}000} \times 4{,}000\right)$	99,000
Profit on sale of 4,000 shares (₹ 1,00,000 Amount Realised—₹ 99,000)	1,000

INVESTMENT IN SUMANA LTD. 12% DEBENTURES ACCOUNT

Date	*Particulars*	*Nominal Value*	*Interest*	*Principal*	*Date*	*Particulars*	*Nominal Value*	*Interest*	*Principal*
		₹	₹	₹			₹	₹	₹
2022 June 1	To Bank	10,00,000	20,000	10,80,000	2022 Oct. 1	To Bank		60,000	
2023 March 31	To Profit & Loss A/c		1,00,000		2023 March 31	By Accrued Interest A/c		60,000	
					"	By Balance c/d	10,00,000		10,80,000
		10,00,000	1,20,000	10,80,000			10,00,000	1,20,000	10,80,000
April 1	To Balance b/d	10,00,000		10,80,000					

Working Note

Calculation of Nominal Value of Shares Acquired

Nominal value of convertible debentures of Salora Ltd. ₹ 4,00,000

For every ₹ 20 value, one share of ₹ 10 is to be given

∴ For ₹ 4,00,000 nominal value of debentures, nominal value of equity shares to be given = $\frac{₹\ 10}{₹\ 20} \times ₹\ 4{,}00{,}000 = ₹\ 2{,}00{,}000$

Number of equity shares acquired is 20,000 (*i.e.* ₹ 2,00,000 ÷ ₹ 10)

SOLUTION (ILLUSTRATION 21)

In the Books of Mr. Brown

12% BONDS

for the year ended 31st March, 2023

Date	Particulars	No.	Interest Income ₹	Amount ₹	Date	Particulars	No.	Interest Income ₹	Amount ₹
2022					2022				
May 1	To Bank A/c	24,000	24,000	19,92,000	Sept. 30	By Bank (Interest)	—	1,44,000	
2023					2023				
March	To P & L A/c (1)	—	—	1,05,000	Mar. 1	By Bank A/c	15,000	75,000	13,50,000
31	To P & L A/c		2,49,000		2023				
					Mar. 31	By Bank (Interest)		54,000	
						By Balance c/d (2)	9,000	—	7,47,000
		24,000	2,73,000	20,97,000			24,000	2,73,000	20,97,000

INVESTMENT IN EQUITY SHARES OF ALPHA LTD.

for the year ended 31st March, 2023

Date	Particulars	No.	Dividend Income ₹	Amount ₹	Date	Particulars	No.	Dividend Income ₹	Amount ₹
2022					2022				
June 15	To Bank A/c	1,50,000	—	38,25,000	Oct. 31	By Bank A/c	80,000	—	17,60,000
Oct. 14	To Bonus Issue	1,00,000	—	—	2023	By Bank A/c			
	(1,50,000/3 × 2)				Jan. 1	—Dividend		2,55,000	
2023						By Balance c/d	1,70,000	—	26,01,000(4)
Mar. 31	To P & L A/c (3)			5,36,000	Mar. 31				
	To P & L A/c		2,55,000						
		2,50,000	2,55,000	43,61,000			2,50,000	2,55,000	43,61,000

INVESTMENT IN EQUITY SHARES OF BEETA LTD.

for the year ended 31st March, 2023

Date	Particulars	No.	Dividend Income ₹	Amount ₹	Date	Particulars	No.	Dividend Income ₹	Amount ₹
2023					2023				
June 10	To Bank A/c	60,000	—	26,92,800	Jan. 15	By Bank A/c (6)	—	—	20,250
2023					Mar. 15	By Bank—Dividend	—	1,18,800	
Jan. 15	To Bank A/c (5)	6,000	—	30,000					
Mar. 31	To P & L A/c	—	1,18,800	—	2023	By Balance c/d			
					Mar. 31	(Bal. fig.)	66,000	—	27,02,550
		66,000	1,18,800	27,22,800			66,000	1,18,800	27,22,800

Working Notes :

(1) Profit on sale of 12% Bonds

Sale Price	₹ 13,50,000
Less : Cost of Bonds Sold = $\frac{19,92,000}{24,000} \times 15,000$	₹ 12,45,000
Profit on Sale	₹ 1,05,000

(2) Closing balance as on 31-3-2023 of 12% Bonds

$\frac{19,92,000}{24,000} \times 9,000 =$ ₹ 7,47,000

(3) Profit on sale of equity shares of Alpha Ltd.

Sales price	₹ 17,60,00
Less : Cost of Bond Sold = $\frac{38,25,000}{2,50,000} \times 80,000$	₹ 12,24,000
Profit on Sale	₹ 5,36,000

(4) Closing balance as on 31-3-2023 of equity shares of Alpha Ltd.

$\frac{38,25,000}{2,50,000} \times 1,70,000 =$ ₹ 26,01,000

(5) Calculation of right shares subscribed by Beeta Ltd.

Right Shares = $\frac{60,000 \text{ shares}}{4} \times 1 = 15,000$ shares

Shares subscribed by Mr. Brown = 15,000 × 40% = 6,000 shares

Value of right shares subscribed = 6,000 shares @ ₹ 5 per share = ₹ 30,000

(6) Calculation of sale of right entitlement by Beeta Ltd.

No. of right shares sold = 15,000 – 6,000 = 9,000 shares

Sale value of right = 9,000 shares × ₹ 2.25 per share = ₹ 20,250

Note : Shares are assumed to be purchased on cum right basis; therefore, amount received from sale of rights is credited to Investment Account.

QUESTIONS

SHORT ANSWER TYPE

1. Discuss the nature and purpose of investment account.
2. What do you mean by Investment Ledger ?
3. Distinguish between Cum-Interest and Ex-Interest.
4. How are investment accounts prepared when there is issue of bonus shares and right shares by the company ?
5. How will you account for sale of rights in the preparation of Investment Accounts ?
6. What is Ex-dividend and cum-dividend quotation ?
7. What is cum-interest-quotation of securities ?
8. On 31st March 2023, Gopal purchased for cash 100 8% ₹ 100 Debentures @ ₹ 106 cum-interest, interest being payable on 30th June and 31st December every year. What is the value of investment to be debited to Investment Account ?

Ans. [₹ 10,400]

9. On 31st March, 2023, Ram purchased through Bank for cash 200 8% ₹ 100 Debentures @ ₹ 104 ex-interest, interest being payable on 30th June and 31st December every year. Bank charges commission of 25 paise per cent on the face value of debentures purchased. What is the value of investment to be debited to Investment Account in the books of Ram ?

Ans. [₹ 20,850]

10. On 1st January 2023, B purchased 20,000 12% Debentures of ₹ 100 each at ₹ 98. Commission on purchase is 1% on face value of debentures. Interest is payable on 30th June and 31st December each year. Prepare Investment Account for the year 2023

Ans. [Balance of Investment A/c at Cost ₹ 19,80,000; Interest credited to Profit and Loss A/c ₹ 2,40,000]

LONG ANSWER TYPE

1. What are the special features of Investment Accounts ? How are stock exchange transactions (sale & purchase of securities) recorded in books ?
2. What do you understand by Investment Account ? How is it prepared ? Explain the terms 'cum-interest' and 'ex-interest' in relation to such account with the help of suitable examples.
3. What benefits an investor gets by preparing an Investment Account ? Is there any difference in preparation of Investment Account for Shares and Debentures ? Explain giving examples.

PRACTICAL PROBLEMS

PURCHASE AND SALE OF SECURITIES

1. Mr. X purchased 1,000, 6% Government Bonds of ₹ 100 each on 31st January, 2023 at ₹ 95 each. Interest is payable on 30th June and 31st December. The price quoted is cum interest. Journalise the transaction.

2. B Ltd. acquires on 31st January ₹ 40,000 6% Government Loan @ 95. On 31st August the company sells ₹ 10,000 of the loan @ 98, Interest on loan is payable at 1st April and 1st October. Books of B Ltd. are closed on 31st December.

   Prepare Loan Account if both the purchases and sales are cum-interest transactions.

Ans. [Profit on Sale on 31st August ₹ 250 ; Balance in Loan A/c ₹ 27,900 ; Interest transferred to P/L A/c ₹ 2,000].

3. On 1-4-2023, Mr. S had 20,000 equity shares in X Ltd. Face value of the shares was ₹ 10 each but their book value was ₹ 16 per share.

   On 1-6-2023, Mr. S purchased 5,000 equity shares more in X Ltd. @ ₹ 14 per share.

   On 1-9-2023, X Ltd. declared 15% dividend for the year 2022-23. Mr. S received the same on 20-9-2023.

   Show Investment Account upto 20-9-2023.

Ans. [Closing Balance ₹ 3,82,500; Dividend (Revenue) ₹ 30,000; Dividend (Capital) ₹ 7,500]

4. In 2021, M/s Wye Ltd. issued 12% fully paid debentures of ₹ 100 each, interest being payable half yearly on 30th September and 31st March of every accounting year.

   On 1st December, 2022, M/s. Bull & Beer purchased 10,000 of these debentures at ₹ 101 cum-interest price, also paying brokerage @ 1% of cum-interest amount of the purchase. On 1st March, 2023 the firm sold all of these debentures at ₹ 106 cum-interest price, again paying brokerage @ 1% of cum-interest amount.

   Prepare Investment Account in the books of M/s. Bull & Bear for the period 1st December, 2022 to 1st March, 2023.

Ans. [Loss on Sale ₹ 700 Interest ₹ 30,000 transferred to Profit & Loss A/c]

5

5. On 1-4-2023, Mr. X had 20,000 equity shares in Y Ltd. Face value of the shares was ₹ 10 each but their book value was ₹ 16 per share.

On 1-6-2023, Mr. X purchased 5,000 equity shares in Y Ltd. more @ ₹ 14 each.

On 30-6-2023, the directors of Y Ltd. announced a bonus issue. Bonus was declared at the rate of one equity share for every five shares held and these shares were received on 2-8-2023.

Show Investment A/c upto 2-8-2023.

Ans. [Closing Balance ₹ 3,90,000 (Nominal Value ₹ 3,00,000)]

6. On 1-1-2023 6% 200 **Debentures** of ₹ 100 each in Y Ltd. were held as investments by X Ltd. at a cost of ₹ 18,200. Interest is payable on 31st December.

On 1-4-2023 ₹ 4,000 of such debentures were purchased by X Ltd. @ ₹ 98 cum-interest and on 1-9-2023 ₹ 6,000 Debentures were sold at ₹ 96 ex-interest. On 1-12-2023 ₹ 8,000 Debentures were sold @ ₹ 99 cum-interest. On 31-12-2023 X Ltd. sold ₹ 10,000 Debentures @ ₹ 95 ex-interest.

Prepare Investment Account for 6% Debentures Y Ltd. in the Books of X Ltd. Ignore Income Tax.

Ans. [Interest transferred to P. & L. A/c ₹ 1,220 ; Profit on All Sales ₹ 680 (*i.e.* ₹ 300 + ₹ 200 + ₹ 180)].

7. Mr. D bought ₹ 12,000 9% **debenture** @ ₹ 84 cum-interest on 1st Feb. On 31st May he disposed half of investment @ ₹ 87 cum-interest. Expenses on purchase etc. amounted to ₹ 100. Brokerage was paid @ 1% of market price. Interest payable on 30th April and 31st October. Books are closed in 30th June, every year. Market price on 30th June ₹ 85.

Prepare Investment A/c for 9% Debentures.

Ans. [Profit on Sale ₹ 118.00; Interest ₹ 405; Balance of Investment ₹ 5,006 (N.V. ₹ 6,000)]

8. Mr. A held on 1st January, 2023, ₹ 1,00,000 of 3.5% **Government Loan** at ₹ 95,000. Three months interest had accrued. On 31st May he purchased a further ₹ 40,000 of the Loan @ ₹ 96 (net) cum-interest. On 31st July, ₹ 30,000 of the Loan was sold at ₹ 94 (net) ex-interest. On 30th November ₹ 20,000 of the Loan was sold at ₹ 96 (net) cum-interest. Interest on the Loan was paid each year on 31st March and 30th September and was collected on 4th April and 5th October. The price of the Loan on 31st December, 2023 was ₹ 96. Draw up Loan Account. Ignore income-tax and paise.

Ans. [Interest transferred to Profit & Loss A/c ₹ 3,822 ; Loss on Sale ₹ 217 *i.e.*, ₹ 300 – ₹ 83].

9. On 1st April, 2022, X, Y and Co. held 9% **debentures** in Banbury Ltd. of the face value of ₹ 10,000 at cost of ₹ 8,000. Market value on that date was ₹ 9,000. Interest is payable on 31st December every year. On 1st December, 2022 debentures of nominal value of ₹ 6,000 were purchased for ₹ 5,000 ex-interest and on 31st December, 2022 debentures of nominal value of ₹ 2,000 were sold cum-interest for ₹ 1,900. On 1st January, 2023 debentures of nominal value of ₹ 6,000 were bought at ₹ 5,800. The market value of the debentures on 31st March, 2023 was at ₹ 90.

Make out Investment Account in the books of X, Y and Co., showing profit or loss on sale of investment. Stocks on 31st March each year are valued at lower of cost (apply FIFO method) and market price.

Ans. [Interest transferred to P. & L. A/c ₹ 1,170 ; Value of Holding ₹ 17,200 ; Profit on Sale ₹ 120].

10. Anik Investments held 600 6% **Debentures** of ₹ 100 each in Tata Ltd on 1-4-2022 at a cost of ₹ 72,000. Interest is payable on 30th June and 31st December every year. On 1st June, 2022, 250 Debentures were purchased cum-interest at ₹ 37,750. On 1st November, 2022, 400 Debentures were sold ex-interest at ₹ 46,250. On 30th November, 2022, 250 Debentures are purchased ex-interest for ₹ 23,250. On 31st December 2022, 350 Debentures are sold cum-interest at ₹ 42,000.

Prepare Investment Account for the year ended 31st March, 2023 valuing closing stock at cost (using FIFO Method) or market price whichever is less. Debenture are quoted at ₹ 140 on 31st March, 2023.

Ans. [Interest transferred to Profit Loss A/c ₹ 3,825; Loss on Sale of Debentures : On 1st November ₹ 1,750 and on 31st December ₹ 5,325; Value of Holding on 31st March, 2023 (Nominal Value ₹ 35,000) ₹ 38,100]

11. On 1st January, 2023, 400 12% **Debentures** of ₹ 100 in A Ltd. were held as investment by B Ltd. at a cost of ₹ 36,800. Interest is payable on 31st December every year.

On 1st May 2023, 50 Debentures were purchased @ ₹ 96 cum-interest and on 1st November 2023, 250 Debentures were sold at ₹ 99 ex-interest. On 1st December 100 Debentures were purchased at ₹ 94 ex-interest. On 31st December 2023, 150 Debentures were sold at ₹ 98 cum-interest.

Prepare Investment Account from the above for the year ending 31st December, 2023, use FIFO Method. Market price of Debentures on 31st December, 2023 is at par.

Ans. [Profit on Sale of Debentures on 1-11-2023 ₹ 1,750; Loss on Sale of Debentures on 31-12-2023 ₹ 900; Interest transferred to Profit and Loss A/c ₹ 4,800; Balance in Investment Account ₹ 14,000 (Dr.)].

12. Mr. Investor furnishes the following details relating to his holding in 6% **Government Bonds** of ₹ 100 each :

Opening balance face value ₹ 60,000 – cost ₹ 59,000

1-3-2023 100 units purchased ex-interest at ₹ 98.

1-7-2023 Sold 200 ex-interest out of the original holding at ₹ 100.

1-10-2023 Purchased 50 units at ₹ 98 cum-interest.

1-11-2023 Sold 200 units ex-interest at ₹ 99 out of the original holdings.

Interest dates are 30th September and 31st March. Mr. Investor closes his books every 31st December. Show Investment Account as it would appear in his books.

Ans. [Interest transferred to P. & L. A/c ₹ 3,375; Value of Holding ₹ 34,367; Profit on 1st Sale ₹ 333 & 2nd Sale ₹ 134].

13. Following information is presented by Mr. Z, relating to his holding in 9% Central **Government Bonds.**

Opening balance (face value) ₹ 1,20,000, Cost ₹ 1,18,000 (Face value of each unit is ₹ 100).

1-3-2023	Purchased 200 units, ex-interest at ₹ 98.
1-7-2023	Sold 500 units, ex-interest out of original holding at ₹ 100.
1-10-2023	Purchased 150 units at ₹ 98, cum interest.
1-11-2023	Sold 300 units, ex-interest at ₹ 99 out of original holdings.

Interest dates are 30th September and 31st March. Mr. Z closes his books every 31st December. Show the investment account as it would appear in his books.

Ans. [Closing Balance ₹ 75,000 (FV) Cost ₹ 73,633; Profit on Sale—July 1, ₹ 833, Nov. 1, ₹ 200; Interest Balance transferred to P&L A/c ₹ 9,938]

14. Jaipur Investment Ltd. holds 1,000 15% **Debentures** of ₹ 100 each in Udaipur Industries Ltd. as on 1st April, 2022, at a cost of ₹ 1,05,000. Interest is payable on 30th June and 31st December each year. On 1st May, 2022, 500 Debentures are purchased-cum-interest at ₹ 53,500. On 1st November, 2022, 600 Debentures are sold ex-interest at ₹ 57,300. On 30th November, 2022, 400 Debentures are purchased ex-interest at ₹ 38,400. On 31st December, 2022, 400 debentures are sold cum-interest for ₹ 55,000.

Prepare Investment Account valuing holding on 31st March, 2023 at cost (applying FIFO method).

Ans. [Interest transferred to P. & L. A/c ₹ 18,625 ; Value of Holding on 31st March ₹ 89,400; Total Profit on Sale of Debentures ₹ 4,300].

15. B. Finance Ltd. held on 1st April, 2022, ₹ 1,00,000 of 12% **units** of *Unit Trust of India* (2024) at ₹ 95,000. Three months' interest had accrued as interest was received half yearly on 30th June and 31st December. All cheques for half yearly interest had been sent by Unit Trust of India in advance and hence bank could credit the Finance Company's Account on the dates of interest themselves.

On 31st August, 2022, the company purchased a further ₹ 40,000 of the Units at ₹ 96 (net) cum-interest. On 31st October, 2022, ₹ 30,000 of the Units were sold at ₹ 94 (net) ex-interest. On 28th February, 2023, ₹ 20,000 of the Units were sold at ₹ 96 (net) cum-interest.

On 31st March, 2023, the marked price of the Unit was ₹ 96. The face value of each unit was ₹ 100. Prepare 12% Units Account for the year ended 31st March, 2023.

Ans. [Loss on Sale of Investment ₹ 500 (net); Closing Balance of Units—Nominal Value ₹ 90,000 at cost ₹ 85,100; Interest Credited to Profit & Loss A/c ₹ 13,100]

16. On July 1, 2022, Madurai Investment Ltd. held ₹ 2,00,000 6% debentures of Chartered Gerald Ltd. which appeared in the books at ₹ 1,93,000. Interest is payable on July 31 and January 31. On October 1, 2022, a further ₹ 1,00,000 debentures in Chartered Gerald Ltd. were bought at ₹ 98 cum-interest and on January 1, 2023, a further ₹ 60,000 debentures were bought at ₹ 97 ex-interest.

On March 31, 2023, ₹ 1,60,000 debentures were sold at ₹ 101 cum-interest and on June 1, 2023, ₹ 1,20,000 debentures were sold at ₹ 102 ex-interest.

Show Investment Account for the period ending on June 30, 2023.

Ans. [Profit on Sale of Debentures on 31-3-2023 ₹ 5,600; Profit on Sale of Debentures on 1-6-2023 ₹ 6,200 ; Interest transferred to Profit & Loss A/c ₹ 15,300 ; Value of Debentures on June 30 (Following FIFO Method) ₹ 77,600 (Nominal Value) ₹ 80,000 ; Accrued Interest for 5 months on ₹ 80,000 Debentures ₹ 2,000]

BONUS SHARES AND RIGHT SHARES

17. On 1st April, 2022, XY Ltd. has 15,000 equity shares of ABC Ltd. at a book value of ₹ 15 per share (face value ₹ 10 per share). On 1st June, 2022, XY Ltd. acquired 5,000 equity shares of ABC Ltd. for ₹ 1,00,000 on cum right basis. ABC Ltd. announced a bonus and right issue.

(1) Bonus was declared, at the rate of one equity share for every five shares held, on 1st July 2022.

(2) Right shares are to be issued to the existing shareholders on 1st September 2022. The company will issue one right share for every 6 shares at 20% premium. No dividend was payable on these shares.

(3) Dividend for the year ended 31-3-2022 was declared by ABC Ltd. @ 20%, which was received by XY Ltd. on 31st October, 2022.

XY Ltd.

(*i*) Took up half the right issue.

(*ii*) Sold the remaining rights for ₹ 8 per share.

(*iii*) Sold half of its share holding on 1st January, 2023 at ₹ 16.50 per share, brokerage being 1%.

You are required to prepare Investment Account of XY Ltd,. for the year ended 31st March, 2023 assuming the shares are being valued at average cost.

Ans. [Profit on Sale of Shares ₹ 50,855 ; Closing value of shares (on average basis) as on 31st March, 2023 ₹ 1,61,500**]**

18. On 1st April 2022, Mr. Neel purchased 5,000 **equity shares** of ₹ 100 each in X Ltd. @ ₹ 120 each from a Broker, who charged 2% brokerage. He incurred $\frac{1}{2}$% as cost of shares transfer stamps. On 31st January, 2023, Bonus was declared in the ratio of 1 : 2. Before and after the record date of bonus shares, the shares were quoted at ₹ 175 per share and ₹ 90 per share respectively. On 31st March, 2023, Mr. Neel sold bonus shares to a broker, who charged 2% brokerage.

Show the Investment Account in the books of Mr. Neel, who held the shares as current assets and closing value of investments shall be made at cost or Market value, whichever is lower.

Ans. [Balance (5,00,000 FV) Cost ₹ 4,10,000; Profit on sale of bonus shares on 31-3-2023 ₹ 15,500; Cost of equity shares purchased on 1-4-2022 ₹ 6,15,000]

19. On 1-5-2023, Mr. Mishra purchased 800 equity shares of 10 each in Fillco Ltd. @ ₹ 50 each from a broker who charged 5%. He incurred 20 paisa per 100 as cost of shares transfer stamps. On 31-10-2023, bonus was declared in the ratio 1 : 4. The shares were quoted at ₹ 110 and ₹ 60 per share before and after the record date of bonus shares respectively. On 30-11-2023, Mr. Mishra sold the bonus shares to a broker who charged 5%. You are required to prepare Investment Account in the books of Mr. Mishra for the year ending 31-12-2023 and closing value of Investment shall be made at cost or market value whichever is lower.

Ans. [Cost of equity shares purchased on 1-5-2023 ₹ 42, 080; Profit on Sale of bonus shares on 30-11-2023 ₹ 2,984 (*i.e.* ₹ 11,400 – ₹ 8,416); Value of equity shares on 31-12-2023 at cost ₹ 33,664]

20. On 1st January, 2023 X Ltd. has 10,000 equity shares of ₹ 10 each in Alpha Ltd. purchased for ₹ 1,25,000, The company unlike investment companies does not make any apportionment of dividends (received or receivable) in between capital and revenue.

On 15th May, 2023, Alpha Ltd. made a *bonus issue* of one fully paid share for every two held. In addition, on the same day right shares were issued at 3 for every 5 held on that date at a premium of ₹ 3, ₹ 7 to be paid on application and balance in one call after a month. These shares are not to rank for dividend for the year ending 30th June, 2023. 2,000 right shares were taken up by X Ltd., balance rights being sold at ₹ 2 each on 25th May, 2023.

On 15th October, 2023, the company declared a dividend of 20% for the year ending 30th June, 2023.

Make out Investment Account in the books of X Ltd. Ignore income tax.

Ans. [Value of Investment on 31st December, 2023 ₹ 1,43,000 (Nominal Value ₹ 1,70,000); Dividend Income ₹ 20,000 transferred to Profit & Loss A/c].

21. On 1st April 2023, Hasan has 20,000 equity shares of Vayu Ltd., at a book value of ₹ 20 per share (face value of ₹ 10 each). He provides the following information :

(*i*) On 10th June 2023, he purchased another 5,000 shares in Vayu Ltd., @ ₹ 15 per share.

(*ii*) On 1st August 2023 Vayu Ltd., issued one bonus share for every five shares held by the shareholders.

(*iii*) On 31st August 2023, the directors of Vayu Ltd. announced a rights issue which entitle the shareholders to subscribe two shares for every six shares held @ of ₹ 15 per share. The shareholders can transfer their rights in full or in part.

Hasan sold 1/4th of his right shares holding to harsh for a consideration of ₹ 3 per share and subscribed the rest of 31st of October 2023.

Prepare Investment A/c in the books of Hasan as on 31st October. 2023.

Ans. [Value of Investments on 31-10-2023 (37,500 shares) ₹ 5,80,000]

Hint. Bonus Shares 5,000 ; Right Shares 10,000 ; Sale of rights ₹ 7,500 ; Rights subscribed ₹ 1,12,500.

Financial Statements of Banking Companies

Banking companies are governed by the Banking Regulation Act, 1949. **Section 5 of the Act defines banking as "the accepting, for the purpose of lending or investment, of deposits of money from the public repayable on demand or otherwise and withdrawable by cheque, draft, order or otherwise".** Therefore, any company which engages itself in the manufacture of goods or carries on any trade and accepts deposits of money from the public for financing its business activities will not be treated as doing business of banking. Section 2 of the Act provides that provisions of Companies Act, 2013 in the absence of special provisions in that regard in Banking Regulation Act, will apply to banks also.

Forms of Business in Which Banking Companies may Engage or Features of a Banking Company

Section 6 of the Act states that in addition to the business of banking, a banking company may engage in any one or more of the following forms of business, namely:

(*i*) the borrowing, raising, or taking up of money;

(*ii*) the lending or advancing of money either upon or without security;

(*iii*) the drawing, making, accepting, discounting, buying, selling, collecting and dealing in bills of exchange, hundies, promissory notes, coupons, drafts, bills of lading, railway receipts, warrants, debentures, certificates, scrips and other instruments, and securities whether transferable or negotiable or not;

(*iv*) the granting and issuing of letters of credit, travellers cheques and circular notes;

(*v*) the buying, selling and dealing in bullion and specie;

(*vi*) the buying and selling of foreign exchange including foreign bank notes;

(*vii*) the acquiring, holding, issuing on commission, underwriting and dealing in stock, funds, shares, debentures, debenture stock, bonds, obligations, securities and investments of all kinds; the purchasing and selling of bonds, scrips, or other forms of securities on behalf of constituents or others;

(*viii*) the receiving of all kinds of bonds, scrips or valuables on deposit or for safe custody or otherwise; the providing of safe deposit vaults;

(*ix*) the collecting and transmitting of money and securities;

(*x*) acting as agents for and Government or local authority or any other person or persons; the carrying on of agency business of any description including the clearing and forwarding of goods, giving of receipts and discharges and otherwise acting as an attorney on behalf of customers;

(*xi*) contracting for public and private loans and negotiating and issuing the same;

(*xii*) the effecting, insuring, guaranteeing, underwriting, participating in managing and carrying out of any issue, public or private, or State, municipal or other loans or of shares, stock, debenture stock of any company, corporation or association and the lending of money for the purpose of any such issue;

(*xiii*) carrying on and transacting every kind of guarantee and indemnity business;

(*xiv*) managing, selling and realising any property which may come into the possession of the company in satisfaction or part satisfaction of any of its claims;

(*xv*) acquiring and holding and generally dealing with any property or any right, title or interest in any such property which may form the security or part of the security for any loans or advances or which may be connected with any such security;

(*xvi*) undertaking and executing trusts;

(*xvii*) undertaking the administration of estates as executor, trustee or otherwise;

(*xviii*) establishing and supporting or aiding in the establishment and support of associations, institutions, funds, trusts and conveniences calculated to benefit employees or ex-employees of the company or the dependents or connections of such persons; granting pensions and allowances and making payments towards insurance; subscribing or to guaranteeing money for charitable or benevolent objects or for any exhibition or for any public-general or useful object;

(*xix*) the acquisition, construction, maintenance and alternation of any building or works necessary or convenient for the purpose of the company;

(*xx*) selling, improving, managing, developing, exchanging, leasing, mortgaging, disposing of or turning into accounts or otherwise dealing with all or any part of the property and rights of the company;

(*xxi*) acquiring and undertaking the whole or any part of the business of any person or company, when such business is of a nature enumerated or described in this sub-section;

(*xxii*) doing all such other things as are incidental or conducive to the promotion or advancement of the business of the company;

(*xxiii*) any other form of business which the Central Government may, by notification in the *Official Gazette,* specify as a form of business in which it is for a banking company to engage.

No banking company shall engage in any form of business other than those referred above. No banking company can directly or indirectly deal in the buying or selling or bartering of goods, except in connection with the realisation of security given to or held by it or engage in any trade or buy or sell or barter goods for others otherwise than in connection with bills of exchange.

Types of Banks

Commercial banks in India are mainly divided into two categories as given below :

1. Scheduled Commercial Banks
2. Scheduled Co-operative Banks

Scheduled commercial banks are again divided into five types and scheduled co-operative banks are divided into two types as given in the following chart :

Scheduled Commercial Banks	Scheduled Co-operative Banks
1. Nationalised Banks such as SBI, PNB, Central Bank of India, etc. 2. Private Sector Banks such as HDFC Bank. 3. Development Banks such as NABARD. 4. Regional Rural Banks or Gramin Banks. 5. Foreign Banks such as CITI Bank.	1. Scheduled State Co-operative Banks such as Punjab State Co-operative Bank. 2. Scheduled U.T. Co-operative Banks such as Chandigarh Co-operative Bank.

A scheduled bank is one that is included in second schedule of the Reserve Bank of India Act, 1934. A scheduled bank must satisfy the following three conditions :

1. **It must have paid-up capital and reserve of an aggregate value of ₹ 5,00,000.**
2. **It must satisfy RBI that any activity of the bank will not be detrimental to the interest of the depositors.**
3. **A sole tradership firm or a partnership firm cannot be a scheduled bank. It must be a company or corporation.**

Reserve Bank of India is the Central Bank of the country. It is a bank of the last resort. When a commercial bank is in trouble, RBI helps it to overcome the trouble. Following are the services provided by RBI to the commercial banks :

1. Making of loans and advances to commercial banks.
2. Purchase and sale of foreign exchange.
3. Purchase and sale and discounting of inland bills of exchange or promissory notes and foreign bills of exchange.
4. Maintenance of accounts of the scheduled banks for services provided to these banks.
5. Remittance of money to different branches of commercial banks through the offices, branches or agencies of RBI free of cost or at nominal rates.

General Information

1. No banking company can carry on business in India unless its subscribed capital is not less than one-half of the authorised capital and its paid up capital is not less than one-half of the subscribed capital. [Section 12 (*i*)].

2. The capital of the banking company shall consist of equity shares only or of equity shares and such preference shares as may have been issued prior to the 1st of July, 1944, [Section 12 (*ii*)]. As per the Finance Act, 2005, banks are allowed to issue preference shares.

3. No banking company shall pay out directly or indirectly by way of commission, brokerage, discount or remuneration in any form in respect of any shares issued by it, any amount exceeding in the aggregate two and one-half per cent of the paid-up value of the said shares. (Section 13).

As per Section 8 of the Banking Regulation Act, 1949, a banking company can neither itself nor on behalf of the others deal in buying or selling or bartering of goods except in connection with the realisation of security given to or held by it.

4. A Banking company cannot create any charge upon its uncalled capital and any such charge shall be void. (Section 14)

5. ***Payment of Dividends.*** **No banking company shall pay any dividend on its shares until all its capital expenses (including preliminary expenses, organisation expenses, share selling commission, brokerage, amounts of losses incurred and any other item of expenditure not represented by tangible assets) have been completely written off. (Section 15).**

However, as per the Act, it is permissible for a banking company to pay dividend on its shares without writing off :

(*i*) The depreciation in the value of its investments in approved securities where such depreciation has not actually been capitalised or otherwise accounted for as a loss.

(*ii*) The depreciation in the value of its investments in shares, debentures or bonds (other than approved securities) where adequate provision for such depreciation has been made to the satisfaction of its auditors ; and

(*iii*) The bad debts where adequate provision for such bad debts has been made to the satisfaction of its auditors.

6. A banking company must have a wholetime chairman appointed for five years at a time. He may become a director of a subsidiary of the banking Company or of a guarantee Company registered under the Companies Act but cannot take up any other appointment. The chairman is appointed by Board of Directors but in the case of nationalised banks, he is appointed by the Central Government. At least 51% of the directors of a banking company must be persons having specialised knowledge and useful to the banking industry. The Reserve Bank of India has the power to order the removal of a director or the Chairman. No banking company incorporated in a state of India shall have as a director any person who is a director of another banking company (Section 16).

However, *w. e. f.* 31st January, 1994 provision has been made for appointment of a whole-time or a part-time chairman for a banking company in place of only whole-time chairman earlier. But where a chairman is appointed on a part-time basis, the management of the whole of the affairs of such a banking company shall be entrusted to a managing director.

7. ***Statutory Reserve.*** **Every banking company incorporated in India shall, before any dividend is declared, transfer a sum equal to 25% of the profit of each year to a Statutory Reserve until the amount of the reserve together with any Securities Premium Account is equal to the paid up capital. Such transfer of profits to Reserve Fund should be continued even after the aggregate amount of Reserve Fund and Securities Premium Account, if any, exceeds its paid up capital. The Central Government may, however, grant an exemption in this regard on the recommendation of the Reserve Bank of India. If a banking company appropriates any sum from the reserve or the securities premium account, it shall, within 21 days from the date of such appropriation report the fact to the Reserve Bank of India explaining the circumstances relating to such appropriation. (Section 17). The Statutory Reserve is shown in the Balance Sheet as a liability under the heading 'Reserves and Surplus'.**

Readers are advised to ensure that 25% of the profit earned during the current year is transferred to Statutory Reserve even if the question is silent on this issue in the examination question.

8. *Cash Reserve and Statutory Liquidity Ratio.* A scheduled bank shall maintain deposit with the Reserve Bank equal to at least 3% of its time and demand liabilities (*i.e.* deposits received for fixed periods as well as of its demand liabilities). A non-scheduled bank has to maintain similar balances either in cash or as deposit with the Reserve Bank. The Reserve Bank of India is empowered to raise this percentage upto 15% (Section 18). Thus, the minimum percentage of cash reserves varies from time to time depending upon the guidelines of the Reserve Bank of India. In addition to above, every bank is required to maintain in India in the form of cash, gold or unencumbered approved securities an amount which is not less than 25% or such other percentage not exceeding 40% (as the RBI may specify from time to time) of the total of its demand and time liabilities in India. It is called statutory liquidity ratio. SLR will be in addition to cash reserve to be maintained by banks. **These ratios have been given statutory recognition to safeguard the interest of depositors and prevent banks from over-extending their resources.**

9. *Demand and Time Liabilities.* Demand liabilities of a bank are those which are payable on demand. These liabilities include current deposits of depositors, demand liabilities portion of saving bank deposits, balances in overdue fixed deposits, cash certificates, outstanding telegraphic transfers, demand drafts, unclaimed deposits, and deposits held as security for advances which are payable on demand. Time liabilities of a bank are those which are not payable on demand but are payable after a certain period. These liabilities include fixed deposits, cumulative and recurring deposits, time liabilities portion of saving bank deposits, margin held against letters of credit, if not payable on demand, staff security deposits etc.

10. *Restriction on Loans and Advances.* **No banking company shall make any loans or advances on the security of its own shares or grant or agree to grant a loan or advance to or on behalf of : (*a*) any of its directors; (*b*) any firm in which any of its directors is interested as partner, manager or guarantor; (*c*) any company of which any of its directors is a director, manager, employee or guarantor or in which he holds substantial interest; or (*d*) any individual in respect of whom any of its directors is a partner or a guarantor. (Section 20).**

11. *Performing and Non-performing Assets.* Loans, advances and discounting and purchasing of bills are the principal assets and the main source of income of a bank. Sometimes some of these assets may become non-performing and may not bring any income to the bank. Keeping in view this banks are required by the Reserve Bank of India to classify their assets into two main categories as given below :

(*a*) Performing assets (or standard assets)

(*b*) Non-performing assets

Performing or Standard Assets. **Assets (such as loans, advances, bills discounted or purchased) in respect of which interest and principal amount due are received regularly on due dates are called performing or standard assets. Such assets do not carry more than the normal risk attached to the business.**

Non-performing Assets. **A non-performing asset (such as a loan, advance etc.) is in respect of which interest and/or instalment of principal due remained overdue for a period of more than 90 days.** Such assets are risky and become a threat to the liquidity and profitability of a bank. Non-performing assets may arise because of defaults on the part of borrowers and bad lending practices followed by the banks to favour their near ones and friends. These assets may also arise because of recession in the market or due to natural calamities. Income from performing assets is recognised on Accrual basis whereas interest income from non-performing assets is recognised on cash basis.

12. Banks in India are under the general supervision of the Reserve Bank of India. The Reserve Bank can order a bank not to accept further deposits. A bank can open a branch only at the permission of the Reserve Bank.

13. ***Limits as to Investments in Shares and Debentures.*** Except in subsidiary companies, no banking company shall hold shares in any other company, whether as pledgee, mortgagee or absolute owner of an amount exceeding 30% of the paid up share capital of that company or 30% of its own paid up share capital and reserves. The Reserve Bank of India has removed the above limit of 30% on investments made by the banks in the equity and debentures issues of all India financial institutions.

14. ***Share Capital.*** To ensure that no banking company commences or carries on business with inadequate capital, section 11 of the Banking Regulation Act, 1949 prescribes the minimum limits of paid up capital and reserves of the banking company which are as follows :

(*a*) For banking companies incorporated outside India :

(*i*) If it has a place of business in Mumbai or Kolkata	₹ 20 lakhs
(*ii*) If the places of business are elsewhere	₹ 15 lakhs

The above sum must be kept deposited with the Reserve Bank of India either in cash or in unencumbered securities.

In addition to the above sum, a further amount equal to 20% of the annual profits in respect of business transacted through its branches in India must be kept deposited with the Reserve Bank of India at the end of each year.

(*b*) For banking companies incorporated in India ;

(*i*) If the places of business are in more than one State and if any place of business is in Mumbai or Kolkata	₹ 10 lakhs
(*ii*) If the places of business are in more than one State and none of the places of business is in Mumbai or Kolkata	₹ 5 lakhs
(*iii*) If the places of business are only in one State and none of the places of business is in Mumbai or Kolkata	₹ 1 lakh for the principal place plus ₹ 10,000 for each additional place of business in the same district and ₹ 25,000 for a place of business outside the district subject to a maximum of ₹ 5 lakhs. But if the place of business is only at one place, the maximum amount required is ₹ 50,000. For a banking company which has commenced business after 15th September 1962, its paid-up capital should be at least ₹ 5 lakhs.

(*iv*) If the places of business are only in one State and if the places of business are also in Mumbai or Kolkata.	₹ 5 lakhs plus ₹ 25,000 for each place of business outside Mumbai and Kolkata subject to a maximum of ₹ 10 lakhs.

A banking company commencing business after the coming in force of the Banking Company (Amendment) Act, 1962, shall have a paid-up capital of not less than ₹ 5 lakhs irrespective of the number of places of its business.

Licensing and General Supervision of Banking Companies

The Reserve Bank of India has the power to exercise general supervision of banks. A bank has to obtain prior permission of the Reserve Bank of India for opening a new branch or for transfer of an existing branch in India or abroad. The Reserve bank determines the policy in relation to advances and rate of interest to be followed on deposits and loans from time to time keeping in view the economic condition of the country. It also determines cash reserve ratio and liquidity ratio to be followed by the banks from time to time and makes changes in these ratios keeping in view the requirements of the country.

Risk-adjusted Assets

For the calculation of capital adequacy ratio, the assets side of the Balance Sheet of a bank is recalculated on the basis of assigning risk weights to each category of assets depending on the degree of risk involved. This is based on the principle of conservatism by considering assets of the bank at their risk adjusted values rather than at their book values for the purpose of calculation of capital adequacy ratio. For example, cash balances are risk free whereas advances are susceptible to credit risks. The risk of loss in case of secured loan is less as compared to an unsecured loan. Recognising the degree of risk involved, the Reserve Bank of India has assigned different risk weights to different categories of assets. For example cash balance with RBI is assigned a risk weight of zero whereas loans and advances not secured have been assigned a risk weight of 100%. The risk adjusted value for any category of assets is calculated by multiplying the value of the category of an asset as per Balance Sheet with the risk weight assigned thereto by RBI.

Capital Adequacy Ratio

The limits as to share capital given above are inadequate because these were fixed a long time back. To strengthen the capital base of the banks, the Reserve Bank of India, on the recommendations of the Narasimham Committee introduced in April, 1992 the risk weighted asset ratio system. According to this system, paid up capital and reserves of a bank after writing off bad debts should form an adequate percentage (8 to 10%) of the assets of the bank, its investments, loans and advances. All these items have been assigned weights according to the prescribed risks for example, cash balances are not susceptible to any risks and are assigned zero weight and loans and advances not guaranteed susceptible to credit risks are assigned 100% weight. Ratio so computed is known as *Capital Adequacy Ratio.*

This ratio is used to protect depositors and promote the stability and efficiency of financial systems around the world. Two types of capital are measured : *Tier one capital* which can absorb losses without a bank being required to cease trading and *tier two capital,* which can absorb losses in the event of winding up and so provides a lesser degree of protection to depositors. CAR is similar to leverage. In the most basic formulation, it is comparable to the inverse of debt-to-equity leverage formulations (although CAR uses equity over assets instead of debt-to-equity, since assets are by definition equal to debt plus equity—a transformation is required). Unlike traditional leverage, however, CAR recognises that assets can have different levels of risk.

Capital Adequacy Ratios (CARs) are a measure of the amount of a bank's core capital expressed as a percentage of its risk-weighted assets and it is known as Capital to Risk Weighted Asset Ratio (CRAR).

Capital Adequacy Ratio is defined as

$$CAR = \frac{\text{Capital Funds (Tier 1 Capital + Tier 2 Capital)}}{\text{Risk Weighted Assets}}$$

Tier 1 Capital

= (paid up capital + statutory reserve + disclosed free reserves)

– (equity investments in subsidiary + intangible assets + current and b/f losses)

Tier 2 Capital = (A) Undisclosed Reserves + (B) General Loss reserves +(C) Hybrid debt capital instrument and subordinated debts where risk can either be weighted assets (*a*) or the respective national regulator's minimum total capital requirement if using risk weighted assets.

Tier 1 Capital Ratio. The Basel rules recognise that different types of equity are more important than others and to recognise *i.e.* Tier 1 capital and Tier 2 capital. Tier 1 capital is actual contributed from equity plus retained earnings. The minimum CAR ratio as per Basel Accord norms ; Tier 1 equity to risk weighted assets is at least 5% while minimum CAR including Tier II is 10%.

Tier 2 Capital includes preference shares plus 50% of subordinated debt. The maximum Tier II capital is 50% of CAR as per Basel norms.

Non-Banking Financial Companies (NBFC) are required to maintain adequate capital. Every NBFC shall maintain a minimum capital ratio consisting of Tier I and Tier II capital which shall not be less than 12% of its aggregate risk-weighted assets. The total of Tier II capital, at any point of time, shall not exceed 100% of Tier I capital.

Capital Adequacy Ratio is a key indicator of a bank's financial strength. Keeping in view the importance of this ratio, all banks in India were to achieve the capital adequacy ratio of 8% by March 31, 1996 and banks were required to raise this ratio to 10% by 2002.

Here Capital Employed = Tier I Capital (including Equity Share Capital, Statutory Reserve, Free Reserves and Capital Reserve Realised in Cash + Tier II Capital (including Preference Share Capital, Debentures Convertible into Shares, Revaluation Reserve at 45%, Capital Reserve not realised in cash at 45% and any Other Provision : maximum 12.5% of assets Further it is provided that Tier II capital should not exceed Tier I capital.

Risk Weighted Assets are calculated as follows :

Assets	*Risk*
Cash in hand	0%
Balance or Deposits with other Bank	20%
Investment in Government Securities guaranteed by Government	0%
Investment in Government approved Securities Bonds of other banks	20%
Other Investments	100%
Loan guaranteed by Government	0%
Loan to Government Companies	100%

Loan covered by ECGC etc.	50%
Other Assets	100%
Acceptance, endorsements and other obligations	100%

ILLUSTRATION 1. Find out the capital adequacy ratio from the following information given by a commercial bank :

	₹ in crores
Equity Share Capital	**1,900.00**
Preference Share Capital (Issued before 1st July, 1944)	**100.00**
Statutory Reserve	**500.00**
Capital Reserve (Of which ₹ 10 crore were due to revaluation of assets and balance due to sale of capital asset)	**50.00**
Assets :	
Cash Balance	**30.00**
Balance with other banks	**50.00**
Other Investments	**100.00**
Loan and advances guaranteed by the Government	**1,700.00**
Premises	**15,000.00**
Furniture and Fixtures etc.	**1,000.00**
Acceptances and Endorsements	**16,000.00**

SOLUTION

Calculation of Capital Employed		₹ in crores
Tier I Capital		
Equity Share Capital		1,900.00
Statutory Reserve		500.00
Capital Reserve Realised in Cash		40.00
Total Tier I Capital		2,440.00
Tier II Capital	₹ in crores	
Preference Share Capital	100.00	
45% of ₹ 10 crores Revaluation Reserve	4.50	
		104.50
Capital Employed		2,544.50

CALCULATION OF RISK WEIGHTED ASSETS

	Amount ₹ in crores	*Weightage*	*Value ₹ in crores*
Cash Balance	30.00	0%	0
Balance with Other Banks	50.00	20%	10.00
Other Investments	100.00	100%	100.00
Loans and Advances Guaranteed by the Govt.	1,700.00	0%	0
Premises	15,000.00	100%	15,000.00
Furniture & Fixtures etc.	1,000.00	100%	1,000.00
Acceptances and Endorsements	16,000.00	100%	16,000.00
			32,110.00

$$\text{Capital Adequacy Ratio} = \frac{\text{Capital Employed}}{\text{Risk Weighted Assets}} \times 100 = \frac{2,544.50}{32,110.00} \times 100 = 7.92\%$$

ILLUSTRATION 2. A commercial bank has the following capital funds and assts. Segregate the capital funds into Tier I and Tier II capitals. Find out the risk adjusted assets and risk weighted assets ratio. State your observation on the risk weighted assets ratio taking 9% as the minimum ratio.

Particulars	Amount (₹ in lakhs)
Equity Share Capital	400.000
Statutory Reserve	250.000
Capital Reserve (of which Reserve ₹ 18 crores were due to revaluation of assets and the balance due to sale of Capital Assets)	86.000
Assets :	
Cash Balance with RBI	12.00
Balance with Other Banks	20.00
Other Investments	40.00
Loans and Advances	
Guaranteed by Government	14.50
Others	5,465.00
Premises, Furniture and Fixtures	74.00
Off Balance Sheet Items :	
(*i*) Guarantees and Other Obligations	700.00
(*ii*) Acceptances, Endorsements and Letter of Credit	4900.00

SOLUTION

Computation of Tier I and Tier II Capital Fund

Particulars		Amount (₹ in crores)
Capital Funds—Tier I		
Equity Share Capital		400.00
Statutory Reserve		250.00
Capital Reserve (arising out of sale of assets) (₹ 86 cr – ₹ 18 cr.)		68.00
		718.00
Capital Fund—Tier-II		
Capital Reserve (Arising Out of Revaluation of Assets)	18.00	
Less : Discount to the extent of 55%	(9.90)	
		8.10
		726.10

Risk Adjusted Assets

Particulars	Amount (₹ in crores)	% of weight	Amount (₹ in crores)
Funded Risk Assets			
Cash Balance with RBI	12.00	0	0.00
Balance with Other Banks	20.00	20	4.00

Other Investments	40.00	100	40.00
Loans & Advances :			
(i) Guaranteed by Government	14.50	0	0.00
(ii) Others	5,465.00	100	5,465.00
Premises, Furniture & Fixtures	74.00	100	74.00
Total (i)			5,583.00
Off Balance Sheet Items			
Guarantees and Other Obligations	700.00	100	700.00
Acceptances, Endorsements and Letter of Credit	4,900.00	100	4,900.00
Total (ii)			5,600.00
Total [(i) + (ii)]			11,183.00

Risk Weighted Assets Ratio :

$$\frac{\text{Capital Funds}}{\text{Risk Adjusted Assets}} \times 100 = \frac{₹\ 726.10 \text{ crores}}{₹\ 11{,}183 \text{ crores}} \times 100 = 6.49\%$$

As minimum Capital Adequacy Ratio is 9%, Bank has to improve the ratio of 6.49% to 9% by introducing further Tier I capital or by reducing Risk Adjusted Assets.

ACCOUNTS AND AUDIT

The provisions of the Act relating to annual accounts and audit of a banking company are given in Sections 29-34A and are as follows :

Preparation of Annual Accounts. On 31st March each and every banking company incorporated in India, in respect of all business transacted by it, and every banking company incorporated outside India, in respect of all business transacted through its branches in India shall prepare with reference to that year a Balance Sheet and Profit and Loss Account as on the working of the year in the Forms set out in third schedule or as near thereto as circumstances admit. Form A in third schedule is the Balance Sheet and Form B is the Profit and Loss Account. Forms A and B have been revised w.e.f. 1st April, 1991. In other words the annual accounts for the year ending 31st March 1992 and onwards are to be prepared in the new formats as given in the book.

The requirements of the Companies Act relating to the Balance Sheet and Statement of Profit and Loss of a company shall, is so far as they are not inconsistent with the Banking Companies Act, apply to the Balance Sheet and Profit and Loss Account of a banking company.

Audit of Accounts. The Balance Sheet and the Profit and Loss Account of a banking company is required to be audited by a Chartered Accountant. The appointment of the auditor of a banking company is made as per the provisions of the Companies Act. His powers, duties and liabilities are also governed by the Companies Act, but the auditor's report on the accounts of a banking company must include certain additional particulars. Every banking company is required to take pervious approval of the Reserve Bank of India before appointing or reappointing auditors. In addition, the Reserve Bank can order special audit of the banking companies Accounts if it thinks fit in the public interest of the banking company or its depositors.

Filing of Accounts. Three copies of the audited Balance Sheet and Profit and Loss Account together with the auditors' report shall be furnished as returns to the Reserve Bank of India within three months from the end of the accounting year to which they relate. This period of three months can be extended by the Reserve Bank for a further period upto three months. Reserve Bank is authorised to call for any further information as it may think proper from a banking company relating to the business of such company.

A banking company is also required to send to the Registrar of Companies three copies of its audited Balance Sheet and Profit and Loss Account and Auditor's Report and when the Reserve Bank requires any additional information in connection with the accounts, a copy of any such additional information shall also be sent to the Registrar.

Publication of Accounts. The Balance Sheet, Profit and Loss Account and the Auditor's Report of every banking company shall be published in any newspaper circulating at the place where it has principal office, within six months from the end of the accounting year.

Pricipal Accounting Policies for Banking Companies in Respect of Foreign Exchange Transactions

(*i*) Monetary assets and liabilities have been translated at the exchange rate prevailing at the close of year. Non-monetary assets have been carried in the books at the historical cost.

(*ii*) Income and Expenditure items in respect of Indian branches have been translated at the exchange rates on the date of transactions and in respect of foreign branches at the close of the year.

(*iii*) Profit or Loss on foreign currency position including pending forward exchange contracts have been accounted for at the exchange rates prevailing at the close of the year.

Accounting System

The accounting system of a banking company is different from that of a trading or manufacturing enterprise. A bank has a large number of customers whose accounts are to be maintained in such a way so that these should be kept up-to-date and checked regularly. Following are the main features of a bank's accounting system:

(*i*) **Voucher posting**—Entries in the personal ledger are made directly from vouchers instead of being posted from the books of prime entry.

(*ii*) **Voucher summary sheets**—The vouchers entered into different personal ledgers each day are summarised on summary sheets, totals of which are posted to the control accounts in the general ledger.

(*iii*) **Daily trial balance**—The general ledger trial balance is extracted and agreed every day.

(*iv*) **Continuos checks**—All entries are checked by persons other than those who have made the entries.

(*v*) **Control accounts**—A trial balance of the detailed personal ledgers is prepared periodically, usually every two weeks, agreed with general ledger control accounts.

(*vi*) **Double voucher system**—Two vouchers are prepared for every transaction not involving cash—one debit voucher and another credit voucher.

Books Required

A banking company is required to maintain a large number of subsidiary books, more important of these are given below :

(*a*) Receiving Cashier's Counter Cash Book.

(*b*) Paying Cashier's Counter Cash Book.

(*g*) Bills Discounted and Purchased Ledger.

(*h*) Loan Ledger.

(*c*) Current Accounts Ledger.
(*d*) Saving Bank Accounts Ledger.
(*e*) Fixed Deposit Accounts ledger.
(*f*) Investment Ledger.
(*i*) Cash Credit Ledger.
(*j*) Customers' Acceptances, Endorsements and Guarantee Ledger.
(*k*) Recurring Deposits Accounts Ledger

The proforma for Loan ledger is given on the next page.

Principal books of accounts are :

1. Cash Book . This book gives the summary of the Receiving Cashier's Counter Cash Book and the Paying Cashier's Counter Cash Book.

2. General Ledger. This ledger contains control accounts for the subsidiary ledgers listed above and accounts of expenses and assets not covered by the subsidiary ledgers.

In addition to the above books, following are the chief registers and memorandum books kept by a bank :

(1) Demand Draft Register.
(2) Bills for Collection Register.
(3) Share Security Register.
(4) Safe Custody Register.
(5) Jewellery Register.
(6) Letter of Credit Register.
(7) Safe Deposit Vault Register.
(8) Standing Order Register.

Proformas of Loan Ledger Bills for Collection (or DD) Register and Share Security Register are given on the next page.

Slip System of Posting

In this system, posting is made from slips prepared inside the organisation itself or from slips filled in by its customers. So entries are not made in the books of original entry or subsidiary books, but posting of entries is done from slips. In a banking company, the main slips are pay-in-slips, withdrawal slips and cheques and all these slips are filled in by clients of the bank. These slips serve the basis of entry in the ledgers and control accounts in the General Ledger are prepared on the basis of analysis of these slips.

Main reasons for the adoption of the slip system of posting by the bank are the following :

1. The bank must have customer's account up-to-date for a customer may present a cheque any time during hours meant for the public. Slip system helps in keeping the accounts up-to-date.
2. The number of transactions in a bank is very large. The adoption of slip system can suitably distribute the work of posting among many persons.
3. It ensures smooth flow of accounting work.

Main advantages of the slip system are :

1. **Saving of time and labour.** The bank saves a lot of time and clerical labour as most of the slips are filled in by its customers.
2. **No need of subsidiary books.** Subsidiary books are avoided as posting is done from slips.
3. **Minium delay.** Entries can be recorded with minimum delay as slips can easily pass from hand to hand among clerks concerned.
4. **Division of labour.** The slip system enables the division of work of posting among employees due to a large number of transactions in a bank.
5. **Smooth accounting.** The writing of the day book and posting of the ledger can be done simultaneously without loss of time.

LOAN LEDGER

Name.................................... Date........................

Address.. Security .... Rate of Interest .... % per annum.

Date	Particulars	Debit ₹	Credit ₹	Dr. Balance ₹	Days	Product	Interest ₹

BILLS FOR COLLECTION (OR D.D.) REGISTER

Date	D.D or (B.C.) No.	From whom Received	Drawn by	Drawee and Station	Bill or D.D.		Favouring	Amount ₹	Date of Realisation	Remarks
					Date	No.				

SHARE SECURITY REGISTER

Name of Party .... Limit ₹ ....

Address .... Margin ....

Serial No.	Date of Pledge	Name of Company	Share Scrip No.	Distinctive Number		Number of Shares Received	Paid Value ₹	Market Value ₹	Class of Shares	Disposal	Remarks
				From	To						

6. **Reliable accounting system.** Slip system provides a basis for reliable accounting system as most of the slips are prepared by customers themselves. Moreover, each transaction is recorded in different books which are maintained on self balancing system.
7. **Perfect basis of auditing.** Individual slips (known as vouchers) are filled up by customers and becomes a proof for a transaction to the satisfaction of the auditor.
8. **Proper evidence.** Slip duly filled by a customer provides evidence of a transaction. When needed slips preserved by the banks can be shown to the customers for their satisfaction.

Disadvantages of the slip system are :

1. **Risk of loss or destruction of slips.** Slips may be lost, destroyed or misappropriated as these are loose.
2. **Difficulty in verification.** Books cannot be verified if subsidiary books are not kept.
3. **Inconvenience to customers.** This system causes great inconvenience to the illiterate and semi-literate customers as slips are to be filled in (especially the amount in words and figures) with the help of other customers and arrogant bank employees.
4. **Risk of manipulation and misappropriation.** Dishonest employees can embazzle the money by destroying the loose and large number of slips and manipulating the amounts.
5. **Expensive system.** Slip system becomes difficult due to large number of daily transactions in a bank and becomes expensive to keep a date-wise record of such slips.

FINAL ACCOUNTS

According to Section 29 of the Banking Regulation Act, banks are required to prepare final accounts for each financial year ending 31st March. Books of banks are closed each year on 31st March. But for internal purpose, banks usually close their books on 30th September.

Profit and Loss Account

A banking company is required to prepare its Profit and Loss Account according to Form B in the Third Schedule to the Banking Regulation Act, 1949. Form B is in a summary form and the details of the various items are given in the schedules. Form B is given as follows :

Form 'B'

FORM OF PROFIT AND LOSS ACCOUNT

PROFIT & LOSS ACCOUNT

for the year ended 31st March (Year) (000's ommitted)

	Schedule No.	Year ended on 31-3... (Current Year)	Year ended on 31-3... (Previous Year)
I. Income			
Interest earned	13		
Other income	14	———	———
	Total :	———	———
II. Expenditure			
Interest expended	15		
Operating expenses	16		
Provisions and contingencies		———	———
	Total :	———	———

III.	**Profit/Loss**		
	Net Profit/Loss (—) for the year		
	Profit/Loss (—) brought forward		
	Total :		
IV.	**Appropriations**		
	Transfer to statutory reserve		
	Transfer to other reserves		
	Transfer to Government/proposed dividend		
	Balance carried over to balance sheet		
	Total :		

SCHEDULED 13 — INTEREST EARNED

(₹ '000)

		Year ended on 31-3... (Current Year)	Year ended on 31-3... (Previous Year)
I.	Interest/discount on advances/bills		
II.	Income on investments		
III.	Interest on balances with Reserve Bank of India and other inter-bank funds		
IV.	Others		
	Total :		

SCHEDULED 14 — OTHER INCOME

		Year ended on 31-3... (Current Year)	Year ended on 31-3... (Previous Year)
I.	Commission, exchange and brokerage		
II.	Profit on sale of investments *Less* : Loss on sale of investments		
III.	Profit on revaluation of investments *Less* : Loss on revaluation of investments		
IV.	Profit on sale of land, buildings and other assets *Less* : Loss on sale of land, buildings and other assets		
V.	Profit on exchange transactions *Less* : Loss on exchange transactions		
VI.	Income earned by way of dividends etc. from subsidiaries/companies and/or joint ventures abroad/in India		
VII.	Miscellaneous Income		
	Total :		

Note : Under items II to V loss figures may be shown in brackets.

SCHEDULED 15 — INTEREST EXPENDED

	Year ended on 31-3... (Current Year)	Year ended on 31-3... (Previous Year)
I. Interest on deposits		
II. Interest on Reserve Bank of India/inter-bank borrowings		
III. Others		
Total :		

SCHEDULED 16 — OPERATING EXPENSES

	Year ended on 31-3... (Current Year)	Year ended on 31-3... (Previous Year)
I. Payments to and provisions for employees		
II. Rent, taxes and lighting		
III. Printing and stationery		
IV. Advertisement and publicity		
V. Depreciation on bank's property		
VI. Directors' fees, allowances and expenses		
VII. Auditors' fees, allowances and expenses (including branch auditors)		
VIII. Law charges		
IX. Postages, telegrams, telephones, etc.		
X. Repairs and maintenance		
XI. Insurance		
XII. Other expenditure		
Total :		

GUIDELINES OF RESERVE BANK OF INDIA FOR PROFIT & LOSS ACCOUNT

Income Side Items

(1) Interest Earned

I. Interest/discount on advances/bills	Includes interest and discount on all types of loans and advances like cash credits, demand loans, overdrafts, exports loans, term loans, domestic and foreign bills purchased and discounted (including those rediscounted), overdue interest and also interest subsidy, if any, relating to such advances/bills.
II. Income on investments	Includes all income derived from the investment portfolio by way of interest and dividend.
III. Interest on balances with Reserve Bank of India and other inter- bank funds	Includes interest on balances with Reserve Bank and other banks, call loans, money market placements, etc.

IV. Others	Includes any other interest/discount income not included in the above heads.

(2) Other Income

I. Commission, exchange and brokerage	Includes all remuneration on services such as commission on collections, commission/exchange on remittances and transfers, commission on letters of credit, letting out of lockers and guarantees, commission on Government business, commission on other permitted agency business including consultancy and other services, brokerage, etc. on securities. It does not include foreign exchange income.
II. Profit on sale of investments *Less:* Loss on sale of investments	
III. Profit on revaluation of investments *Less:* Loss on revaluation of investments	Includes profit/loss on sale of securities, furniture, land and buildings, motor vehicles, gold, silver, etc. Only the net position should be shown. If the net position is a loss, the amount should be shown as a deduction. The net profit/loss on revaluation of assets may also be shown under this item.
IV. Profit on sale of land, buildings and other assets *Less:* Loss on sale of land, buildings and other assets	
V. Profit on exchange transactions *Less:* Loss on exchange transactions	Includes profit/loss on dealing in foreign exchange, all income earned by way of foreign exchange, commission and charges on foreign exchange transactions excluding interest which will be shown under interest. Only the net position should be shown. If the net position is a loss, it is to be shown as a deduction.
VI. Income earned by way of dividends etc. from subsidiaries, companies, joint ventures abroad/in India	
VII. Miscellaneous income	Includes recoveries from constituents for godown rents, income from bank's properties, security charges, insurance etc. and any other miscellaneous income. In case any item under this head exceeds one percentage of the total income, particulars may be given in the notes.

Expenditure Side

(1) Interest Expended

I. Interest on deposits	Includes interest paid on all types of deposits including deposits from banks and other institutions.
II. Interest on Reserve Bank of India/ inter bank borrowings	Includes discount/interest on all borrowings and refinance from Reserve Bank of India and other banks.

III. Others	Includes discount/interest on all borrowings/refinance from financial institutions. All other payments like interest on participation certificates, penal interest paid, etc. may also be included here.
(2) Operating Expenses	
I. Payments to and provisions for emp-loyees	Includes staff salaries/wages, allowances, bonus, other staff benefits like provident fund, pension, gratuity, liveries to staff, leave fare concessions, staff welfare, medical allowance to staff, etc.
II. Rent, taxes and lighting	Includes rent paid by the banks on buildings and municipal and taxes paid (excluding income-tax and interest tax) electricity and other similar charges and levies. House rent allowance and other similar payments to staff should appear under the head 'Payments to and provisions for employees'.
III. Printing and statio-nery	Includes books and forms and stationery used by the bank and other printing charges which are not incurred by way of publicity expenditure.
IV. Advertisement and publicity	Includes expenditure incurred by the bank for advertisement and publicity purposes including printing charges of publicity matter.
V. Depreciation on bank's property	Includes depreciation on bank's own property, motor cars and other vehicles; furniture, electric fittings, vaults, lifts, leasehold properties, non-banking assets, atc.
VI. Directors' fees, allo-wances and expenses	Includes sitting fees and all other items of expenditure in-curred on behalf of directors. The daily allowance, hotel charges, conveyance charges, etc. which though in the nature of reimbursement of expenses incurred may be included under this head. Similar expenses of local Committee members may also be included under this head.
VII. Auditors' fees and expenses (including branch auditors' fees and expenses)	Includes the fees paid to the statutory auditors and branch auditors for professional services rendered and all expenses for performing their duties, even though they may be in the nature of reimbursement of expenses. If external auditors have been appointed by banks themselves for internal inspections and audits and other services, the expenses incurred in that context including fees may not be included under this head but shown under 'other expenditure'.
VIII. Law charges	All legal expenses and reimbursement of expenses incurred in connection with legal services are to be included here.
IX. Postage, telegrams, telephones, etc.	Includes all postal charges like stamps, telegrams, telephones, teleprinter, etc.

X. Repairs and maintenance	Includes repairs to bank's property, their maintenance charges, etc.
XI. Insurance	Includes insurances charges on bank's property, insurance premia paid to Deposit Insurance & Credit Guarantee Corporation, etc. to the extent they are not recovered from the concerned parties.
XII. Other expenditure	All expenses other than those not included in any of the other heads, like, licence fees, donations, subscriptions to papers, periodicals, entertainment expenses, travel expenses, etc. may be included under this head. In case any particular item under this head exceeds one percentage of the total income particulars may be given in the notes.
(3) Provisions and contingencies	Includes all provisions made for bad and doubtful debts, provisions for taxation, provisions for diminution in the value of investments, transfers to contingencies and other similar items.

ILLUSTRATION 3. From the following information prepare Profit and Loss Account of Thrifty Bank for the year ended on 31st March, 2023.

	₹ ('000)		₹ ('000)
Interest on Loans	**2,590**		
Interest on Fixed Deposits	**3,170**	**Interest on Overdrafts**	**1,540**
Rebate on Bills Discounted	**490**	**Directors' Fees, Allowances and Expenses**	**30**
Commission	**82**	**Auditors' Fees and Expenses**	**12**
Payment to Employees	**540**	**Interest on Savings Bank Deposits**	**680**
Discount on Bills Discounted (Gross)	**1,550**	**Postage, Telegrams & Telephones**	**14**
Interest on Cash Credits	**2,230**	**Printing and Stationery**	**29**
Rent, Taxes and Lighting	**180**	**Sundry Charges**	**17**

Additional information :

(*i*) Provide for Contingencies ₹ 2,00,000

(*ii*) Transfer ₹ 15,57,000 to Reserves and

(*iii*) Transfer ₹ 2,00,000 to Central Govt.

SOLUTION

Thrifty Bank

PROFIT & LOSS ACCOUNT

for the year ended 31st March, 2023

	Schedule No.	*Year ended* 31-3-2023
I. *Income*		₹ ('000)
Interest Earned	13	7,420
Other Income	14	82
Total		7,502

II. *Expenditure*		
Interest Expended	15	3,850
Operating Expenses	16	822
Provisions & Contingencies		200
Total		4,872
III. *Profit/Loss*		₹ ('000)
Net Profit for the year		2,630
Profit brought forward		—
		2,630
IV. *Appropriations :*		
Transfer to Statutory Reserve (25% of ₹ 2,630)		658
Transfer to Other Reserves		1,557
Transfer to Central Govt.		200
Balance carried over to B/S		215
		2,630

Working Notes :

SCHEDULE 13—INTEREST EARNED

	₹ ('000)
1. Interest/discount on advances/bills (2,590 + 1,550 + 2,230 + 1,540 – 490)	7,420
2. Interest on investments	—
3. Interest on balances with RBI & other interbank funds	—
4. Others	—
	7,420

SCHEDULE 14 — OTHER INCOME

	₹ ('000)
Commission	82
	82

SCHEDULE 15—INTEREST EXPENDED

	₹ ('000)
1. Interest on Fixed Deposits	3,170
2. Interest on Saving Bank Deposits	680
Total	3,850

SCHEDULE 16 — OPERATING EXPENSES

	₹ ('000)
I. Payments to Employees and Provision for Employees	540
II. Directors' Fees, Allowances and Expenses	30
III. Rent, Taxes & Lighting	180
IV. Postage, Telegrams & Telephones	14
V. Auditors' Fees & Expenses	12
VI. Printing and Stationery	29
VII. Sundry Charges	17
	822

ILLUSTRATION 4. **Some of the items in the Trial Balance of CANHC Bank Limited as on March 31, 2023 were as follows :**

	₹		₹
Loans and Advances	71,50,000	Printing and Stationery	5,000
Current Accounts (including Overdrafts of ₹ 15,00,000)	66,00,000	Interest on Saving Bank Deposits	75,000
Bills Discounted and Purchased	19,20,000	Auditor's Fees	5,000
Interest on Fixed Deposits	1,55,000	Interest on Overdrafts	95,000
Interest on Loans	2,25,000	Provision for Doubtful Debts, April 1, 2022	42,000
Discount (subject to unexpired discount ₹ 30,000)	2,01,000	Bad Debts	21,000
Interest on Cash Credits	1,05,000	Provision for Income Tax, April 1, 2022	66,000
Commission earned	47,000	Income Tax paid for 2022-2023	54,000
Loss on Investment	34,000		
Salaries and Allowances	82,000		

Required : Prepare the Profit and Loss Account of the Bank maintaining the provision for Income tax at ₹ 84,000 and Provision for Doubtful Debts at ₹ 52,000 for the year ended March 31, 2023.

SOLUTION

CANHC Bank Ltd.
PROFIT & LOSS ACCOUNT
for the year ended 31st March, 2023

Particulars	Schedule No.	Year ended 31st March 2023 (₹ '000)	Year ended 31st March 2022 (₹ '000)
I. Income			
Interest earned	13	626	
Other Income	14	13	
Total		639	
II. Expenditure			
Interest Expended	15	230	
Operating Expenses	16	92	
Provisions and Contingencies ₹ [72 (2) + 31 (1) + 30 Unexpired Discount] (₹ '000)		133	
Total		455	
III. Profit/Loss			
Net Profit for the year		184	
Profit/Loss brought forward		—	
Total		184	
IV. Appropriations			
Transfer to Statutory Reserve @ 25% of ₹ 184 (₹ '000)		46	
Balance carried over to Balance Sheet		138	
Total		184	

SCHEDULE 13—INTEREST EARNED

Particulars	Year ended 31st March 2023 (₹ '000)	Year ended 31st March 2022 (₹ '000)
I. Income/Discount [225 + 201 + 105 + 95] (₹ '000)	626	
II. Interest on Investment	—	
III. Interest on Balances with RBI and Other Inter Bank Funds	—	
	626	

SCHEDULE 14—OTHER INCOME

Particulars	Year ended 31st March 2023 (₹ '000)	Year ended 31st March 2022 (₹ '000)
I. Commission, Exchange and Brokerage	47	
II. Loss on Sale of Investment	(–) 34	
	13	

SCHEDULE 15—INTEREST EXPENDED

Particulars	Year ended 31st March 2023 (₹ '000)	Year ended 31st March 2022 (₹ '000)
I. Interest on Deposits [0.75 + 1.55] lakhs	230	
II. Interest on RBI/Inter Bank Borrowings	—	
	230	

SCHEDULE 16—OPERATING EXPENSES

Particulars	Year ended 31st March 2023 (₹ '000)	Year ended 31st March 2022 (₹ '000)
I. Payments to and Provisions for Employees	82	
II. Printing & Stationery	5	
III. Auditors' Fees	5	
	92	

Working Notes :

(1) **PROVISION FOR DOUBTFUL DEBTS ACCOUNT**

Particulars	₹ '000	Particulars	₹ '000
To Bad Debts	21	By Balance b/d	42
To Balance c/d	52	By Profit & Loss A/c	31
	73		73

(2) **PROVISION FOR TAXATION ACCOUNT**

Particulars	₹ '000	Particulars	₹ '000
To Bank A/c	54	By Balance b/d	66
To Balance c/d	84	By Profit & Loss A/c	72
	138		138

ILLUSTRATION 5. From the following information relating to Global Finance Bank Ltd., prepare Profit and Loss Account for the year ended 31-3-2023. Also show schedules 13, 14, 15 & 16 as necessary.

Information for the year ending 31-3-2023 :

	₹ *(in '000)*		₹ *(in '000)*
Interest/discount on advances/bills	1,58,140	Depreciation on bank's property	1,460
Income on investments	59,050	Directors' fees, allowances & expenses	35
Interests on balances with R.B.I.	21,215	Auditor's fees and expenses	205
Commission, exchange & brokerage	14,535	Law charges	110
Profit on sale of investments	570	Postage, telephone, etc.	1,560
Interest on deposits	1,57,020	Repairs and maintenance	455
Interest on R.B.I. borrowings	16,810	Insurance	4,575
Payment to employees	48,585	Other expenditure	4,420
Rent, taxes, lighting	4,775	Balance of Profit & Loss A/c b/f	7,620
Printing and stationery	1,065	Advertisement and publicity	435

Following adjustments are to be made :

(*a*) Provide for Income Tax (including surcharge) @ 51.75%

(*b*) Every year the bank transfers 25% of profit to statuary reserve and 5% of profit of revenue reserve.

(*c*) Dividend amounting to ₹ 10,00,000 for the year ended 31-3-2023 is proposed by the Board of Directors.

SOLUTION

Global Finance Bank Ltd.
PROFIT AND LOSS ACCOUNT
for the year ending 31st March, 2023

	Schedule	*Year ended 31-3-2023*
		₹ (in '000)
I. *Income*		
Interest Earned	13	2,38,405
Other Income	14	15,105
		2,53,510
II. *Expenditure*		
Interest Expended	15	1,73,830
Operating Expenses	16	67,680
Provisions & Contingencies		
(Income tax @ 51.75% on profit before tax of ₹ 12,000 thousands)		6,210
		2,47,720

III.	*Profit/Loss*		
	Net Profit for the year		5,790
	Profit brought forward		7,620
			13,410
IV.	*Appropriations* :		
	Transfer to Statutory Reserve (25% of ₹ 5,790 thousands)		1,448
	Transfer to Other Reserves (5% of ₹ 5,790 thousands)		290
	Proposed Dividend		1,000
	Balance c/d to Balance Sheet		10,672
			13,410

SCHEDULE 13—INTEREST EARNED

		₹ '000
1.	Interest/Discount on Advances/Bills	1,58,140
2.	Income on Investments	59,050
3.	Interest on Balances with RBI	21,215
4.	Others	—
		2,38,405

SCHEDULE 14—OTHER INCOME

		₹ '000
1.	Commission, Exchange and Brokerage	14,535
2.	Profit on Sale of Investments	570
		15,105

SCHEDULE 15—INTEREST EXPENDED

		₹ '000
1.	Interest on Deposits	1,57,020
2.	Interest on RBI Borrowings	16,810
		1,73,830

SCHEDULE 16—OPERATING EXPENSES

		₹ '000
1.	Payment to Employees	48,585
2.	Rent, Taxes & Lighting	4,775
3.	Printing & Stationery	1,065
4.	Advertisement & Publicity	435
5.	Depreciation on Bank's Property	1,460
6.	Directors' Fees, Allowances and Expenses	35
7.	Auditors' Fees	110
8.	Law Charges	205
9.	Postage, Telephone, etc.	1,560
10.	Sundry Charges	9,450
		67,680

ILLUSTRATION 6. **Following figures have been obtained from the books of the Rana Bank Ltd. for the year ending 31st March, 2023 :**

	₹ (in '000)		₹ (in '000)
Issued and subscribed capital	1,000	Postage and telegrams	61
Interest and discount earned	3,800	Profit on sale of investments	240
Commission and exchange earned	195	Loss on sale of investments	38
Interest paid	2,000	Rent received	62
Salaries and wages	210	Depreciation	31
Directors' fees	35	Stationery	60
Rent and taxes	70	Auditors' fees	8

Additional information **:**

(*i*) The Profit and Loss Account had a balance of ₹ 10,00,000 on 1st April, 2022.

(*ii*) An advance of ₹ 12,00,000 has become doubtful and it is expected that only 50% of the amount due can be recovered from the security.

(*iii*) The provision of tax be made at 25%.

(*iv*) A dividend of 10% is proposed.

Prepare Profit and Loss Account of the Rana Bank Ltd. for the year ending 31st March, 2023.

SOLUTION

Rana Bank Ltd.

PROFIT AND LOSS ACCOUNT

for the year ending 31st March, 2023

	Schedule No.	*Year ending 31-3-2023*	*Year ending 31-3-2022*
I. *Income*	₹ (in '000)	₹ (in '000)	
Interest Earned	13	3,800	
Other Income	14	459	
		4,259	
II. *Expenditure*			
Interest Expended	15	2,000	
Operating Expenses	16	475	
Provisions and Contingencies (1)		896	
		3,371	
III. Net Profit for the year		888	
Profit brought forward		1,000	
Total		1,888	
IV. *Appropriations*			
Transfer to Statutory Reserve			
(25% of ₹ 222 thousands)		222	
Transfer to Other Reserves		—	
Proposed Dividend		100	
Balance carried over to Balance Sheet		1,566	
Total		1,888	

SCHEDULE 13—INTEREST EARNED

	Year ending 31-3-2023	Year ending 31-3-2022
	₹ in '000	₹ in '000
Interest/Discount on Advances/Bills	3,800	
	3,800	

SCHEDULE 14—OTHER INCOME

		Year ending 31-3-2023	Year ending 31-3-2022
		₹ in '000	₹ in '000
Commission and Exchange		195	
Profit on Sale of Investments	240		
Less : Loss on Sale of Investments	38		
		202	
Miscellaneous Income (Rent Received)		62	
		459	

SCHEDULE 15—INTEREST EXPENDED

	Year ending 31-3-2023	Year ending 31-3-2022
	₹ in '000	₹ in '000
Interest on Deposits	2,000	
	2,000	

SCHEDULE 16—OPERATING EXPENSES

	Year ending 31-3-2023	Year ending 31-3-2022
	₹ in '000	₹ in '000
Payments to and Provisions for Employees	210	
Rent, Taxes and Lighting	70	
Printing and Stationery	60	
Depreciation on Bank's Property	31	
Directors' Fees, Allowances and Expenses	35	
Audit Fees and Expenses	8	
Postage, Telegrams and Telephones	61	
	475	

(1) *Calculation of Provisions and Contingencies*

	₹
Provision for Bad and Doubtful Debts 50% of ₹ 12,00,000 =	6,00,000
Provision for Tax @ 25% of ₹ 11,84,000 (2)	2,96,000
Total	8,96,000
Provision and Contingencies in ₹ '000	896

(2) Provision for Tax has been calculated as follows :

		In ₹ '000
Interest Earned		3,800
Other Income		459
		4,259
	₹ '000	
Less : Interest Expended	2,000	
Operating Expenses	475	
Provision for Bad and Doubtful Debts	600	
		3,075
Profit before Tax		1,184
Provision for Tax @ 25%		2,96,000

Or Provision for Tax ₹ 2,96,000.

ILLUSTRATION 7. From the following information, prepare Profit and Loss Account of South India Bank Ltd. as on 31st March, 2023.

	₹ ('000)		₹ ('000)
Interest and discount	3,045	Rent, taxes and lighting	210
Income from investments	115	Printing and stationery	180
Interest on balance with RBI	180	Advertisement and publicity	95
Commission, exchange and brokerage	820	Depreciation	92
		Directors' fees	220
Profit on sale of investments	110	Auditors' fees	120
Interest on deposits	1,225	Law charges	230
Interest to RBI	161	Postage, telegrams and telephone	70
Payment to and provision for employees	1,044	Insurance	56
		Repairs and maintenance	48

Other Informations :

(*i*) **Interest and discount mentioned above is after adjustment for the following :**

	₹ ('000)
Tax provision for the year	220
Provision during the year for doubtful debts	102
Loss on sale of investments	12
Rebate on bills discounted	58
	392

(*ii*) **25% of profit is transferred to statutory reserve.**

5% of profit is transferred to revenue reserve.

Profit brought forward from the last year ₹ 16,000.

SOLUTION

South India Bank Ltd.
PROFIT & LOSS ACCOUNT
for the year ended 31st March, 2023

	Schedule No.	Year ended 31st March 2023
I. *Income*		₹ ('000)
Interest Earned	13	3,674
Other Income	14	918
Total		4,592
II. *Expenditure*		
Interest Expended	15	1,386
Operating Expenses	16	2,365
Provisions and Contingencies ₹ (220 + 102) (₹ in '000)		322
Total		4,073
III. *Profit/Loss*		
Net Profit for the year		519
Profit-brought forward		16
		535
IV. *Appropriations*		
Transfer to Statutory Reserve (25% of ₹ 519) (₹ in '000)		130
Transfer to Other Reserves (5% of ₹ 519) (₹ in '000)		26
Balance carried to B/S		379
		535

Working Notes :

SCHEDULE 13—INTEREST EARNED

	₹ ('000)
1. Interest/discount ₹ (3,045 + 220 + 102 + 12) (₹ in '000)	3,379
2. Income from investments	115
3. Interest on balances with RBI & other inter bank fund	180
4. Others	—
Total	3,674

SCHEDULE 14— OTHER INCOME

		₹ (000)
I. Commission, Exchange & Brokerage		820
II. Profit on Sale of investments	110	
Less : Loss on sale of investments	12	98
Total		918

SCHEDULE 15—INTEREST EXPENDED

	₹ ('000)
I. Interest on Deposits	1,225
II. Interest on RBI/Inter Bank Fund	161
Total	1,386

SCHEDULE 16 — OPERATING EXPENSES

	₹ ('000)
I. Payments to and Provisions for Employees	1,044
II. Rent, Taxes and Lighting	210
III. Printing and Stationery	180
IV. Advertisement and Publicity	95
V. Depreciation on Bank Property	92
VI. Directors' Fees, Allowances & Expenses	220
VII. Auditors' Fees & Expenses	120
VIII. Postage, Telegrams & Telephones	70
IX. Law Charges	230
X. Repairs & Maintenance	48
XI. Insurance	56
Total	2,365

ILLUSTRATION 8. **Following figures are extracted from the books of the New Bank Ltd. as on 31st March, 2023 :**

	₹ ('000)		₹ ('000)
Interest and Discount received	3,695	Payments to Employees	200
Interest paid on Deposits	2,032	Directors' Fees and Allowances	30
Issued and Subscribed Capital	1,000	Rent and Taxes paid	100
Statutory Reserve under Sec. 17	800	Postage and Telegrams	50
Commission, Exchange & Brokerage	200	Depreciation on Bank's Property	30
Rent received	55	Stationery etc.	50
Profit on Sale of Investments	200	Advertisement and Publicity	10
Audit Fees	5	Preliminary Expenses	5

The further information is given : (*a*) A customer to whom a sum of ₹ 10,00,000 has been advanced has become insolvent and it is expected only 50% can be recovered from his estate. Interest due at 18% on his debt has not been provided in the books. (*b*) There were also other debts for which a provision of ₹ 1,50,000 was found necessary by the auditors. (*c*) Rebate on bills discounted as on 1st April, 2022 ₹ 16,000. Rebate on bills discounted as on 31st March, 2023 ₹ 12,000. (*d*) Provide ₹ 6,50,000 for income tax. (*e*) The Directors desire to declare 10% dividend. (*f*) Write off all preliminary expenses.

Prepare Profit and Loss Account in accordance with the Law. Make necessary assumptions. Figures of previous year need not be given.

SOLUTION

THE NEW BANK LTD.
PROFIT & LOSS ACCOUNT
For the year ended 31st March, 2023

₹ ('000)

	Schedule No.	*Year ended 31-3-2023*
I. Income		
Interest Earned	13	3,879
Other Income	14	455
		4,334
II. Expenditure		
Interest Expended	15	2,032
Operating Expenses	16	480
Provisions and Contingencies	—	(1) 1,300
		3,812
III. Profit/Loss		
Net Profit for the year		522
Profit brought forward		—
		522
IV. Appropriations		
Transfer to Statutory Reserve (25% of 522)		130.5
Transfer to Other Reserves		—
Transfer to Govt./Proposed Dividend		100.0
Balance carried over to Balance sheet		291.5
		522.0

SCHEDULE 13—INTEREST EARNED

₹ ('000)

	Year ended 31-3-2023
I. Interest/Discount on Advances/Bills (3,695 + 180 Interest Outstanding + 16 Rebate on Bills Discounted on 1-4-2022 –12 Rebate on Bills Discounted as on 31-3-2023)	3,879
II. Income on Investments	—
III. Interest on Balances with RBI and Other Inter-bank Funds	—
IV. Others	—
	3,879

SCHEDULE 14—OTHER INCOME

₹ ('000)

I. Commission, Exchange and Brokerage	200
II. Lockers Rent	55
III. Transfer Fees	—
IV. Profit on Sale of Investments	200
	455

Working Note (1) : *Calculation of Provisions & Contingencies*

	₹
Provision for Bad Debts : 50% of (₹ 10,00,000) + ₹ 1,50,000	6,50,000
Provision for Income Tax	6,50,000
Provisions and Contingencies	13,00,000

SCHEDULE 15—INTEREST EXPENDED

	₹ ('000)
I. Interest on Deposits	2,032
	2,032

SCHEDULE 16—OPERATING EXPENSES

	₹ ('000)
I. Payments to Employees	200
II. Rent, Taxes & Lighting	100
III. Printing and Stationery	50
IV. Advertisement & Publicity	10
V. Depreciation on Bank's Property	30
VI. Directors' Fees & Allowances	30
VII. Audit Fees	5
VIII. Law Charges	—
IX. Postage, Telegrams & Telephones	50
X. Preliminary Expenses	5
	480

Balance Sheet

Balance Sheet of a Banking Company is drawn up according to Form A in the Third Schedule. From A is reproduced as follows :

Form 'A'

Form of Balance Sheet

BALANCE SHEET OF ...... **(here enter name of the Banking company)**

as on 31st March **(Year)**

(000's omitted)

Capital and Liabilities	*Schedule*	*as on 31-3... (Current Year)*	*as on 31-3... (Previous Year)*
Capital	1		
Reserves & Surplus	2		
Deposits	3		
Borrowings	4		
Other Liabilities and Provisions	5		
Total			
Assets			
Cash and Balances with Reserve Bank of India	6		
Balances with Banks and Money at Call and Short Notice	7		

	Schedule		
Investments	8		
Advances	9		
Fixed Assets	10		
Other Assets	11	———	———
Total :		———	———
Contingent Liabilities	12		
Bills for Collection			

SCHEDULE 1 — CAPITAL

	as on 31-3... (Current Year)	as on 31-3... (Previous Year)
I. For Nationalised Banks		
Capital (Fully owned by Central Government)	———	———
	———	———
II. For Banks Incorporated Outside India		
Capital :		
(*i*) (The amount brought in by banks by way of start-up capital as prescribed by RBI should be shown under this head)		
(*ii*) Amount of deposit kept with the RBI under Section 11 (2) of the Banking Regulation Act, 1949	———	———
Total	———	———
III. For Other Banks		
Authorised Capital		
(Shares of ₹ each)		
Issued Capital		
(Shares of ₹ each)		
Subscribed Capital		
(Shares of ₹ each)		
Called-up Capital		
(Shares of ₹ each)		
Less : Calls unpaid		
Add : Forfeited Shares	———	———
	———	———

SCHEDULE 2 — RESERVES & SURPLUS

	as on 31-3... (Current Year)	As on 31-3... (Previous Year)
I. Statutory Reserves		
Opening Balance		
Additions during the year		
Deductions during the year		
II. Capital Reserves		
Opening Balance		
Additions during the year		
Deductions during the year		

III. Share Premium
Opening Balance
Additions during the year
Deductions during the year
IV. Revenue and other Reserves
Opening Balance
Additions during the year
Deductions during the year
V. Balance in Profit and Loss Account

Total
(I, II, III, IV and V)

SCHEDULE 3 — DEPOSITS

	as on 31-3... *(Current Year)*	*as on 31-3...* *(Previous Year)*
A. I. Demand Deposits		
(*i*) From Banks		
(*ii*) From others		
II. Saving Bank Deposits		
III. Term Deposits		
(*i*) From Banks		
(*ii*) From others		
Total (I, II and III)		
B. (*i*) Deposits of branches in India		
(*ii*) Deposits of branches outside India		
Total :		

SCHEDULE 4 — BORROWINGS

	as on 31-3... *(Current Year)*	*as on 31-3...* *(Previous Year)*
I. Borrowings in India		
(*i*) Reserve Bank of India		
(*ii*) Other banks		
(*iii*) Other institutions and agencies		
II. Borrowings outside India		
Total : (I and II)		
Secured borrowings included in I & II above —₹		

SCHEDULE 5 — OTHER LIABILITIES AND PROVISIONS

	as on 31.3... *(Current year)*	*as on 31.3...* *(Previous year)*
I. Bills payable		
II. Inter-office adjustments (net)		
III. Interest accrued		
IV. Others (including provisions)		
Total :		

SCHEDULE 6 — CASH AND BALANCES WITH RESERVE BANK OF INDIA

	as on 31-3... (Current Year)	As on 31-3... (Previous Year)
I. Cash in hand (including foreign currency notes)		
II. Balances with Reserve Bank of India		
(*i*) in Current Account		
(*ii*) in Other Accounts		
Total : (I and II)		

SCHEDULE 7 — BALANCES WITH BANKS & MONEY AT CALL & SHORT NOTICE

	as on 31-3... (Current Year)	As on 31-3... (Previous Year)
I. In India		
(*i*) Balances with banks		
(*a*) in Current Accounts		
(*b*) in Other Deposit Accounts		
(*ii*) Money at call and short notice		
(*a*) With banks		
(*b*) With other institutions		
Total: (*i*) and (*ii*)		
II. Outside India		
(*i*) in Current Accounts		
(*ii*) in Other Deposit Accounts		
(*iii*) Money at call and short notice		
(*i*), (*ii*) and (*iii*) Total:		
Grand Total : (I) and (II)		

SCHEDULE 8— INVESTMENTS

	as on 31-3... (Current Year)	as on 31-3... (Previous Year)
I. Investments in India in		
(*i*) Government securities		
(*ii*) Other approved securities		
(*iii*) Shares		
(*iv*) Debentures and Bonds		
(*v*) Subsidiaries and / or joint ventures		
(*vi*) Others (to be specified)		
Total :		
II. Investments outside India in		
(*i*) Government securities (including local authorities)		
(*ii*) Subsidiaries and / or joint ventures abroad		
(*iii*) Other investments (to be specified)		
Total :		
Grand Total : (I & II)		

SCHEDULE 9— ADVANCES

	as on 31.3... *(Current Year)*	*as on 31.3...* *(Previous Year)*
A. (*i*) Bills purchased and discounted		
(*ii*) Cash credits, overdrafts and loans repayable on demand		
(*iii*) Term loans		
Total :		
B. (*i*) Secured by tangible assets		
(*ii*) Covered by Bank/Government guarantees		
(*iii*) Unsecured		
Total :		
C. I. Advances in India		
(*i*) Priority Sectors		
(*ii*) Public Sector		
(*iii*) Banks		
(*iv*) Others		
Total :		
II Advances outside India		
(*i*) Due from banks		
(*ii*) Due from others		
(*a*) Bills purchased and discounted		
(*b*) Syndicated loans		
(*c*) Others		
Total :		
Grand Total : (C I and II)		

SCHEDULE 10— FIXED ASSETS

	as on 31-3... *(Current Year)*	*as on 31-3...* *(Previous Year)*
I. Premises		
At cost as on 31st March of the preceding year		
Additions during the year		
Deductions during the year		
Depreciation to date		
II. Other Fixed Assets (including furniture and fixtures)		
At cost as on 31st March of the preceding year		
Additions during the year		
Deductions during the year		
Depreciation to date		
Total :		
(I and II)		

SCHEDULE 11— OTHER ASSETS

	as on 31-3... (Current Year)	as on 31-3... (Previous Year)
I. Inter-office adjustments (net)		
II. Interest accrued		
III. Tax paid in advance/tax deducted at source		
IV. Stationery and stamps		
V. Non-banking assets acquired in satisfaction of claims		
VI. Others @		
Total :		

@ In case there is any unadjusted balance of loss, the same may be shown under this item with appropriate footnote.

SCHEDULE 12— CONTINGENT LIABILITIES

	as on 31-3... (Current Year)	as on 31-3... (Previous Year)
I. Claims against the bank not acknowledged as debts		
II. Liability for partly paid investments		
III. Liability on account of outstanding forward exchange contracts		
IV. Guarantees given on behalf of constituents (*a*) In India (*b*) Outside India		
V. Acceptances, endorsements and other obligations		
VI. Other items for which the bank is contingently liable		
Total :		

GUIDELINES OF THE RESERVE BANK OF INDIA FOR BALANCE SHEET

CAPITAL AND LIABILITIES SIDE

CAPITAL

Nationalised Banks

Capital (fully owned by Central Government)	The Capital owned by Central Government as on the date of the Balance Sheet including contribution from Government, if any, for participating in World Bank Projects should be shown
Banking Companies Incorporated outside India.	(*i*) The amount brought in by banks by way of start up capital as prescribed by RBI should be shown under this heading. (*ii*) The amount of deposit kept by RBI, under sub-section 2 of section 11 of the Banking Regulation Act, 1949, should also be shown.
Other Banks (Indian) Authorised Capital (...Shares of ₹ each) Issued Capital (... Shares of ₹ each) Subscribed Capital (...Shares of ₹ each) Called up Capital	Authorised, Issued, Subscribed, Called-up Capital should be given separately. Calls-in-arrears will be deducted from Called up Capital while the paid-up value of forfeited shares should be added thus arriving at the paid-up capital. Where necessary, items which can be combined should be shown under one head for instance 'Issued and Subscribed Capital'.

(...Shares of ₹ each) *Less*: Calls unpaid *Add*: Forfeited Shares Paid up Capital	**Notes—General** The changes in the above items, if any, during the year, say, fresh contribution made by Government, fresh issue of capital, capitalisation of reserve, etc. may be explained in the notes.
Reserves and Surplus	
I. Statutory Reserves	Reserves created in terms of Section 17 or any other section of Banking Regulation Act must be separately disclosed.
II. Capital Reserves	The expression 'capital reserves' shall not include any amount regarded as free for distribution through the profit & loss account. Surplus on revaluation should be treated as Capital Reserves. Surplus on translation of the financial statements of foreign branches (which includes fixed assets also) is not a revaluation reserve.
III. Securities Premium	Premium on issue of share capital may be shown separately under this head.
IV. Revenue and Other Reserves	The expression 'Revenue Reserve' shall mean any reserve other than capital reserve. This item will include all reserves, other than those separately classified. The expression 'reserve' shall not include any amount written off or retained by way of providing for depreciation, renewals or diminution in value of assets or retained by way of providing for any known liability.
V. Balance of Profit	Includes Balance of Profit after appropriations. In case of loss the balance may be shown as a deduction. **Notes—General** Movement is various categories of reserves should be shown as indicated in the schedule.
Deposits	
A. I. Demand Deposits	Includes all bank deposits repayable on demand.
(*i*) from banks (*ii*) from others	Includes all demand deposits of the non-bank sectors. Credit balances in overdrafts, cash credit accounts, deposits payable at call, overdue deposits, inoperative current accounts, matured time deposits and cash certificates, certificates of deposits, etc. are to be included under this category.
II. Saving Banks Deposits	Includes all savings banks deposits (including inoperative saving bank accounts).
III. Term Deposits (*i*) from banks	Includes all types of bank deposits repayable after a specified term.
(*ii*) from others	Includes all types of deposits of the non-bank sector repayable after a specified term. Fixed deposits, cumulative and recurring deposits, cash certificates, certificates of deposits, annuity deposits, deposits mobilised under various schemes, ordinary staff deposits, foreign currency non-resident deposits accounts, etc. are to be included under this category.

B.(*i*) Deposits of branches in India (*ii*) Deposits of branches outside India	The total of these two items will agree with the total deposits.
	Notes—General (*a*) Interest payable on deposits which is accrued but not due should not be included but shown under other liabilities. (*b*) Matured time deposits and cash certificates, etc. should be treated as demand deposits. (*c*) Deposits under special schemes should be included under term deposits if they are not payable on demand. When such deposits have matured for payment they should be shown under demand deposits. (*d*) Deposits from banks will include deposits from the banking system in India, co-operative banks, foreign banks which may or may not have a presence in India.
Borrowings	
(I) Borrowings in India (*i*) Reserve Bank of India	Includes borrowings/refinance obtained from Reserve bank of India.
(*ii*) Other Banks	Includes borrowings/refinance obtained from commercial banks (including co-operative banks).
(*iii*) Other institutions and agencies	Includes borrowings/reference obtained from Industrial Development Bank of India, Export-Import Bank of India, National Bank for Agricultural and Rural Development and other institutions, agencies (including liability against participation certificates, if any).
(II) Borrowings outside India	Includes borrowings of Indian branches abroad as well as borrowings of foreign branches.
Secured borrowings included above.	This item will be shown separately. Includes secured borrowings/refinance in India and outside India.
	Notes—General (*i*) The total of I & II will agree with the total borrowings shown in the balance sheet. (*ii*) Inter-office transactions should not be shown as borrowings. (*iii*) Funds raised by foreign branches by way of certificates of deposits, notes, bonds, etc. should be classified depending upon documentation, as 'deposits', 'borrowings', etc. (*iv*) Refinance obtained by banks from Reserve Bank of India and various institutions are being brought under the head 'Borrowings'. Hence, advances will be shown at the gross amount on the assets side.

Other Liabilities and Provisions

(I) Bills payable	Includes drafts, telegraphic transfers, traveller cheques, mail transfers payable, pay slips, bankers cheques and other miscellaneous items.
(II) Inter-office adjustments (net)	The inter-office adjustments balance, if in credit, should be shown under this head. Only net position of inter-office accounts, inland as well as foreign, should be shown here.
(III) Interest accrued	Includes interest accrued but not due on deposits and borrowings.
(IV) Others (including provisions)	Includes net provision for income tax and other taxes like interest tax (less advance payment, tax deducted at source, etc.), surplus in aggregate in provisions for bad debts account, surplus in aggregate in provisions for depreciation in securities, contingency funds which are not disclosed as reserves but are actually in the nature of reserves, proposed dividend/transfer to Government, other liabilities which are not disclosed under any of the major heads such as unclaimed dividend, provisions and funds kept for specific purposes, unexpired discount, outstanding charges like rent, conveyance, etc. Certain types of deposits like staff security deposits, margin deposits, etc. where the repayment is not free should also be included under this head.

Notes—General

(*i*) For arrival at the net balance of inter-office adjustments all connected inter-office accounts should be aggregated and the net balance only will be shown, representing mostly items in transit and unadjusted items.

(*ii*) The interest accruing on all deposits, whether the payment is due or not, should be treated as a liability.

(*iii*) It is proposed to show only pure deposits under the head 'deposits' and hence all surplus provisions for bad and doubtful debts, contingency funds, secret reserves, etc. which are not netted off against the relative assets, should be brought under the head 'Others (including provisions)'.

Contingent Liabilities

I. Claims against the bank not acknowledged as debts.	
II. Liability for partly paid investments	Liabilities on partly paid shares, debentures, etc. will be included in this head.
III. Liability on account of outstanding forward exchange contracts	Outstanding forward exchange contracts may be included here.

IV. Guarantees given on behalf of constituents (*i*) In India (*ii*) Outside India.	Guarantees given for constituents in India and outside India may be shown separately.
V. Acceptances, endorsements and other obligations.	This item will include letters of credit and bills accepted by the bank on behalf of customers.
VI. Other items for which the Bank is contingently liable	Arrears of cumulative dividends, bills rediscounted under underwriting contracts, estimated amounts of contracts remaining to be executed on capital account and not provided for, etc. are to be included here.

Assets Side

Cash and Balances with the Reserve Bank of India

I. Cash in hand (including foreign currency notes)	Includes cash in hand including foreign currency notes and also of foreign branches in the case of banks having such branches.
II. (*i*) in Current Account (*ii*) in other Accounts	

Balances with Banks and Money at Call and Short Notice

I. In India (*i*) Balances with banks (*a*) in current accounts (*b*) in other Deposit accounts	Includes all balances with banks in India (including co-operative banks). Balances in current accounts and deposits accounts should be shown separately.
(*ii*) Money at call and short notice (*a*) with banks (*b*) with other institutions	Includes deposits repayable within 15 days or less than 15 days notice lent in the inter-bank call money market.
II. Outside India (*i*) Current accounts (*ii*) Deposit accounts	Includes balances held by foreign branches and balances held by Indian branches of the banks outside India. Balance held with foreign branches by other branches of the bank should not be shown under this head but should be included in inter-branch accounts. The amounts held in 'current accounts' and 'deposit accounts' should be shown separately.
(*iii*) Money at call and short notice	Includes deposits usually classified in foreign countries as money at call and short notice.

Investments

I. Investments in India (*i*) Government securities	Includes Central and State Government securities and Government treasury bills. These securities should be shown at the book value. However, the difference between the book value and market value should be given in the notes to the balance sheet.
(*ii*) Other approved securities	Securities other than Government securities, which according to the Banking Regulation Act, 1949 are treated as approved securities, should be included here.

(iii) Shares	Investments in shares of companies and corporations not included in items *(ii)* should be included here.
(iv) Debentures and Bonds	Investments in debentures and bonds of companies and corporations not included in item *(ii)* should be included here.
(v) Investments in subsidiaries/joint ventures	Investments in subsidiaries/joint ventures (including RRBs) should be included here.
(vi) Others	Includes residual investments, if any, like gold, commercial paper and other instruments in the nature of shares/debentures/bonds.
II. Investments outside India *(i)* Government securities (including local authorities)	All foreign Government securities including securities issued by local authorities may be classified under this head.
(ii) Subsidiaries and/or joint ventures abroad	All investments made in the share capital of subsidiaries floated outside India and/or joint venture abroad should be classified under this head.
(iii) Others	All other investments outside India may be shown under this head.

The Reserve Bank of India has revised the existing guidelines on classification and valuation of the investments with effect from 30th September, 2000. Now the banks are required to classify their entire investment portfolio under three categories :

(i) Held to maturity ; *(ii)* Available for Sale and *(iii)* Held for Trading. In balance sheet the investments will continue to be shown as per the existing six classifications as given under the heading of Investments. The securities acquired by the banks with the intention to hold them to maturity will be classified under 'Held to Maturity'. The securities acquired by the banks with the intention to trade by taking advantage of the short-term price/interest rate movements will be classified under 'Held for Trading'. The securities which do no fall within the above two categories will be classified under 'Available for Sale'.

Advances

A. *(i)* Bills purchased and discounted *(ii)* Cash credits, over-drafts and loans repayable on demand	In classification under Section 'A', all outstandings—in India as well as outside—less provisions made, will be classified under three heads as indicated and both secured and unsecured advances will be included under these heads.
(iii) Term loans	Including over due instalments.
B. *(i)* Secured by tangible assets	All advances or part of advances which are secured by tangible assets may be shown here. The item will include advances in India and outside India.
(ii) Covered by Bank/ Government Guara-ntee	Advances in India and outside India to the extent they are covered by guarantees of Indian and foreign governments and Indian and foreign banks and DICGC & ECGC are to be included.

(*iii*) Unsecured	All advances not classified under (*i*) and (*ii*) will be included here. Total of 'A' should tally with total of 'B'.
C. I. Advances in India (*i*) Priority sectors (*ii*) Public sector (*iii*) Banks (*iv*) Others	Advances should be broadly classified into 'Advances in India' and 'Advances outside India'. Advances in India will be further classified on the sectoral basis as indicated. Advances to sectors which for the time being are classified as priority sectors according to the instructions of the Reserve Bank are to be classified under the head 'Priority sectors'.
C. II. Advances outside India (*i*) Due from banks (*ii*) Due from others (*a*) Bills purchased and discounted (*b*) Syndicated loans (*c*) Others	Such advances should be excluded from item (*ii*) *i.e.* advances to public sector. Advances to Central and State Governments and other Government undertakings including Government companies and corporations which are, according to the statutes to be treated as public sector companies are to be included in the category "Public Sector". All advances to the banking sector including co-operative bank will come under the head 'Banks'. All the remaining advances will be included under the head 'Others' and typically this category will include non-priority advances to the private, joint and co-operative sectors. **Notes—General** (*i*) The gross amount of advances including refinance and rediscounts but excluding provisions made to the satisfaction of auditors should be shown as advances. (*ii*) Term loans will be loans not repayable on demand. (*iii*) Consortium advances would be shown net of share from other participating banks/institutions.
Fixed Assets	
I. Premises (*i*) At cost at on 31st March of the preceding year (*ii*) Additions during the year (*iii*) Deductions during the year (*iv*) Depreciation to date	Premises wholly or partly owned by the banking company for the purpose of business including residential premises should be shown against 'Premises'. In the case of premises and other fixed assets, the previous balance, additions there to and deductions therefrom during the year as also the total depreciation written off should be shown. Where sums have been written off on reduction of capital or revaluation of assets, every balance sheet after the first balance sheet subsequent to the reduction or revaluation should show the revised figures for a period of five years with the date and amount of revision made.
II. Other Fixed Assets (including furniture and fixtures) (*i*) At cost on 31st March of the preceding year	Motor vehicles and all other fixed assets other than premises but including furniture and fixtures should be shown under this head.

(*ii*) Additions during the year	
(*iii*) Deductions during the year	
(*iv*) Depreciation to date.	
Other Assets	
I. Inter/office adjust-ments (net)	The inter-office adjustments balance, if in debit, should be shown under this head. Only net position of inter-office accounts, inland as well as foreign, should be shown here. For arriving at the net balances of inter-office adjustment accounts, all connected inter-office accounts should be aggregated and the net balance, if in debit, only should be shown representing mostly items in transit and unadjusted items.
II. Interest accrued	Interest accrued but not due on Investments and advances and interest due but not collected on investments will be the main components of this item. As banks normally debit the borrowers' accounts with interest due on the balance sheet date, usually there may not be any amount of interest due on advances. Only such interest as can be realised in the ordinary course should be shown under this head.
III. Tax paid in advance/ tax deducted at source	The amount of tax deducted at source on securities, advance tax paid etc. to the extent that these items are not set off against relative tax provisions should be shown against this item.
IV. Stationery and stamps	Only exceptional items of expenditure on stationery like bulk purchase of security paper, loose leaf or other ledgers, etc. which are shown as quasi-assets to be written off over a period of time should be shown here. The value should be on a realistic basis and cost escalation should be taken into account, as these items are for internal use.
V. Non-banking assets acquired in satisfac-tion of claims	Immovable properties/tangible assets acquired in satisfaction of claims are to be shown under this head.
VI. Others	This will include items like claims which have not been met, for instance, clearing items, debit items, representing addition to assets or reduction in liabilities which have not been adjusted for technical reasons, want of particulars, etc., advances given to staff by a bank as employer and not as a banker, etc. Items which are in the nature of expenses which are pending adjustments should be provided for and the provision netted against this item so that only realisable value is shown under this head. Accrued income other than interest may also be included here.
Bills for Collection	Bills and other items in the course of collection and not adjusted will be shown against this item in the summary version only. No separate schedule is proposed.

Explanation of Some Terms relating to Balance Sheet

Bills Payable. Bank provide the facility of remitting funds from one place to another place to their customers by means of pay orders, bank drafts, telegraphic transfers, traveller cheques etc. Customers desirous of remitting money deposit the necessary amounts with the bank and receives in exchange the bank drafts, pay orders, traveller cheques etc. which are sent to the payees and they encash these. If some of these pay orders, bank drafts and traveller cheques remain encashed upto the day of preparation of final accounts of the bank should be shown as a liability in the Balance Sheet under heading of "Other Liabilities and Provisions" as an item of Bills Payable.

Money at Call and Short Notice. This item appears on the assets side of a Bank Balance Sheet and represents temporary loans to Bill Brokers, Stock Brokers and other banks. If the loan is given for one day, it is called 'money at call' and if the loan cannot be called back on demand and will require at least a notice of three days for calling back, it is called 'money at short notice'. It also includes deposits repayable within 10 days or less than 15 days notice lent in the inter bank call money market. The rate of interest on which money is lent fluctuates every day, sometimes very sharply (more than 30%), depending on the demand and supply of money.

Advances

Advances appear on the assets side as fourth head and include loans, cash credits, bank overdrafts and bills discounted and purchased. Banks generally advance money to their customers in the form of loans, cash credits, overdrafts and purchasing and discounting of bills. **Provisions in respect of doubtful advances are deducted from advances to the extent necessary and the excess provision for doubtful debts is included under "Other Liabilities and Provisions".**

(*i*) Cash Credit. It is an arrangement by which the customer is granted the right to borrow money from time to time upto a certain limit. Cash credit is usually given on hypothecation or pledge of stock. The bank usually charges a higher bank interest on the actual amount withdrawn than that charged on loan because the bank has to keep the amount allowed as cash credit always ready under the fear that money allowed may be demanded at any time. Further, in case of cash credit arrangement, the customer is required to pay a minimum interest whether the customer draws any amount or not.

A cash credit overdraft account is treated as NPA if it remains out of order for a period of more than 90 days. An account is treated as 'out of order' if any of the following conditions is satisfied :

(*a*) The outstanding balance remains continuously in excess of the sanctioned limit/drawing power.

(*b*) Though the outstanding balance is less than the sanctioned limit/drawing power—

- (*i*) there are no credits continuously for more than 90 days as on the date of Balance Sheet; or
- (*ii*) credits during the aforesaid period are not enough to cover the interest debited during the same period.

(*c*) Further any amount due to the bank under any credit facility is 'overdue' if it is not paid on the due date fixed by the bank.

(*ii*) Overdraft. This facility is available to a customer who operates a current account with the bank. This facility is granted to customers who have high goodwill and name for honest dealings. In case of bank overdraft, customer is permitted to overdraw money upto a certain level. The facility of overdraft is beneficial to the customer as he has to pay interest only upon the sum overdrawn by him and not upon the maximum limit of the overdraft.

***(iii)* Loan.** Loan is advance of a fixed amount to a customer to be withdrawn in lump sum by him. Interest is charged on the total amount of the loan agreed to be paid to a customer whether he uses the full amount of the loan or not. So, customers prefer to take cash credit and pay interest at a little higher rate as they find it inconvenient to use the whole amount of the loan immediately.

***(iv)* Discounting of Bills.** Discounting of a bill means making the payment of the bill before the maturity date of the bill. While making payment of the bill, the bank deducts discount for the unexpired period for the amount of the bill discounted. The bank keeps the bill with it till the maturity date and gets its payment for the customer on the due date.

***(v)* Purchasing and Discounting of Bills.** The bank may purchase or discount clean or documentary bills at the current rate of interest.

Clean Bills. These are the bills to which no documents such as bill of lading, insurance policy etc. are attached.

Documentary Bills. These bills are supported by documents such as bills of lading, insurance policy etc. These bills are secured as in case of non-payment of the bill, the bank can attach the goods.

Bills for Collection. These are drafts and bills drawn by sellers of goods on the purchasers of goods and sent to the bank for collection against delivery documents (*i.e.* railway receipts, truck receipts, bill of lading). The bank hands over the documents authorising the delivery of the goods to the borrower only after the collection of the amount of the bill. **If some bills are left uncollected at the end of the year, they are shown in the summary version only. These are not shown in any schedule. They appear at the foot of the Balance Sheet.** An alternative method for making a record of bills for collection is that a separate register known as Bills for Collection Register is maintained. Two accounts are to be maintained which are mirror images of each other. They are Bills for Collection (Assets) Account and Bills for Collection (Liability) Account.

ILLUSTRATION 9. From the following details, prepare Bills for Collection (Asset) Account and Bills for Collection (Liability) Account :

	₹
On 1-4-2022, Bills for Collection were	**10,20,000**
During the year 2022-23, Bills Received for Collection amounted to	**15,00,000**
Bills Collected during the year 2022-23	**19,69,400**
Bills dishonoured and returned during the year	**5,42,000**

SOLUTION

BILLS FOR COLLECTION (ASSET) ACCOUNT

		₹			₹
1-4-2022	To Balance b/d	10,20,000	2022-23	By Bills for Collection (Liability) A/c	19,69,400
2022-23	To Bills for Collection (Liability) A/c	15,00,000	2022-23	– do –	5,42,000
			31-3-2023	By Balance c/d	8,600
		25,20,000			25,20,000
1-4-2023	To Balance b/d	8,600			

BILLS FOR COLLECTION (LIABILITY ACCOUNT

		₹			₹
2022-23	To Bills for Collection (Asset) A/c	19,69,400	1-4-2022	By Balance b/d	10,20,000
2022-23	To Bills for Collection (Asset) A/c	5,42,000	2022-23	By Bills for Collection (Asset) A/c	15,00,000
31-3-23	To Balance c/d	8,600			
		25,20,000			25,20,000
			1-4-23	By Balance b/d	8,600

Acceptances, Endorsements and Other Obligations. A bank can accommodate its customers by accepting and endorsing bills on their behalf. This is usually done in the case of foreign bills to facilitate negotiations and foreign business dealings. In such cases, the bank is liable towards third parties to whom bills are given or endorsed guarantee of payment is given in case of non-payment of the promised amount. On the other hand, customers are liable to the bank for such claims. The bank enters such bills in the Bills Accepted Register. ***Outstanding amount of acceptances, endorsements and other obligations at the end of the year has to be shown as contingent liabilities in Schedule 12 in the Balance Sheet.***

ILLUSTRATION 10. From the following details prepare "Acceptances, Endorsements and Other Obligations A/c" as would appear in the general ledger.

On 1-4-2022 acceptances not yet satisfied stood at ₹ 22,30,000. Out of which ₹ 20 lacs were subsequently paid off by clients and bank had to honour the rest. A scrutiny of the Acceptance Register revealed the following :

Client	*Acceptances/Guarantees*	*Remarks*
	₹	
A	**10,00,000**	**Bank honoured on 10-6-2022**
B	**12,00,000**	**Party paid off on 30-9-2022**
C	**5,00,000**	**Party failed to pay and bank had to honour on 30-11-2022**
D	**8,00,000**	**Not satisfied up to 31-3-2023**
E	**5,00,000**	**— do —**
F	**2,70,000**	**— do —**
Total	**42,70,000**	

SOLUTION **ACCEPTANCES, ENDORSEMENTS AND OTHER OBLIGATIONS ACCOUNT**

		₹				₹
2022-23	To Constituents' Liabilities for Acceptances/ Guarantees etc. (Paid off by Clients)	20,00,000	1-4-2022	By Balance b/d		22,30,000
"	To Constituents' Liabilities for Acceptances/ Guarantees etc. (Honoured by bank)	2,30,000	2022-23	By Constitutents' Liabilities for Acceptances/ Guarantees etc.	₹	
				A	10,00,000	
				B	12,00,000	
				C	5,00,000	
				D	8,00,000	

Date	Particulars	₹	Date	Particulars	₹	₹
10-6-2022	To Constituents' Liabilities for Acceptances/ Guarantees etc. (Honoured by bank)	10,00,000		E	5,00,000	
				F	2,70,000	42,70,000
30-9-2022	To Constituents' Liabilities for Acceptances/ Guarantees etc.	12,00,000				
30-11-2022	To Constituents' Liabilities for Acceptances/ Guarantees etc. (Honoured by bank on party's failure to pay)	5,00,000				
31-3-2023	To Balance c/d (Acceptances not yet satisfied)	15,70,000				
		65,00,000				65,00,000
			1-4-2023	By Balance b/d		15,70,000

ILLUSTRATION 11. The following figures were also available for Assured Bank Limited:

- **On 1st April, 2022 Acceptances, Endorsements etc. not yet satisfied amounted to ₹ 29,00,000.**
- **During the year, Acceptances, Endorsements, Guarantees, etc. were ₹ 88,00,000.**
- **The Bank honored acceptances of ₹ 55,00,000 and a client paid off ₹ 20,00,000 against the guaranteed liabilities.**
- **The Bank paid ₹ 2,00,000 which clients failed to pay.**

Pass necessary Journal Entries with narrations and prepare "Acceptances, Endorsements and other Obligations Account" in the General Ledger.

SOLUTION

JOURNAL ENTRIES IN THE BOOKS OF ASSURED BANK LTD.

	Particulars			***Debit*** (₹)	***Credit*** (₹)
2022-23	Constituents' Liabilities for Acceptances, Endorsements A/c	Dr.		88,00,000	
	To Acceptances, Endorsements and Other Obligations A/c				88,00,000
	(Being liability accepted during the year)				
2022-23	Acceptances, Endorsements & Other Obligations A/c	Dr.		55,00,000	
	To Constituents' Liabilities for Acceptances, Endorsements A/c				55,00,000
	(Being Bank honoured acceptances against guaranteed bills)				
2022-23	Acceptances, Endorsements & Other Obligations A/c	Dr.		20,00,000	
	To Constituents' Liabilities for Acceptances, Endorsements A/c				20,00,000
	(Being client paid off against guaranteed bills)				
2022-23	Acceptances, Endorsements & Other Obligations A/c	Dr.		2,00,000	
	To Constituents' Liabilities for Acceptances, Endorsements A/c				2,00,000
	(Being Bank paid off against guaranteed bill which clients failed to pay)				

ACCEPTANCES, ENDORSEMENT AND OTHER OBLIGATIONS ACCOUNT IN THE GENERAL LEDGER

		₹			₹
2022-23	To Constituents' Liabilities for Acceptance, Endorsement, etc.	55,00,000	2022 April 1	By Balance b/d	29,00,000
2022-23	To Constituents' Liabilities for Acceptances, Endorsement, etc.	20,00,000	2022-23	By Constituents' Liabilities for Acceptances, Endorsements, etc.	88,00,000
2022-23	To Constituents' Liabilities for Acceptances, Endorsements, etc. (amount paid on failure of clients)				
2023 April 1	To Balance c/d	40,00,000			
		1,17,00,000			1,17,00,000

Inter-office Adjustments. A bank having several branches will receive periodical statements from them regarding the inter-branch transactions. It is possible that some entries may remain unadjusted in the head office of the bank at the close of the financial year. Such entries are recorded in the Balance Sheet under the sub-heading 'Branch Adjustments' and may appear on the assets side under the heading 'Other Assets' if it has a debit balance and on the liabilities side under the heading 'Other Liabilities' if it has a credit balance.

Non-banking Assets. A banking company is not allowed to deal directly or indirectly in the purchase or sale or barter of goods except in connection with its legitimate banking business. But a bank can always lend against the security of the assets. The bank may have to take possession of the asset given as security if the loanee fails to repay the loan. In that case, the asset acquired in satisfaction of the claim of the bank will be shown as Non-banking Assets in the Balance Sheet under the heading 'Other Fixed Assets'. Such assets acquired should be disposed of within seven years as a banking company is not allowed to hold such assets for any period exceeding seven years from the date of their acquisition. Profit or loss on sale of such assets is required to be shown separately in the Profit and Loss Account of the Bank. Reserve Bank may in any particular case extend the aforesaid period of seven years by such period not exceeding five years, where it is satisfied that such extension would be in the interest of the depositors of the Banking company. It may be noted that if bank lends against such assets as are allowed to be held by bank, say Government Securities, it can continue to hold them if the loanee (loan taker) fails to pay his loan obligation. Such assets cannot be treated as non-banking assets.

Interest on Doubtful Debts

While closing its books for an accounting year, a bank takes credit for interest accrued on term loan, cash credits, overdrafts, bills purchased and discounted etc. But it must not take such a credit for interest accrued on Non-Performing Assets (NPAs)/Doubtful Assets. The guiding principle in line with International Accounting Standards, is that the income on NPA (doubtful debts) should not be recognized on accrual basis and should be treated as income only when actually received. Hence, no entry need be passed and, therefore, no credit for interest can be taken.

While finalising accounts of a bank some advances may be doubtful for collection. Interest on such advances cannot be treated as income. Interest on doubtful debts is debited to Loan Account and credited to Interest Suspense Account. The proportionate amount of interest received in cash is transferred to Interest Account and the balance to the Loan Account. The Loan Account is closed by transferring the balance to Bad Debts Account.

ILLUSTRATION 12. On 31st March 2023 Loan Account in the books of a bank showed a debit balance of ₹ 3,00,000 including ₹ 24,000 due from a merchant which is doubtful. The interest accrued on this loan upto 31-3-2023 was ₹ 15,000 including ₹ 3,000 on doubtful debts.

The merchant became insolvent and the official receiver paid a dividend of 50 paise in the rupee on 30-4-2023.

Pass necessary journal entries relating to Merchant's Loan Account which is doubtful in the books of the bank on 31-3-2023 and 30-4-2023 and prepare Merchant's Loan Account.

SOLUTION

JOURNAL

			₹	₹
2023 March 31	Merchant's Loan Account	Dr.	3,000	
	To Interest Suspense Account			3,000
	(Interest on doubtful loan credited to Interest Suspense Account)			
April 30	Cash Account	Dr.	13,500	
	To Merchant's Loan Account			13,500
	(Receipt of 50% of the amount due from merchant on 30-4-2023)			
April 30	Interest Suspense Account	Dr.	3,000	
	To Merchant's Loan Account			1,500
	To Interest Account			1,500
	(50% of Merchant's Loan Account transferred to Interest Account, the balance to Loan Account)			
"	Bad Debts Account	Dr.	12,000	
	To Merchant's Loan Account			12,000
	(Amount Irrecoverable)			

LOAN LEDGER

MERCHANT'S LOAN ACCOUNT

		₹			₹
2023 March 31	To Balance b/d	24,000	2023 March 31	By Balance c/d	27,000
"	To Interest Suspense A/c	3,000			
		27,000			27,000
2023 April 1	To Balance b/d	27,000	2023 April 30	By Cash A/c	13,500
			"	By Interest Suspense A/c	1,500
			"	By Bad Debts A/c	12,000
		27,000			27,000

Rebate on Bills Discounted or Unexpired Discounts. This item is like interest received in advance and represents unearned discounts for those bills which will mature after the closing of the financial accounts.

When a bank discounts a bill, the following entry is recorded :

Bills Discounted Account	Dr.	(with full value of the bill)
To Customers Account		(with the amount of present cash value)
To Discount Account		(Discount deducted by the bank)

The bank will deduct discount for the period for which it has to wait to get payment of the bill on the maturity date. At the close of the financial year, some of the bills discounted may not have matured; consequently, the total discount credited in respect of such bills cannot be treated as earned during the current year. Therefore, discount for the unexpired period is debited to Discount Account to cancel the credit given previously and credited to Rebate on Bills Discounted Account or Unexpired Discount Account or Discount Received in Advance Account. In the Profit and Loss Account, this item is deducted from Interest and Discount to get the net income of the year. In the Balance Sheet, this item appears under the heading 'other liabilities' as unexpired discounts. At the commencement of the next year, reverse entry is passed as follows :

Rebate on Bills Discounted Account Dr.
To Discount Account
(Being unexpired discount of the previous year expiring this year and becoming income)

ILLUSTRATION 13. Following is an extract from the Trial Balance of a Bank as at 31st March, 2023 :

	₹	₹
Bills discounted	**51,50,000**	
Rebate on bills discounted not yet due, April 1, 2022		**30,501**
Discount received		**1,45,500**

An analysis of the bills discounted as shown above shows the following :

Date of Bills	***Amount ₹***	***Term Months***	***Discounted @ % p.a.***
2023			
January 13	**7,50,000**	**4**	**12**
February 17	**6,00,000**	**3**	**10**
March 6	**4,00,000**	**4**	**11**
March 16	**2,00,000**	**2**	**10**

Find out the amount of discount received to be credited to Profit and Loss Account and pass appropriate Journal Entries for the same. How the relevant items will appear in the Bank's Balance Sheet ?

SOLUTION

The amount to be credited to Profit and Loss Account is ascertained from the Discount Account as follows :

DISCOUNT ACCOUNT

		₹			₹
2023			2022		
Mar. 31	To Profit and Loss A/c (Bal. fig. transferred)	1,41,700	April 1	By Rebate on Bills Discounted (on 1-4-2022)	30,501
Mar. 31	To Rebate on Bills Discounted (on 31-3-2023)	34,301	2023 Mar. 31	By Sundries	1,45,500
		1,76,001			1,76,001

SOLUTION

CALCULATION OF UNEXPIRED DISCOUNTS OR REBATE ON BILLS DISCOUNTED

Date of Bill	*Date of Maturity including three days*	*No.of days after March 31*	*Amount* ₹	*Rate of Discount % p.a.*	*Total Annual Discount*	*Proportionate Discount for days after 31st March*	
2023 Jan. 13	2023 May 16	46	7,50,000	12	₹ 90,000	₹ 11,342	$\left(₹\ 90{,}000 \times \frac{46}{365}\right)$
Feb. 17	May 20	50	6,00,000	10	60,000	8,219	$\left(₹\ 60{,}000 \times \frac{50}{365}\right)$
March 6	July 9	100	4,00,000	11	44,000	12,055	$\left(₹\ 44{,}000 \times \frac{100}{365}\right)$
March 16	May 19	49	2,00,000	10	20,000	2,685	$\left(₹\ 20{,}000 \times \frac{49}{365}\right)$
						34,301	

JOURNAL ENTRIES

				₹	₹
2022 April 30	Rebate on Bills Discounted Account To Discount Account (Being unexpired discount brought forward from the previous year, credited to Discount Account)	Dr.		30,501	30,501
2023 March 31	Discount Account To Rebate on Bills Discounted Account (Being provision for unexpired discount required at the end of the year)	Dr.		34,301	34,301
" 31	Discount Account To Profit and Loss Account (Being discount earned for the year 2022-23 transferred)	Dr.		1,41,700	1,41,700

BALANCE SHEET
as on 31-3-2023

	Schedule	₹
Liabilities		
Other Liabilities		
Rebate on Bills Discounted	5	34,301
Assets		
Advances		
Bills Discounted	9	51,50,000

ILLUSTRATION 14. **On 31st March, 2022, Upkeep Bank Ltd. had a balance of ₹ 27 crores in 'Rebate on Bills Discounted Account. During the year ended 31st March, 2023, Upkeep Bank Ltd. discounted bills of exchange of ₹ 12,000 crores charging interest @ 18%, per annum the average period of discount being 73 days. Of these, bills of exchange of ₹ 1,800 crores were due for realisation from the acceptors/customers after 31st March, 2023, the average period outstanding after 31st March, 2023 being 36.5 days.**

Upkeep Bank Ltd. asks you to pass journal entries and show the ledger accounts pertaining to: (*i*) Discounting of bills of exchange and (*ii*) Rebate on bills discounted.

SOLUTION

UPKEEP BANK LTD.
JOURNAL ENTRIES

Date	*Particulars*		*L.F.*	*In crores (₹)*	*In crores (₹)*
2022 April 1	Rebate on Bills Discounted A/c To Discount on Bills A/c (Being transfer of opening balance of Rebate on Bills Discounted A/c to Discount on Bills A/c)	Dr.		27	27
2022-23	Bills Purchased and Discounted A/c To Discount on Bills A/c To Clients A/c (Being bills discounted during the year and discount earned @ 18% p.a. on ₹ 12,000 crores for 73 days average period)	Dr.		12,000	432 11,568

2023 March 31	Discount on Bills A/c Dr. To Rebate on Bills Discounted A/c (Being unexpired discount in respect of ₹ 1,800 crores @ 18% p.a. for 36.5 days average period)		32.4	32.4
March 31	Discount on Bills A/c Dr. To Profit and Loss A/c (Being income on bills discounted for the year transferred to Profit and Loss A/c)		426.6	426.6

DISCOUNT ON BILLS ACCOUNT

		In crores (₹)			In crores (₹)
2023 March 31	To Rebate on Bills Discounted A/c	32.4	2022 April 1	By Rebate on Bills Discounted A/c	27.0
" 31	To Profit and Loss A/c	426.6	2022-23	By Bills Purchased and Discounted A/c	432.0
		459.0			459.0

REBATE ON BILLS DISCOUNTED ACCOUNT

		In crores (₹)			In crores (₹)
2022 April 1	To Discount on Bills A/c	27.0	2022 April 1	By Balance b/d	27.0
2023 March 31	To Balance c/d	32.4	2023 March 31	By Discount on Bills A/c	32.4
		59.4			59.4
			2023 April 1	By Balance b/d	32.4

ILLUSTRATION 15. **Following balances have been extracted from the books of a banking company as on 31st March, 2023 :**

Bad Debts	**₹ 5,00,000**	**Required Provision for Bad Debts**	**₹ 7,00,000**
Advances	**₹ 74,50,000**	**Provision for Taxation to be made**	**25% of Net Profit**
Profit before charging Bad Debts	**₹ 21,50,000**		

Show how the above items will appear in the banking company's Profit and Loss Account and Balance Sheet.

SOLUTION

PROFIT AND LOSS ACCOUNT
for the year ending 31st March, 2023

	Schedule No.	₹
I. Income	13	21,50,000
II. Expenditure		
Provisions and Contingencies (1)		14,37,500
III. Profit/Loss		
Net Profit for the year		7,12,500

BALANCE SHEET
as on 31-3-2023

		Schedule No.	₹
Capital & Liabilities			
Other Liabilities & Provisions :	(2)	5	2,37,500
Assets			
Advances	(3)	9	67,50,000

Working Notes :

(1) Provisions and Contingencies

	₹
Bad Debts	5,00,000
Provision for Bad Debts	7,00,000
Provision for Taxation (₹ 21,50,000 – ₹ 5,00,000 – ₹ 7,00,000) × 25%	2,37,500
	14,37,500

(2) Provision for Taxation has been shown under the heading of "Other Liabilities and Provisions in the Balance Sheet".

(3) The figure of Advances in the Balance Sheet is after deducting Provision for Bad Debts. Bad debts must have already been deducted from advances.

ILLUSTRATION 16. **(*Particulars of Loans and Advances*) From the books of accounts of New Bank Ltd. as on 31st March, 2023 the following particulars regarding loans and advances given by the Bank in India are available :**

		₹
(*i*)	**Loans to corporate sector fully secured (excluding banks but including companies in which directors are interested)**	**10,00,000**
(*ii*)	**Loan to Vijay Bank Ltd.—fully secured**	**3,00,000**
(*iii*)	**Debts due by officers (excluding directors—fully secured)**	**2,00,000**
(*iv*)	**Loans to non-corporate sector—fully secured**	**9,00,000**
(*v*)	**Loans to Nagrik Bank Ltd.—fully secured**	**4,00,000**
(*vi*)	**Debts due by Manogk, director of the Bank—fully secured**	**1,00,000**
(*vii*)	**Debts considered good which are unsecured**	**5,00,000**
(*viii*)	**Debts due by companies in which the directors are interested, fully secured**	**6,00,000**
(*ix*)	**Maximum amount of debts at any time during the year**	**15,00,000**
(*x*)	**Doubtful debts**	**50,000**
(*xi*)	**Provision for Bad and Doubtful Debts**	**75,000**
(*xii*)	**Maximum amount of debts due by officers and directors at any time during the year**	**5,00,000**

You are required to show how the items are statutorily required to be entered in the Balance Sheet of the Bank.

SOLUTION

New Bank Ltd.
SCHEDULE 9—ADVANCES

(₹ in '000)

A.	(1)	Bills purchased and discounted	
	(2)	Cash credits, overdrafts and loan payable on demand	
	(3)	Term Loans	3,400
		Total	3,400

B.	(1)	Secured by transferable assets	2,900
	(2)	Covered by Bank/Govt. guarantees	—
	(3)	Unsecured	500
		Total	3,400
C.	*(i)*	Advances in India	—
		(1) Priority sectors	—
		(2) Public Sector	700
		(3) Banks	2,700
		(4) Others	3,400
D.	*(ii)*	Advances outside India	—
		(1) Due from banks	—
		(2) Due from others	—
		(*a*) Bills purchased and discounted	—
		(*b*) Syndicated loans	—
		(*c*) Others	—
		Total	
		Grand Total of (*i*) & (*ii*)	3,400

Income Recognition

Bank advances can also be classified as performing assets and non-performing assets (NPA). Interest income from NPA is considered as income as and when it is received rather than on accrual basis.

The above general rule, however, does not apply in case of advances against term deposits, NSCs, IVPs, KVPs and Life Policies provided adequate margin is available.

In case of banks, interest on non-performing assets is not recognised as income and taken to the Profit and Loss Account. An asset becomes non-performing when it ceases to generate income for the bank. Non-performing asset means a credit facility in respect of which interest and/or principal repayment instalment is in arrears for more than 90 days. There is no promise of recovering the dues in full having regard to the value of security or current net worth of the borrower guarantor, hence the possibility of loss in realsing such debts. Further, if one of the accounts of a borrower comes under the category of non-performing asset, all the accounts of that borrower (other than loans with a liability of less than ₹ 25,000) will be treated as non-performing assets. The identification of non-performing assets is done on the basis of the position as on the Balance Sheet date. If an account is regularised before the Balance Sheet date by payment of overdue amount, the account may not be treated as a non-performing asset. Now-a-days banks are evaluated on the basis of percentages of their non-performing assets. Therefore, banks make their best possible efforts to reduce the percentages of their NPAs.

ILLUSTRATION 17. On 31st March, 2023 Lakshmi Bank Ltd. finds that :

(1) On a term loan of ₹ 2 crores, interest for the last three quarters is in arrears beyond the due date.

(2) The amount of ₹ 10 lakhs of a discounted bill was due on 1st January, 2023 but the same has not been received.

(3) On a term loan of ₹ 1 crore, interest for the last one quarter is due.

Which of the above items will be treated as non-performing assets (NPA) on 31st March, 2023.

SOLUTION

(1) A term loan is treated as NPA if interest on it remains due for a period of exceeding 90 days. In the present case, interest is in arrears for the last 3 quarters beyond the due 90 days. Hence the term loan is NPA.

(2) To be treated as NPA the discounted bill must remain overdue for a period of more than 90 days. But in the present case, bill has remained overdue for 89 days (*i.e.* January 1, 2023 to March 31, 2023). Hence the discounted bill is not to be treated as NPA.

(3) The term loan of ₹ 1 crore is not to be treated as NPA because interest is due for not more than 90 days.

Provision for Taxation

Provision for taxation is charged to the Profit and Loss Account under the heading "Provisions and Contingencies" and in the Balance Sheet, it is shown under the heading "Other Liabilities and Provisions" on the liabilities side. **Provision for taxation is to be made after making provision for doubtful debts.**

ILLUSTRATION 18. Given below is interest on advances of a commercial bank

(₹ in lakhs)

	Performing Assets		*NPA*	
	Interest earned	*Interest received*	*Interest earned*	*Interest received*
Term Loans	**200**	**150**	**140**	**10**
Cash Credits & Overdrafts	**1,400**	**1,200**	**300**	**25**
Bills purchased and discounted	**300**	**300**	**150**	**40**

Calculate the amount of interest to be recognised as income.

SOLUTION

Interest on performing assets should be recognised on accrual basis but interest on NPA should be recognised on receipt basis.

		₹ in Lakhs
Interest on Term Loans	(200 + 10)	210
Interest on Cash Credit & Overdrafts	(1,400 + 25)	1,425
Income from bills purchased & discounted	(300 + 40)	340
Interest to be recognised as Income		1,975

Classification of Bank Advances

The banks are required to classify their advances into following four broad groups :

(*i*) Standard Assets
(*ii*) Sub-standard Assets
(*iii*) Doubtful Assets and
(*iv*) Loss Assets.

The above classification is done after taking into consideration the degree of well defined credit worthiness and the extent of dependance on the collateral security for realisation of dues. Each broad category is discussed as under :

(*i*) Standard Assets. These assets do not disclose any problem and also do not carry more than normal risk attached to the business. These are known as performing assets. The banks have to make a general provision of 0.40% on standard assets. **As per prudential norms of RBI, provisions towards standard assets need not be netted from gross advances but shown separately as Contingent Provisions against Standard Assets under 'Other Liabilities and Provisions—Others' in Schedule 5 of Balance Sheet.**

(*ii*) Sub-standard Assets. Such assets have been classified as non-performing assets (*i.e.* NPA) for a period not exceeding one year. The current net worth of the borrower/guarantor or the current market value of the security charged under such cases is not enough to ensure recovery of the dues to the bank in full. Such an asset will have well defined weaknesses that jeopardise the liquidation of the debt and perhaps the bank will have to sustain some loss if deficiencies are not corrected. Where instalments of term loans are overdue for a period not exceeding one year should be treated as sub-standard asset.

(*iii*) Doubtful Assets. An asset which has remained NPA for a period of one year. In term loans if the instalments of the principal have remained overdue for a period of one year should be treated as doubtful. A loan is classified as doubtful if all the weaknesses inherent in that classified as sub-standard with the added characteristics that weaknesses make collection or liquidation in full on the basis of currently known facts, conditions and values highly questionable and improbable.

(*iv*) Loss Assets. Where the loss on an asset has been identified by bank or internal auditor or the RBI inspector but the amount has not been written off wholly or partly is known as loss asset. Such an asset is uncollectable and is of such little value that it is not desirable to show it as bank's asset though it may have some salvage or recovery value. **According to the Prudential Norms of the Reserve Bank of India, the entire loss asset has to be written off. If such assets are permitted to remain in the books for any reason, 100% of the outstanding need be provided for.**

The above classification is done to provide a basis for determining provisions on loans, investments and other assets and determining losses to arrive at correct profitability of banks.

Provision Norms for Doubtful Assets According to RBI

(*i*) 100 per cent of the extent to which the advance is not covered by the realisable value of the security to which the bank has a valid recourse and the realisable value is estimated on a realistic basis.

(*ii*) In regard to the secured portion, provision may be made on the following bases, at the rates ranging from 25 per cent to 100 per cent of the secured portion (as given later in this chapter) depending upon the period for which the asset has remained doubtful.

Treatment of Interest Suspense Account

Amounts held in Interest Suspense Account is not to be reckoned as part of provisions. Amounts lying in the Interest Suspense Account is to be deducted from the relative advances and thereafter, provisioning as per the norms, should be made on the balances after such deduction.

Advances Covered by ECGC/DICGC Guarantee

In the case of advances guaranteed by DICGC/ECGC provision can be made only for the balance in excess of the amount guaranteed by these Corporations. Further, while arriving at the provision required to be made for doubtful assets, realisable value of the securities should first be deducted from the outstanding balance in respect of the amount guaranteed by these Corporations and then provision made.

Advance Covered by CGTSI Guarantee

In case the advance covered by CGTSI guarantee becomes non-performing, no provision need be made towards the guaranteed portion. The amount outstanding in excess of the guaranteed portion should be provided for as per the guidelines on provisioning for non-performing advances.

Agricultural Advance

(*a*) A loan granted for short duration crops will be treated as NPA, if the instalment of principal or interest thereon remains overdue for two crop seasons. A loan granted for long duration crops will be treated as NPA, if the instalment of principal or interest thereon remains overdue for one crop season.

(*b*) A loan granted for short duration crops will be treated as NPA, if the instalment of principal or interest thereon remains overdue for two crop seasons. A loan granted for long duration crops will be treated as NPA, if the instalment of principal or interest thereon remains overdue for one crop season. For the purpose of these guidelines, "long duration" crops would be crops with crop season longer than one year and crops, which are not "long duration" crops, would be treated as "short duration" crops. The crop season for each crop, which means the period upto harvesting of the crops raised, would be as determined by the State Level Bankers' Committee in each State. Depending upon the duration of crops raised by an agriculturist, the above NPA norms would also be made applicable to agricultural term loans availed of by him.

Provisions

The banks should make provisions against sub-standard assets, doubtful assets and loss assets on the following bases but after taking into account the time lag between an account becoming doubtful of recovery, its recognition as such, realisation of the security and the erosion over time in value of security charged to the banks.

***(i)* Loss Assets.** The entire assets should be written off. If the assets are to remain in the books for any reason, then 100% of the outstanding should be provided.

***(ii)* Doubtful Assets.**

(*a*) 100% of the extent to which the advance is not covered by the realisable value of the security in the possession of the bank. The realisable value is estimated on realistic basis.

(*b*) Over and above item (*a*) above, depending on the period for which the assets remained doubtful 25% to 100% of the secured portion (*i.e.* estimated realisable value of the outstandings) on the following basis :

Period for which the advance has been considered as doubtful	% of provision
Upto one year	25
One to three years	40
More than three years	100

(*iii*) Sub-standard Assets. A general provision of 15 per cent on total outstanding is required to be made without making any allowance for DICGC/ECGC guarantee cover and securities available. The 'unsecured exposures' which are identified as 'substandard' would attract additional provision of 10 per cent, *i.e.*, a total of 25 per cent on the outstanding balance. In case of unsecured infrastructure loan where certain safeguards such as escrow accounts are available, 20% provision on the outstanding balance is required. Unsecured exposure is defined as an exposure where the realisable value of the security, as assessed by the bank approved valuers and Reserve Bank's inspecting officers is not more than 10 per cent, *abinitio* of the outstanding exposure.

RBI vide its notification No. DBOD No. B.P.B.C. 94/21.4.048/2011-12 dated 18th May 2011 has increased the provisioning rates for secured sub-standard assets from 10% to 15% for secured doubtful assets upto 1 year from 20% to 25% and for secured doubtful assets of 1 year to 3 years the provisioning rate has been increased from 30% to 40%.

(*iv*) Standard Assets. A general provision of a minimum of 0.40% of total standard assets should be made. It has been clarified by RBI that the provision should be made on global loan basis and not on domestic advances alone.

Provisions for Other Purposes. Normally banks have two retirement benefits *i.e.* Provident Fund and Gratuity. Some banks have pension schemes also. Most of the banks have set up recognised gratuity or pension funds in order to cover up related liability. It is necessary that such liabilities are estimated on accrual basis and full provision is made for the purpose forthwith.

Table showing Provisioning Norms for Loans and Advances

Category	*Provisioning Norms*	*Rate %*
1. Standard Assets	(*a*) Direct advances to agriculture and small micro enterprises	0.25
	(*b*) Advances to commercial real estate	1.00
	(*c*) Restructured Loan and Advance A/c	2.00
	(*d*) All other advances and loans not included in (*a*), (*b*) and (*c*) above	0.40
2. Sub-standard Assets	(*a*) Secured portion of loans and advances	15
	(*b*) Unsecured portion in respect of infrastructure loan accounts where certain safeguards such as Escrew Accounts are available	20
	(*c*) Unsecured portion of loans and advances	25
3. Doubtful Assets	(*a*) Unsecured portion of loans and advances	100
	(*b*) Secured portion of loans and advances :	
	(*i*) For doubtful debts upto one year	25
	(*ii*) Exceeding one year but not 3 years	40
	(*iii*) Exceeding 3 years	100
4. Loss Assets	The entire amount should be written off	100

ILLUSTRATION 19. A Loan Account remains out of order as on the date of Balance Sheet of a Bank. The account has been classified as doubtful asset (upto 3 years). Details of the account is :

Outstanding	₹ 7,24,000	
ECGC Cover	30% of outstanding (Subject to maximum of ₹ 1,50,000)	
Value of security :		₹
As per valuation on the date of grant of loan		2,25,000
As per realisable value as on date of Balance Sheet		1,75,000

Compute the necessary provision to be made by bank as per applicable rate.

SOLUTION

COMPUTATION OF PROVISION TO BE MADE BY A BANK

	₹
Outstanding Value of Doubtful Assets (upto 3 years)	7,24,000
Less : Value of Security (excluding ECGC cover)	(1,75,000)
Sub Total	5,49,000
Less : ECGC Cover (subject to ₹ 1,50,000 maximum)	(1,50,000)
Unsecured Portion	3,99,000
Provision :	₹
For unsecured portion @ 100% of ₹ 3,99,000	3,99,000
For secured portion @ 40% of ₹ 1,75,000	70,000
Total Provision	4,69,000

ILLUSTRATION 20. From the following information of STP Bank Ltd. pertaining to the year 2022-23, compute the provision to be made in the Profit and Loss Account :

	₹ in lakhs
Assets	
Standard	30,000
Sub-standard	20,000
Doubtful :	
For one year (secured)	8,000
for two years and three years (secured)	2,500
For more than three years (secured by mortgage of Plant & Machinery ₹ 500 lakhs)	2,000
Loss Assets	1,700

SOLUTION

Calculation of Provision to be made in the Profit and Loss Account

Classification of Assets	*Amount of Advances ₹ in lakhs*	*% of Provision*	*Provision ₹ in lakhs*
Standard Assets	30,000	0.40	120
Sub-standard assets	20,000	15	3,000

Doubtful Assets :			
For one year (secured)	8,000	25	2,000
For two to three years (secured)	2,500	40	1,000
For more than 3 years : Secured	500	100	500
Unsecured	1,500	100	1,500
Loss Assets	1,700	100	1,700
Total Provision to be made			9,820

ILLUSTRATION 21. From the following information, find out the amount of provision to the shown in the Profit and Loss Account of a commercial bank :

	₹ in lakhs		₹ in lakhs
Assets		**Doubtful (fully secured) :**	
Standard	**8,000**	**for one year**	**1,000**
Sub-standard		**for three years**	**1,600**
(Value of Security ₹ 5,000 lakhs)	**6,000**	**for more than three years**	**400**
Loss Assets	**1,200**		

SOLUTION

CALCULATION OF PROVISION

Assets		*Amount* ₹ in lakhs	*% of Provision*	*Provision* ₹ in lakhs
Standard		8,000	0.40	32
Sub-standard		6,000	(15% of 6,000 lakhs + 10% of 1,000 lakhs which is unsecured)	1,000
Doubtful :	for one year	1,000	25	250
	for 3 years	1,600	40	640
	for more than 3 years	400	100	400
Loss Assets		1,200	100	1,200
				3,522

ILLUSTRATION 22. Rajatapeeta Bank Ltd. had extended the following credit lines to a Small Scale Industry, which had not paid any interest since March, 2017 :

	Term Loan	***Export Loan***
Balance outstanding on 31-3-2023	**₹ 35 lakhs**	**₹ 30 lakhs**
DICGC/ECGC Cover	**40%**	**50%**
Securities held	**₹ 15 lakhs**	**₹ 10 lakhs**
Realisable Value of Securities	**₹ 10 lakhs**	**₹ 08 lakhs**

Compute necessary provisions to be made for the year ended 31st March, 2023.

SOLUTION

	Term Loan *₹ in lakhs*	*Export Credit* *₹ in lakhs*
Balance Outstanding on 31-3-2023	35	30
Less : Realisable Value of Securities	10	8
Unsecured Amount	25	22

Provision for Unsecured Portion @ 100%	25	22
Add : Provision for Secured Portion @ 100% (1)	10	8
	35	30
Less : DICGC Cover @ 40% of ₹ 35 lakhs	14	
ECGC Cover @ 50% of ₹ 30 lakhs		15
Total Provision Required	21	15

Alternate Solution

		Term Loan ₹ in lakhs		*Export Credit ₹ in lakhs*
Balance Outstanding on 31-3-2023		35.0		30.0
Less : Realisable Value of Securities		10.0		8.0
		25.0		22.0
Less : DICGC Cover @ 40% of ₹ 25 lakhs		10.0		
ECGC Cover @ 50% of ₹ 22 lakhs				11.0
Unsecured Balance		15.0		11.0
Required :				
100% for Unsecured Balance		15.0		11.0
Add : 100% for Secured Portion	10.0		8.0	
Less : Covered under DICGC @ 40%	4.0	6.0		
Covered under ECGC @ 50%			4.0	4.0
Total Provision Required		21.0		15.0

ILLUSTRATION 23. From the following information, compute the amount of provisions to be made in the Profit and Loss Account of a Commercial Bank for the year ending on 31-3-2023.

Assets (Category of Advances)	(₹ in lakhs)
Standard Advances	7,000
Sub-standard Advances	3,500
(Include secured exposures ₹ 1,000 lakhs and balances unsecured exposures ₹ 2,500 lakhs includes ₹ 1,500 lakhs in respect of infrastructure loan accounts where escrow accounts are available)	
Doubtful Advances—Unsecured portion	1,500
Doubtful Advances—Secured portion	
For Doubtful upto to 1 year	500
For Doubtful more than 1 year and upto 3 years	600
For Doubtful more than 3 years	300
Loss Advances	200

SOLUTION

CALCULATION OF AMOUNT OF PROVISION TO BE MADE IN THE PROFIT AND LOSS ACCOUNT

	Assets	*Amount*	*% of Provision*	*Provision*
		₹ in lakhs	% of Provision	₹ in lakhs
1.	Standard Advances	7,000	0.40	28
2.	Sub-standard Advances :			
	(*a*) Secured Portion	1,000	15	150
	(*b*) Unsecured Portion in respect of infrastructure loan accounts where escrow accounts are available	1,500	20	300
	(*c*) Unsecured Portion	1,000	25	250
3.	Doubtful Advances :			
	(*a*) Unsecured Portion	1,500	100	1,500
	(*b*) Secured Portion :			
	For one year	500	25	125
	More than 1 year and upto 3 years	600	40	240
	More than 3 years	300	100	300
4.	Loss Advances	200	100	200
	Total Provision against Advances			3,093

ILLUSTRATION **24. From the following information find out the amount of provisions required to be made in the Profit & Loss Account of a commercial bank for the year ended 31st March, 2023.**

(*i*) Packing credit outstanding from Food Processors ₹ 60 lakhs against which the bank holds securities worth ₹ 15 lakhs. The above advance has remained doubtful for more than 3 years.

(*ii*) Other advances :

Assets classification	₹ in lakhs	Doubtful (fully secured) :	₹ in lakhs
		For one year	900
Standard	3,000	For two years	600
Sub-standard	2,200	For three years	400
Loss assets	600	For more than 3 years	300

SOLUTION

(*i*) ***Provision Required Against Packing Credit***

	₹ in lakhs
Amount outstanding (Packing Credit)	60
Less : Realisable value of securities	15
Advance doubtful for more than 3 years	45
Required Provision (100% to the extent not secured)	45
Add: Provision for secured portion (100% of ₹ 15 lakhs outstanding for more than 3 years)	15
	60

(ii) ***Provision Required Against Other Advances***

Assets	*Amount ₹ in lakhs*	*% of Provision*	*Provision ₹ in lakhs*
Standard	3,000	0.40	12
Sub-standard	2,200	15%	330
Doubtful (fully secured)			
For one year	900	25%	225
For two years	600	40%	240
For three years	400	40%	160
For more than 3 years	300	100%	300
Loss assets	600	100%	600
			1,867

Total Provision Required (60 + 1,867) = ₹ 1,927 lakhs

Note : Doubtful advances have been given to be fully secured. In case no security cover is available against these advances, provision will be made @ 100%.

Export Project Finance

In respect of export project finance, there could be instances where the actual importer has paid the dues to the bank abroad but the bank in turn is unable to remit the amount due to political developments such as war, strife, UN embargo, etc.

In such cases as per RBI norms, where the lending bank is able to establish through documentary evidence that the importer has cleared the dues in full by depositing the amount in the bank abroad before it turned into NPA in the books of the bank, but the importer's country is not allowing the funds to be remitted due to political or other reasons, the asset classification may be made after a period of one year from the date the amount was deposited by the importer in the bank abroad.

Advances Under Rehabilitation Approved by BIFR/TLI

As per prudential norms of RBI, banks are not permitted to upgrade the classification of any advance in respect of which the terms have been re-negotiated unless the package of re-negotiated terms has worked satisfactorily for a period of one year. While the existing credit facilities sanctioned to a unit under rehabilitation packages approved by BIFR/term lending institutions will continue to be classified as substandard or doubtful as the case may be, in respect of additional facilities sanctioned under the rehabilitation packages, the Income Recognition, Asset Classification norms will become applicable after a period of one year from the date of disbursement.

Government Guaranteed Advances

Government guaranteed advances : With effect from 31st March, 2001, in respect of advances sanctioned against State Government guarantee, if the guarantee is invoked and remains in default for more than 90 days the banks are required to make normal provisions as discussed above.

Advances granted under rehabilitation packages approved by BIFR/term lending institutions.

(i) In respect of advances under rehabilitation package approved by BIFR/term lending institutions, the provision should continue to be made in respect of dues to the bank on the existing credit facilities as per their classification as sub-standard or doubtful asset.

(*ii*) As regards the additional facilities sanctioned as per package finalized by BIFR and/or term lending institutions, provision on additional facilities sanctioned need not be made for a period of one year from the date of disbursement.

Advances against term deposits, NSCs eligible for surrender, IVPs, KVPs, and life policies would attract provisioning requirements as applicable to their asset classification status. Advances against gold ornaments, government securities and all other kinds of securities are not exempted from provisioning requirements.

Categories of Investments

The investment portfolio of a bank can broadly be divided into categories *i.e.*

(*i*) Approved Securities. These are predominantly government securities. These securities are further bifurcated into permanent and current investments. *Permanent investments* are those where the bank's intention is to hold till maturity. Current investments are those where the bank's intention is to deal in *i.e.* buy and sell on day to day basis. To begin with the bank should keep not more than 70% of its investments in the permanent category from the accounting year 1992-93. This ratio has to be brought down to 50% in due course.

(*ii*) Others i.e., Shares, Debentures and Bonds. There is no objection to banks interchanging the investments from one category to another with prior authorisation of the Board of Directors in which case depreciation, if any, will have to be fully provided for. **Depreciation on permanent investments need not be provided as it is not likely to affect their realisable value but depreciation on current investments should be fully provided for.** Permanent investments could be valued at cost unless it is more than the face value, in which case the premium has to be amortised over the period remaining for maturity of the security. Banks generally are not expected to sell securities in permanent category but if they do so then any loss on such transaction in securities has to the written off but if there is only gain that should be transferred to Capital Reserve Account.

Classification of Investments

The investment portfolio of a Bank would normally consists of both approved securities (predominantly government securities) and other securities (shares, debentures, bonds, etc.) Banks are requires to classify their entire investment portfolio into three categories.

(*i*) **Held-to-maturity :** Securities acquired by bank with the intention to hold them upto maturity should be classified as 'held-to-maturity'.

(*ii*) **Held-for-maturity/trading :** Securities required by bank with the intention to trade by taking advantage of short-term price interest rate movements should be classified as held-for-maturity/trading.

(*iii*) **Available-for-sale :** Securities which do not fall within the above two categories should be classified as available-for-sale.

ILLUSTRATION 25. From the following information, you are required to prepare Profit and Loss Account of Popular Bank for the year ended 31st March 2023.

Particulars	₹
Interest on Cash Credit	**13,65,000**
Interest on Overdraft	**5,62,500**

Interest on Term Loans	11,55,000
Income on Investments	6,30,000
Interest on Balance with RBI	1,12,500
Commission on Remittances and Transfer	56,250
Commission on Letters of Credit	88,500
Commission on Government Business	61,500
Profit on Sale of Land and Building	20,250
Loss on Exchange Transactions	39,000
Interest paid on Deposit	20,40,000
Auditors' Fees and Allowances	90,000
Directors' Fees and Allowances	1,87,500
Advertisements	1,35,000
Salaries, Allowances and Bonus to Employees	9,30,000
Payment to Provident Fund	2,10,000
Printing and Stationery	1,05,000
Repairs and Maintenance	37,500
Postage, Telegrams, Telephones	60,000

Other Information :

(*i*) Interest on NPA is as follows :

	Earned (₹)	*Collected* (₹)
Cash Credit	6,15,000	3,00,000
Overdraft	3,37,500	75,000
Term Loans	5,62,500	1,87,500

(*ii*) Classification of Non-Performing Advances :

	₹
Standard	22,50,000
Sub-standard	8,40,000
Doubtful Assets not covered by Security	1,50,000
Doubtful Assets covered by Security for one year	37,500
Loss Assets	1,50,000

(*iii*) Investments ₹ 20,62,500

Bank should not keep more than 25% of its investments as 'Held-to Maturity.

The market value of its rest 75% investments is ₹ 14,81,250 as on 31st March, 2023.

SOLUTION

PROFIT AND LOSS ACCOUNT OF POPULAR BANK

for the year ended 31st March, 2023

	Schedule No.	*Year ended 31-3-2023*
		₹
I. Income		
Interest Earned	13	28,72,500
Other Income	14	1,87,500
Total		30,60,000
II. Expenditure		
Interest Expended	15	20,40,000
Operating Expenses	16	17,55,000
Provisions and Contingencies [See Working Note (1)]		5,10,000
Total		43,05,000
III. Profit/Loss		
Net Loss for the year (II – I)		12,45,000
IV. Appropriations		—

SCHEDULE 13—INTEREST EARNED

		₹
1.	Interest/Discount on Advances/Bills :	
	Interest on Cash Credit (₹ 13,65,000 – ₹ 3,15,000 not yet collected)	10,50,000
	Interest on Overdraft (₹ 5,62,500 – ₹ 2,62,000 not yet collected)	3,00,000
	Interest on Term Loans (₹ 11,55,000 – ₹ 3,75,000 not yet collected)	7,80,000
2.	Interest on Investments	6,30,000
3.	Interest on Balance with RBI	1,12,500
		28,72,500

Note: Interest on Non Performing Assets (NPA) is recognised on cash collected basis and not an earned (*i.e.* accrual) basis. Hence interest not yet collected in cash has been reduced.

SCHEDULE 14—OTHER INCOME

		₹	₹
1.	Commission, Exchange and Brokerage :		
	Commission on Remittances and Transfer	56,250	
	Commission on Letter of Credit	88,500	
	Commission on Government Business	61,500	2,06,250
2.	Profit on Sale of Land and Building		20,250
			2,26,500
3.	*Less* : Loss on Exchange Transactions		39,000
			1,87,500

SCHEDULE 15—INTEREST EXPENDED

		₹
1.	Interest on Deposits	20,40,000

SCHEDULE 16—OPERATING EXPENSES

		₹	₹
1.	Payment to and Provision for Employees :		
	Salaries, Allowances and Bonus	9,30,000	
	Provident Fund Contribution	2,10,000	11,40,000
2.	Printing and Stationery		1,05,000
3.	Advertisement and Publicity		1,35,000
4.	Directors' Fees and Allowances		1,87,500
5.	Auditors' Fees and Allowances		90,000
6.	Postage, Telegrams and Telephones		60,000
7.	Repairs and Maintenance		37,500
			17,55,000

Working Note :

(1) Calculation of Provisions and Contingencies

		₹
Provision for Non-performing Assets		
Standard Assets @ 0.4% of ₹ 22,50,000		9,000
Sub-standard Assets @ 15% of ₹ 8,40,000		1,26,000
Doubtful Assets not covered by Security @ 100% of ₹ 1,50,000		1,50,000
Doubtful Assets covered by Security of one year @ 25% of ₹ 37,500		9,375
Loss Assets @ 100% of ₹ 1,50,000		1,50,000
		4,44,375
Depreciation on Current Investments :		
Cost of Investments (75% of ₹ 20,62,500 of Total Investment)	15,46,875	
Less : Market Value	14,81,250	65,625
		5,10,000

Note: 25% of the total investments are held to maturity. In the case of investments held to maturity (*i.e.* long-term investments), valuation is done at cost. Therefore, depreciation on investments has been calculated only on 75% investments which are not held to maturity.

ILLUSTRATION 26. Arrange the following balances and information in the serial order of the statutory form under the heading "Capital and Liabilities", as given in Form A in the Third Schedule of the Banking Regulation Act, 1949. The balances refer to the position of the Sound Bank Ltd. as at 31st March, 2023 :

The Authorised Capital of the Bank is ₹ 5,50,00,000, divided into 5,00,000 shares of ₹ 100 each and 1,00,000 shares of ₹ 50 each.

All the shares have been issued and subscribed for.

The 1,00,000 shares of ₹ 50 each are shares issued as fully paid bonus shares.

In respect of the shares of ₹ 100 each, ₹ 50 per share has been called up and paid.	**₹ '000**
Securities Premium	**15,000**
Reserve Fund	**12,500**
Dividend Equalisation Reserve	**3,500**
Fixed Deposits	**3,09,399**
Saving Bank Deposits	**1,01,834**

Current Accounts	**2,92,039**
Contingency Accounts	**1,22,760**
Borrowings from other Banking Companies in India (This has been secured by bills discounted)	**15,000**
Unexpired Discounts	**178**
Bills Payable	**3,684**
Branch Adjustments	**6,511**
Profit and Loss	**4,602**
Unclaimed Dividends	**342**
Bills for Collection being Bills Receivable, Payable in India	**6,710**
Bills for Collection being Bills Receivable, Payable outside India	**10,782**
Acceptances, Endorsements and Other Obligations	**49,918**

SOLUTION

Sound Bank Ltd.
BALANCE SHEET
as on 31st March, 2023

		Schedule	*₹ '000*
Capital and Liabilities			
Share Capital		1	30,000
Reserves and Surplus		2	31,000
Deposits		3	8,26,032
Borrowings		4	15,000
Other Liabilities and Provisions		5	10,715
			9,12,747
Contingent Liabilities		12	49,918
Bills for Collection :	₹ '000		
Payable in India	6,710		
Payable Outside India	10,782		
	17,492		

Schedules to Balance Sheet
SCHEDULE 1—SHARE CAPITAL

	₹ '000
Authorised, Issued and Subscribed	
5,00,000 Shares of ₹ 100 each	50,000
1,00,000 Shares of ₹ 50 each	5,000
	55,000
Called up and Paid-up Capital	
5,00,000 shares of ₹ 100 each, ₹ 50 per share called up and paid up	25,000
1,00,000 shares of ₹ 50 each fully paid up	5,000
(Of these 1,00,000 shares of ₹ 50 each have been issued as fully paid up bonus shares)	
	30,000

SCHEDULE 2—RESERVES AND SURPLUS

	₹ '000
Reserve Fund	12,500
Securities Premium Account	15,000
Dividend Equalisation Reserve	3,500
	31,000

SCHEDULE 3—DEPOSITS

	₹ '000
Current Accounts and Contingency Accounts (₹ 2,92,039 + ₹ 1,22,760)	4,14,799
Saving Bank Deposits	1,01,834
Fixed Deposits	3,09,399
	8,26,032

SCHEDULE 4—BORROWINGS

	₹ '000
Borrowings from Other Banks in India (Secured by Bills Discounted)	15,000

SCHEDULE 5—OTHER LIABILITIES AND PROVISIONS

	₹ '000
Bills Payable	3,684
Branch Adjustments	6,511
Unexpired Discounts	178
Unclaimed Dividends	342
	10,715

SCHEDULE 12—CONTINGENT LIABILITIES

	₹ '000
Acceptances, Endorsements and Other Obligations	49,918

ILLUSTRATION 27. **Following information is furnished to you by Sound Bank Ltd. for the year ended 31st March, 2023 :**

	(₹ *in thousands*)
Interest and Discount—(Income)	8,860
Interest on Public Deposits—(Expenditure)	2,720
Operating Expenses	2,662
Other Incomes	250
Provisions and Contingencies (it includes provision in respect of Non-performing Assets (NPAs) and tax provisions)	2,004
Rebate on Bills Discounted to be provided for as on 31-3-2023	30
Classification of Advances :	
Standard Assets	5,000
Sub-standard Assets (fully secured)	1,120

Doubtful Assets—fully unsecured	**200**
Doubtful Assets—fully secured	
Less than 1 year	**50**
More than 1 year but less than 3 years	**300**
More than 3 years	**300**
Loss Assets	**200**

You are required to prepare :

(*i*) Profit and Loss Account of the Bank for the year ended 31st March, 2023.

(*ii*) Provision in respect of advances.

SOLUTION

Sound Bank Ltd.
PROFIT AND LOSS ACCOUNT
for the year ended 31st March, 2023

	Schedule No.	*(₹ in thousands)*
I. *Income* :		
Interest and Discount (8,860 – 30)	13	8,830
Other Income	14	250
		9,080
II. *Expenditure* :		
Interest Expenses	15	2,720
Operating Expenses	16	2,662
Provision and Contingencies		2,004
		7,386
Net Profit/Loss for the year (I – II)		1,694

CALCULATION OF PROVISIONS

(₹ in thousands)

Assets	*Value*	*% of Provision*	*Provision*
Standard Assets	5,000	0.40	20.00
Sub-standard Assets	1,120	15	168.00
Doubtful Assets			
100% Unsecured	200	100	200.00
Secured :			
Less than 1 year	50	25	12.50
More than 1 year but less than 3 years	300	40	120.00
More than 3 years	300	100	300.00
Loss Assets	200	100	200.00
Total Provision			1,020.50

QUESTIONS

SHORT ANSWER TYPE

1. (*a*) Describe the principal accounting policies for a Banking Company in respect of foreign exchange transactions.

   (*b*) What are non-banking assets ?

2. Distinguish money at call from money at short notice.
3. What is slip system of posting ?
4. State the special features of a bank's final accounts.
5. Explain the main provisions governing the preparation of annual accounts of a banking company.
6. What do you mean by Statutory Reserve ?
7. What is rebate on bills discounted ?

OR

Explain rebate on bills discounted along with suitable examples. Give Journal Entries in the books of the bank.

8. Give four examples of Schedule 16 of Bank's Final Accounts.
9. How do you show bills for collection in bank accounts ?
10. Give four examples of Schedule 14 of Bank's Final Accounts.
11. What is Section 17 as per B.R. Act 1949 ?
12. What are standard assets ?
13. What are loss assets ?
14. What are non-performing assets of Banks ?
15. What are branch adjustments in bank accounts ?
16. Give two examples of Schedule 12 forming part of a Balance Sheet of a banking company.
17. Give three examples of Schedule 9 forming part of a Balance Sheet of a banking company.
18. Write a short note on classification of advances in case of Bank ?
19. Write the different types of bank deposits.
20. What is banking company ?
21. Write the items appearing in each schedule forming part of Profit & Loss Account of a bank.
22. Explain the term 'Bills purchased and discounted'.
23. How are the following items treated in Bank Final Accounts ?

    (*a*) Bad Debts ; (*b*) Reserve for Bad Debts ; (*c*) Unexpired Discount ; (*d*) Interest on Doubtful Debts.
24. State the different items shown under other liabilities and provisions in Bank Balance Sheet.
25. Mention the conditions when a cash credit overdraft is treated as out of order.
26. Describe how the classification of investment is done by a banking company.
27. What is cash reserve ratio ?
28. What are the restrictions imposed by the Banking Regulations Act, 1949 on payment of dividend in case of banking companies ?
29. Following facts are given for your information. You are required to give Journal Entries for recording : (*i*) The transaction of discounting. ; (*ii*) The transaction of collecting the bill.

    Bill discounted on 1-11-2023 at 4% p.a. ; for three months : ₹ 90,000 ; Interest and discount ₹ 32,20,000.
30. How will you **classify** the following items for the purpose of **Balance Sheet** of a scheduled bank ?

    Bills payable ₹ 100 lakhs ; Unclaimed dividends ₹ 50 lakhs ; Depreciation fund ₹ 100 lakhs ; Liability for bills discounted ₹ 150 lakhs ; Liability for foreign exchange contract ₹ 50 lakhs ; Bullion ₹ 20 lakhs; Bills purchased and discounted ₹ 80 lakhs ; Cash Credits and Overdraft ₹ 100 lakhs

PROVISION FOR DOUBTFUL DEBTS ON ADVANCES

31. From the following information find out the amount of **provisions** to be shown in the Profit and Loss Account of a Commercial Bank as on 31st March, 2023 :

Assets—Standard ₹ 4,000 lakhs ; Sub-standard ₹ 2,000 lakhs ; Doubtful upto one year ₹ 900 lakhs ; Doubtful upto three years ₹ 400 lakhs ; Doubtful more than three years ₹ 300 lakhs ; Loss Assets ₹ 500 lakhs

Ans. [₹ 1,316 lakhs]

32. The following information for the year ended 31st March, 2023 is available for Seva Bank Ltd.

		₹
Standard Assets		5,50,00,000
Sub-standard Assets		31,50,000
Doubtful Assets but secured—	₹	
Up to one year	29,00,000	
One to three years	17,00,000	
More than three years	7,00,000	
		53,00,000
Loss Assets		21,00,000

You are required to ascertain the amount of provision required to be made by the Bank.

Ans. [₹ 48,97,500]

33. From the following information of a Commercial Bank on 31st March 2023, calculate the amount of provision to be made for NPAS :

	₹
(*i*) Standard Assets	20,60,500
(*ii*) Sub-standard Assets	1,10,000
(*iii*) Doubtful Assets (secured)	
upto 1 year	40,000
1-3 years	25,000
more than 3 years	10,500
(*iv*) Doubtful Assets (Unsecured)	22,500
(*v*) Loss of Assets	15,500

Ans. [₹ 93,242]

REBATE ON BILLS DISCOUNTED

34. Following balances appeared in the books of a bank on 31st March, 2023 :

	₹
Rebate on bills discounted (1-4-22)	16,000
Discount Received	2,30,000
Bills discounted and purchased	15,77,350

Journalise, assuming that :

(1) The rate of discount was 18% p.a. and

(2) Average due date for bills discounted and purchased is 15 May, 2023.

Ans. [Rebate on Bills Discounted (31-3-2023) ₹ 35,004]

35. Following particulars are extracted from the Trial Balance of M/s State Bank of India for the year ending 31-3-2023 :

(*i*) Interest and Discounts ₹ 1,96,62,400 ; (*ii*) Rebate on Bills Discounted (Balance on 1-4-2022) ₹ 65,040 ; (*iii*) Bills Discounted and Purchased ₹ 67,45,400

It is ascertained that proportionate discount not yet earned on the bills discounted which will mature during 2022-23 amounted to ₹ 92,760. Pass necessary Journal entries and show Rebate on Bills Discounted A/c.

36. As on 31st March 2022, Strong Bank Ltd. has a balanced of ₹ 27 crores in "rebate on bills discounted" account. The bank provides you the following further information :

1. During the financial year ending 31st March 2023, Strong Bank Ltd. discounted bills of exchange of ₹ 4,000 crores charging interest @ 15% p.a. and the average period of discount being 146 days.
2. Bills of exchange of ₹ 600 crores were due for realisation from the acceptors/customers after 31st March 2023, the average period outstanding after 31st March 2023, being 73 days.

You are required to pass necessary journal entries in the books of Strong Bank Ltd. for the above transactions.

Ans. [Unexpired Discount ₹ 18 crore]

37. The Trial Balance of National Bank Limited as on 30th June, 2023 shows the following balances :

	₹
(*i*) Interest and discount	45,40,600
(*ii*) Rebate on bill discounted (1-7-2022)	4,750
(*iii*) Bills discounted and purchased	3,37,400

The amount of unexpired discount on 30th June, 2023 is ₹ 5,560. Write necessary adjustment entries and calculate the amount of 'Interest and Discount' to be credited to Profit & Loss Account.***(B.Com. Panjab)***

Ans. [₹ 45,39,790 being Discount Earned transferred to Profit t& Loss A/c]

INTEREST ON DOUBTFUL DEBTS

38. While closing the books of a bank on 31st March 2022, you find in the loan ledger an unsecured balance of ₹ 5,00,000 in the account of one customer Mr. Z whose financial condition is reported to you as bad. Interest on the same amounted to ₹ 50,000 during the year but yet to be recovered. During 2022-23, the bank is able to realise only 80 paise in a rupee on account of customer's bankruptcy. Show the necessary journal entries to record the above.

Ans. [Bad Debts ₹ 1,00,000 ; Interest Credited ₹ 40,000]

39. A loan outstanding of Rs. 50,00,000 has DICGC cover. The loan guaranteed by DICGC is assigned a risk weight of 50%. What is the value of Risk-adjusted Asset ?

Ans. [₹ 25,00,000]

BALANCE SHEET

40. From the following particulars of XY Bank Ltd., prepare a Balance Sheet as on 31-3-2023 in the Revised format.

	(₹ in thousands)		(₹ in thousands)
Authorised Capital	4,000	Telegraphic Transfers Payable	800
Subscribed Capital	2,000	Bank Drafts Payable	1,200
Investments	7,000	Short Loans	40

Bills Discounted	15,000	Rebate on Bills Discounted	10
Profit and Loss A/c (Cr.)	850	Acceptances for Customers	5,000
Endorsement on Bills for Collection	100	Loans and Advances	10,000
Liability of Customers for Acceptances	5,000	Cash Credit	10,000
Money at Call and Short Notice	9,000	Overdraft	1,000
Cash in hand	2,000	Bills Purchased	1,000
Cash with RBI	4,000	Current and Deposit Accounts	56,000
Statutory Reserve	3,000	Investment Fluctuation Fund	100
Cash with State Bank of India	4,000	Bills for Collection	100
Letters of Credit Issued	500	Buildings	1,000

Ans. [B/S Total—₹ 6,40,00,000]

Hint. Letters of credit is a contingent liability.

LONG ANSWER TYPE

1. List out the form of business in which a Banking Company may engage as detailed in Section 6 of the Banking Regulations Act, 1949.
2. What are the main features of a bank's accounting system?
3. Explain the Chief Registers, Memorandum Books, Subsidiary Books required by a banking company.
4. Explain slip system of posting. What are its special features ? What are its advantages and disadvantages?
5. Give in brief the various provisions of the Banking Regulation Act, 1949 relating to the annual accounts of the Banking Company.
6. How does rebate on bills discounted arise and how it is brought into record ? Explain this with a suitable example.
7. What is banking company ? Give the classification of assets for a banking company along with income recognition and provision norms for various categories of assets.
8. Show by means of imaginary figures the following assets and liabilities in the Balance Sheet of a banking company:
   (*a*) Investments, (*b*) Advances, (*c*) Deposits (*d*) Contingent Liabilities; (*e*) Profit and Loss Account.
9. Describe the particulars of advances which must be given either in the Balance Sheet or in a separate schedule to and forming part of the Balance Sheet of a Banking Company in India.
10. Describe in brief the undermentioned items appearing in the Balance Sheet of a Bank :
    (*i*) Rebate on bills discounted; (*ii*) Cash credits and overdrafts; (*iii*) Endorsements and Guarantees; (*iv*) Money at Calls and Short Notice (*v*) Performing Assets and (*iv*) Non-Performing Assets.
11. Write short notes on the following items :
    (*a*) Statutory Reserve (*b*) Non-banking Assets (*c*) Current Accounts (*d*) Bills for Collection. (*e*) Statutory Liquidity Ratio. (*f*) Rebate on Bills Discounted (*g*) Provision for Bad and Doubtful Debts.
12. What are non-performing assets ? Discuss the accounting policy to the followed regarding recognition of income in relation to non-performing assets.
13. Define : (*a*) Standard Assets (*b*) Sub-standard Assets (*c*) Doubtful Assets (*d*) Loss Assets in case of a bank.
14. State the guidelines given by the R.B.I. regarding making provisions of different categories of bank advances.

15. Write a note on classification of investments.
16. Briefly explain the salient features of the directives issued by RBI to scheduled banks on the concept of income recognition and provision for bad and doubtful debts
17. Write a short note on classification of assets in case of a banking company.
18. What are the restrictions imposed by the Banking Regulation Act, 1949 on loans and advances in case of banking companies ?
19. Distinguish between Statutory Reserve and Cash Reserve in respect of Banking Companies.
20. Draw a proforma of Profit and Loss Account of a banking company.

PRACTICAL PROBLEMS

PREPARATION OF PROFIT & LOSS ACCOUNT

1. From the following particulars, prepare Profit and Loss Account of the Safety Bank for the year ended 31st March, 2023.

	₹ ('000)		₹ ('000)
Interest on Deposits	3,200	Discount on Bills Discounted	1,490
Commission (Cr.)	100	Interest on Overdrafts	1,600
Interest on Loans	2,490	Interest on Cash Credits	2,320
Sundry Charges (Dr.)	100	Auditors' Fees	35
Rent and Taxes	200	Directors' Fees	16
Payment to Employees	500	Bad Debts to be written off amounted to	300

Ans. **[Profit ₹ 36,49,000].**

2. Prepare Profit and Loss Account for the year ended 31st March, 2023 of the Very Sound Bank Ltd. from the following particulars :

	₹ ('000)		₹ ('000)
Interest on Loans	250	Discount on Bills Discounted	40
Interest on Saving A/cs	150	Rent, Taxes, Insurance and Lighting	5
Interest on Cash Credits	160	Commission, Exchange and Brokerage	15
Interest on Fixed Deposits	190	Auditors' Fees and Expenses	10
Interest on Overdrafts	70	Directors' Fees and Expenses	20
Payment to Employees	150		

Ans. **[Net Profit ₹ 10,000].**

3. Prepare Profit and Loss Account in respect of the World Bank, incorporated under the Banking Regulation Act from the following balances as on 31st March, 2023. The management decides to make a provision of ₹ 1,00,000 for Bad and Doubtful Debts.

	₹ ('000)	₹ ('000)
Interest received		400
Interest paid on Deposits	210	
Payment to Employees	268	
Commission received		300
Brokerage		150
Advertising	15	
Printing and Stationery	48	

Postage, Telegrams and Telephones	29	
Interest on Borrowings	250	
Directors' Fees and Allowances	30	
Rent	40	
Taxes	30	
Discount		210
Exchange		180
Lockers Rent		110
Transfer Fees		150
Depreciation Written off on Bank Property	30	
Audit Fees	20	
Provision for Diminution in the Value of Govt. Securities	5	
Misc. Expenses	25	
Balance	500	
	1,500	1,500

Ans. [Net Profit ₹ 4,00,000].

4. From the following information, prepare the Profit and Loss Account of German Bank Ltd. for the year 31st March, 2023 :

	₹		₹
Interest on Loans	2,56,000	Directors' Fees	3,000
Interest on Fixed Deposits	2,75,000	Auditors' Fees	1,200
Commission	5,200	Interest on Savings Bank	
Establishment	54,000	Deposits	68,000
Discount on Bills Discounted	1,46,000	Postage and Telegrams	1,400
Interest on Cash Credit	2,23,000	Printing and Stationary	2,900
Interest on Current Accounts	42,000	Sundry Charges	1,700
Rates and Taxes	18,000	Income from Investments	2,000
Interest on Overdrafts	1,54,000	Profit on Sale of Investment	4,000

Bad Debts to be written off amounted to ₹ 40,000 provision for taxation may be made @ 55%.

Ans. [Net Profit ₹ 127.35 lakhs]

5. From the following information, prepare Profit and Loss Account of the Vasari Bank Ltd. for the period ended on 31st March, 2023. Working should form part of your answer :

	(₹ '000)		(₹ '000)
Interest on loans	300	Interest on saving bank deposits	87
Interest on fixed deposits	275	Postage, telegrams and stamps	10
Commission	10	Printing and stationery	20
Exchange and brokerage	20	Sundry expenses	10
Salaries and allowances	150	Rent	15
Discount on bills (gross)	152	Taxes and licences	10
Interest on cash credits	240	Audit fees	10
Interest on temporary overdrafts in current accounts	30		

Additional Information : (*i*) Rebate on bills discounted ₹ 30,000 ; (*ii*) Salary of managing director ₹ 30,000 ; (*iii*) Provision for bad debts ₹ 40,000 ; (*iv*) Provision for income tax is to be made @ 55% (round off to the nearest thousands) ; (*v*) Interest of ₹ 4,000 on doubtful debts was wrongly credited to interest on loan account ; (*vi*) Provide ₹ 15,000 as dividend.

Ans. [Net Profit ₹ 27,000].

6. Following figures are extracted from the books of K. Bank Ltd. as on 31-3-2023 :

	₹ (000)		₹ (000)
Interest and discount received	4,060	Rent paid	108
Interest paid on deposits	2,404	Stationery	48
Capital	1,000	Postage	40
Commission and exchange	180	Audit fee	8
Rent received	60	Depreciation on Bank's properties	25
Profit on sale of investment	190	Director's fee	34
Salaries	210	Preliminary Expenses	10

Further information :

(*a*) A customer to whom a sum of ₹ 5,00,000 has been advanced has become insolvent and 40% recovered from his estate, (*b*) Provision for bad and doubtful debts necessary ₹ 1,00,000, (*c*) Rebate on bill discounted as on 31-3-2022, ₹ 10,000 and Rebate on bills discounted as on 31-3-2023, ₹ 15,000, (*d*) Provide ₹ 7,00,000 for income-tax, (*e*) The directors desire to declare 10% dividend. (*f*) write off all preliminary expenses.

Prepare Profit & Loss A/c in accordance with law.

Ans. [N.P. ₹ 5,08,000; Surplus carried to B/S ₹ 2,81,000]

Hint. Transfer ₹ 1,27,000 of Profit to Statutory Reserve.

7. How will you disclose the following Ledger balances in the Final Accounts of DVD bank :

	(₹ in lakhs)
Current Accounts	700
Saving Accounts	500
Fixed Deposits	700
Cash Credits (doubtful for more than 5 years)	600
Term Loans	500
Bills Discounted and Purchased	800

Additional Information :

(*i*) Included in the current accounts ledger are accounts overdrawn to the extent of ₹ 250 lakhs.

(*ii*) One of the cash credit account of ₹ 10 lakhs (including interest ₹ 1 lakh) is doubtful.

(*iii*) 60% of term loan are secured by government guarantees, 20% of cash credits are unsecured, other portion is secured by tangible assets.

8. On the basis of the following information of Hi-Tech. Bank Ltd. for the period ended 31st March, 2023; prepare—

(*i*) Schedule 13—Interest Earned.

(*ii*) Schedule 14—Other Income.

	₹ in '000
(*i*) Interest and Discount	17,060
(*ii*) Interest on Balances with RBI	60

(*iii*) Income on Investments	4,720
(*iv*) Profit on Exchange Transactions	1,460
(*v*) Loss on Sale of Investments	100
(*vi*) Profit on Sale of Investments	540
(*vii*) Commission, Exchange and Brokerage	3,040
(*viii*) Profit on Sale of Land, Buildings & Other Assets	1,680

Ans. [Schedule 13—₹ 2,18,40,000 ; Schedule 14—₹ 66,20,000].

REBATE ON BILLS DISCOUNTED

9. Given below is an extract from the Trial Balance of a Bank as on March 31, 2023 :

	Dr.	Cr.
	₹ ('000)	₹ ('000)
Bills discounted	1,264	
Rebate on bills discounted on April 1, 2022		8
Discount received		85

An analysis of the Bills discounted as shown above show the following :

Amount	*Due date*	*Rate of Discount*
₹	2023	% p.a.
1,40,000	June 4	5
4,36,000	June 10	4.5
2,82,000	June 24	6
3,80,000	July 5	4

Show with the aid of working, how the relevant items will appear in the Bank's Balance Sheet as at 31st March, 2023 and in the Bank's P & L A/c for the period to 31st March, 2023. Also pass appropriate journal entries.

Ans. [Rebate on Bills Discounted shown as Liability in the Balance Sheet ₹ 13,000. Discount Credited to the Profit and Loss Account ₹ 80,000].

10. On 31st March, 2022, Uncertain Bank Ltd., had a balance of ₹ 9 crores in "Rebate on Bills Discounted Account". During the year ended 31st March, 2023, Uncertain Bank Ltd. discounted bills of exchange of ₹ 4,000 crores charging interest at 18% per annum, the average period of discount being for 73 days. Of these, bills of exchange of ₹ 600 crores were due for realisation from the acceptors/customers after 31st March, 2023, the average period outstanding after 31st March, 2023 being 36·5 days. Uncertain Bank Ltd. asks you to pass journal entries and show the ledger accounts pertaining to :

(*i*) Discounting of bills of exchange and

(*ii*) Rebate on bills discounted.

Ans. [Discount on Bills Discounted ₹ 144 Crores ; Rebate on Bills Discounted on 31-3-2023 ₹ 10·80 Crores]

11. Following Bills have been discounted by a bank during year 2022 @ 5% p.a. :

	Date of Bill	*Amount (₹)*	*Period in Months*
(*i*)	Dec. 28, 2022	50,000	1
(*ii*)	July 27, 2022	1,00,000	4
(*iii*)	Oct. 27, 2022	4,00,000	6
(*iv*)	Dec. 20, 2022	30,000	2

Find out the amount of unexpired discount and make its entry.

Ans. [Unexpired Discount ₹ 7,009]

12. On 31st March, 2023 a bank held the following bills discounted by it earlier :

	Date of Bill 2023	*Terms of Bill (months)*	*Discounted @ % p.a.*	*Amount of Bill ₹*
1	Jan. 17	4	17	3,65,000
2	February 7	3	18	7,30,000
3	March 9	3	17.5	1,82,000

You are required to calculate the Rebate on Bill Discounted. Also show necessary journal entry for the rebate.

Ans. [Rebate on Bills Discounted ₹ 29,270].

13. Following balances are extracted from the Trial Balance as at 31-3-2023; Interest/Discount on Advances/Bills(Cr.) ₹ 98,00,000; Rebate for Bill Discounted (Cr.) ₹ 20,000 and Bills Discounted and Purchased ₹ 4,00,000. It is ascertained that the proportionate discounts not yet earned for bills to mature in 2022-23 amounts to ₹ 14,000. Prepare Ledger Accounts.

Ans. [Interest/Discount ₹ 98,06,000 transferred to Profit & Loss Account]

INTEREST ON DOUBTFUL DEBTS

14. On 31st December 2022, loan ledger of a Bank showed an unsecured loan of ₹ 4,00,000 on which ₹ 20,000 has accrued as interest. The financial position of customer was doubtful. During the year 2023 bank accepted 75 paise in a rupee on account of total debt. Prepare necessary accounts and journal to record the transactions.

Ans. [Bad Debts ₹ 1,00,000 ; Amount Received ₹ 3,15,000]

15. On 31st March, 2023 the loan account in the books of a bank showed a debit balance of ₹ 2,00,000 including ₹ 40,000 due from a merchant which is doubtful. The interest accrued on this loan upto 31-3-2023 was ₹ 10,000 including ₹ 2,000 on doubtful debts.

The merchant became insolvent and the official receiver paid a dividend of 25 paise in the rupee on 30-4-2023.

Pass necessary journal entries in the books of the bank on 31-3-2023 and 30-4-2023 and prepare merchant's loan account.

Ans. [Amount realised from merchant ₹ 10,500 ; Bad Debts ₹ 30,000].

ADVANCES

16. From the books of accounts of a bank as on 31st March, 2023 the following particulars regarding loans and advances given by the bank are available :

Advances to Priority Sector ₹ 3,15,00,000 ; Advances to Public Sector ₹ 90,00,000 ; Advances to Other Banks in India ₹ 45,00,000 ; Advances (Others) ₹ 3,60,00,000

The details of the above advances are as follows :

Bills Purchased and Discounted (Including ₹ 18,00,000 outside India) ₹ 1,10,00,000 ; Cash Credits, Overdrafts and Loans payable on demand ₹ 4,30,00,000 ; Term Loans ₹ 2,70,00,000

Of the above advances ₹ 6,75,00,000 were secured by tangible assets while those of ₹ 45,00,000 were secured by bank and Govt. guarantees and the rest were unsecured.

How are these items to be shown in the Balance Sheet of the bank ?

ACCEPTANCES, ENDORSEMENTS AND OTHER OBLIGATIONS A/C

17. From the following particulars prepare as would appear in the General Ledger.

On 1-4-2022 acceptances not yet satisfied stood at ₹ 44,60,000. Out of which ₹ 40 lacs were subsequently paid off by clients and bank had to honour the rest. Bank register revealed the following :

Client	*Acceptances/Guarantees*	*Remarks*
	₹	
X	20,00,000	Bank honoured on 10-6-2022
Y	12,00,000	Party paid off on 30-9-2022
Z	10,00,000	Party failed to pay and bank had to honour on 30-11-2022
A	8,00,000	Not Satisfied up to 31-3-2023
B	10,00,000	—Do—
C	5,40,000	—Do—
	65,40,000	

Ans. [Balance on 1-4-2023 ₹ 23,40,000]

BILLS FOR COLLECTION

18. From the following details, prepare Bills for Collection (Asset) Account and Bills for Collection (Liability) Account :

On 1-4-2022, Bills for Collection were ₹ 51,00,000 ; During the year 2022-23, Bills Received for Collection Amounted to ₹ 75,00,000 ; Bills Collected during the year 2022-23 ₹ 98,47,000 ; Bills dishonoured and returned during the year ₹ 27,10,000.

Ans. [Balance ₹ 43,000]

PREPARATION OF BALANCE SHEET

19. Prepare Balance Sheet of Bharat Bank Ltd. as at 31st March, 2023 from the following particulars:

	₹ ('000)		₹('000)
Paid up Capital	1,000	Customers' Liability for	
Authorised Capital	5,000	Acceptances and Endorsements	200
Money at Call and Short Notice	500	Furniture and Fixtures	100
Investments	3,000	Land and Building	1,700
Acceptances and Endorsements for		Loans	800
Customers	200	Cash Credits	300
Bills Discounted and Purchased	400	Current Accounts	2,500
Bills Payable	500	Fixed Deposits	1,400
Saving Bank Accounts	1,000	Profit for the year	400
		Cash in hand and with RBI	1,000

The Statutory Reserve is equal to paid up capital. The profit for the year is arrived at before making adjustment for unexpired discount ₹ 5,000 on bills discounted during the year not matured on 31st March, 2023.

Investments include 5,000 shares of the face value of ₹ 100 each on which ₹ 50 is paid up. Claims against the Bank not acknowledged as debts amounted to ₹ 50,000.

Ans. [B/S Total ₹ 78,00,000; Advances ₹ 15,00,000].

20. From the following particulars prepare Balance Sheet of Progressive Bank Ltd. as on 31st March, 2023 :

	Dr. ₹ ('000)	Cr. ₹ ('000)
Share capital	—	1,000
Reserve fund	—	1,600
Fixed deposits	—	4,000
Saving bank deposits	—	6,000
Current accounts	—	22,000
Money at call and short notice in India	200	—
Bills discounted and purchased in India	900	—
Investments at cost :		
Central and State Govt.		
— securities	10,000	—
— debentures	400	—
— bullion	2,400	—
Reserve for buildings	—	1,000
Premises at cost	10,000	
Addition to premises	2,000	—
Depreciation fund on premises	—	8,000
Cash with Reserve Bank of India	3,400	—
Cash with State Bank of India	1,200	—
Unclaimed dividend	—	24
Unexpired discount	—	50
Loans, advances, overdrafts and cash credits in India	10,000	—
Branch adjustment	5,794	—
Silver	200	—
Advance payment to tax	110	—
Interest accrued on investments	260	—
Non-banking assets acquired	70	—
Borrowings from banks in India	—	250
Bills payable	—	2,000
Profit & loss account including ₹ 2,10,000 for the year	—	410
Dividend fluctuation fund	—	600
	46,934	46,934

The bank has bills for collection for its constituents ₹ 3,00,000 and acceptances ₹ 4,00,000.

There was a claim of ₹ 2,00,000 against the bank but not acknowledged as debt. The liability for bills rediscounted was ₹ 32,000. Liability for forward exchange contract was ₹ 20,00,000.

The directors decided to reserve ₹ 2,000 for unexpired discount and transfer reserve for building to depreciation fund.

Ans. [B/S Total ₹ 4,69,34,000].

PREPARATION OF PROFIT AND LOSS ACCOUNT AND BALANCE SHEET

21. Following ledger balances of ABC Bank Ltd. as at 31st March, 2023, are furnished to you. Prepare Profit and Loss Account and Balance Sheet as per requirements of law :

	₹ ('000)		₹ ('000)
Statutory Reserve	1,200	Cash	225
Bad Debts written off	128	Interest earned	550
Operating Expenses	182	Balance with Reserve Bank	2,030
Current Accounts	20,245	Balance with Foreign Banks	1,206
Interest Paid	160	Bills for Collection	1,500
Deposits Accounts	6,920	Borrowings from Banks	6,482
Profit and Loss Account, Balance B/F	229	Cash Credits and Overdrafts	15,457
Bills Receivable for Customers	1,500	Investments	9,882
Discount	244	Bills Discounted	6,228
Endorsements and Guarantees	575	Premises	2,217
Commission	45	Share Capital	2,000

Following further information is furnished :

(1) Rebate on Bills Discounted to be provided ₹ 64,000.

(2) The Bank had paid an interim dividend of ₹ 2,00,000 during the year.

Ans. **[Net Profit ₹ 3,05,000; B/S Total ₹ 3,72,45,000].**

Hint. Adjustment (2) can be a part or separate because it is just information. Interim dividend had already been paid. Cash has already been paid, so it cannot be adjustment.

22. From the following ledger balances of Laxmi Bank Limited, prepare Profit and Loss Account and Balance Sheet as on 31st March, 2023 :

			₹('000)
Share Capital :		Interest, Discount and Commission	245
12,500 Equity Shares of ₹ 100 each	1,250	Cash in hand and with Reserve	
Statutory Reserve	600	Bank of India	1,584
Current Accounts and Deposit A/cs	7,732	Money at call and short notice	274
P & L Account (balance)	15	Bills discounted	379
Interest paid	27	Loans and Advances	4,665
Government Securities	600	Bank Premises and Furniture	418
Other Securities	825	Non-banking Assets	337
Payment to Employees	74	Shares and Stock	637
Depreciation on Premises	22		

Make a provision for rebate on Bills discounted ₹ 3,000.

Ans. **[Profit ₹ 1,19,000; B/S Total ₹ 97,19,000].**

23. Following balances were extracted on the closing date, 31st March, 2023 from the books of Adarsh Bank Ltd. You are required to prepare Balance Sheet and Profit and Loss Account of the Bank.

	₹ ('000)		₹('000)
Current Deposits	45,500	Cash in hand and with RBI	487
Saving Bank Accounts	14,520	Cash with Banks	6,869
Fixed Deposits	37,180	Money at Call	1,500
Sundry Creditors Accounts	454	Investments in Govt. Securities	45,200

Deposits due to Other Banks secured by Investments	12,200	Interest Accrued on Investments	875
Bills for Collection being Bills Receivable	22,100	Investments in Shares	4,700
Acceptances and Endorsements for Customers	11,168	Cash Credit and Loans	44,100
Rebate on Bills Discounted	15	Bills Discounted	33,100
Branch Adjustment (Cr.)	4,555	Furniture, Fixtures and Equipment	500
Statutory Reserve	10,000	Postage & Telegrams	500
Dividend Equalisation Fund	2,500	Interest paid	1,200
Capital : 2 lakh shares of ₹ 100 each , ₹ 50 paid up	10,000	Law Charges	100
Interest and Discount received	5,800	Payment to Employees	2,400
Exchange and Commission (Cr.)	1,700	Directors' Fees	100
General Charges Recovered	55	Stationery and Advertisements	400
Profit and Loss A/c— Balance on 1-4-2022	852	Miscellaneous Expenses	300
		Land and Building	3,500
		Depreciation Reserve	500

Provide for (*a*) Reserve for Taxation ₹ 5 lakhs (*b*) Transfer to General Reserve ₹15 lakhs, and (*c*) Transfer to Dividend Equalisation Fund ₹ 5 lakhs.

Ans. [Net Profit ₹ 20,55,000; B/S Total 14,08,31,000]

24. Following figures are available of New York Bank Ltd. as on 31-3-2023 :

	₹		₹
Loan, Cash Credit & Overdrafts	2,85,000	Cash in hand	1,93,000
Premises	50,000	Money at call	80,000
Govt. Securities	4,00,000	Reserve Fund	2,50,000
Salaries	28,000	Share Capital (50,000 shares of ₹ 10 each)	5,00,000
General Expenses	27,400		
Rent	2,300	Current Deposits	1,00,000
Director's Fee	1,800	Fixed Deposits	1,25,000
Stock of Stationery	8,500	Saving Bank Deposits	50,000
Bills Purchased	46,000	Profit & Loss A/c (1-4-2022)	16,000
Interim Dividend Paid	17,000	Interest A/c	1,28,000
Shares	50,000	Recurring Deposits	20,000

Other information :

(*i*) Provision for bad and doubtful debts is required amounting to ₹ 5,000; (*ii*) Interest accrued on investment was ₹ 8,000, (*iii*) Unexpired discount amounted to ₹ 380, (*iv*) Interim dividend declared was 4% actual, (*v*) Endorsement made on behalf of customers ₹ 1,15,000, (*vi*) Authorised capital was 80,000, Equity Shares of ₹ 10 each, (*vii*) ₹ 10,000 was entered to the premises during the year. Depreciation at 5% on the opening balance is required, (*viii*) Market value of Government Security was ₹ 3,90,000.

Prepare Profit & Loss Account and Balance Sheet for the year ended 31-3-2023 in the prescribed form.

Ans. [N.P. ₹ 59,120; B/S Total ₹ 11,18,500]

25. From the following ledger balances of Hyderabad Bank Limited as on 31st March, 2023 prepare Profit and Loss Account and Balance Sheet :

	₹ ('000)		₹('000)
Fixed Deposits	325	*Share Capital* :	
Saving Deposits	1,775	5,000 Equity Shares of ₹ 100 each,	
Current Accounts	3,875	₹ 50 paid	250
Money at Call and Short Notice	240	Statutory Reserve	150
Investments	1,550	Profit and Loss Account	
Interest accrued and paid	100	(Cr.) (on 1-4-2022)	130
Payment to Employees	40	Bills Payable	400
Rent, Taxes & Lighting	10	Unclaimed Dividends	5
General Expenses	5	Sundry Creditors	225
Dividend for 2022-23	25	Bills for Collection	70
Premises (after ₹ 50,000		Acceptances on behalf of Customers	100
depreciation upto 31-3-2022)	600	Non Banking Assets	120
Cash in hand	75	Bills Discounted and Purchased	250
Cash at Reserve Bank	705	Loans, Overdrafts and Cash Credits	3,500
Cash at other Banks	520	Interest and Discount	325
Borrowed from Banks	280		

Rebate on Bills Discounted amounted to ₹ 2,500. Allow 5% Depreciation on Premises on original cost. Provide ₹ 25,000 for Doubtful Debts.

Ans. [Net Profit ₹1,10,000; B/S Total ₹ 75,27,500].

26. Following is the Trial Balance of B. Bank Ltd. as on 31st March, 2023.

	Dr. (₹ '000)	Cr. (₹ '000)
Share Capital Account (Authorised and paid up) : 10,000 shares of ₹ 100 each, ₹ 50 paid up		500
Statutory Reserve		800
Fixed Deposit Account		3,000
Saving Bank Deposits		2,000
Current Accounts		11,000
Money at Call and Short Notice	150	
Bills Discounted and Purchased	550	
Investments at cost :		
Government and Trust Securities	6,100	
Shares	650	
Debentures	200	
Pakistan Government Securities	600	
Reserve for Buildings		500
Interest and Discount		650
Commission, Brokerage and Exchange		60
Lockers Rent		20
Interest on Deposits	200	
Payment to Employees	215	

Postage and Telegrams	5	
Rents, Rates, Insurance, etc.	11	
Legal Charges	2	
Directors' Fees	2	
Auditors' Fees	1	
Miscellaneous Receipts		61
Premises—at cost	5,000	
Addition to Premises	1,000	
Depreciation Fund on Premises		4,000
Repairs to Premises	60	
Stationery, Printing and Advertisements	72	
Stamps in hand	3	
Other Expenses of Business	15	
Cash in hand	62	
Cash with Reserve Bank of India	1,200	
Cash with other Banks	1,100	
Unclaimed Dividends		12
Unexpired Discounts		25
Loans, Overdrafts and Cash Credits	5,800	
Inter Office Adjustments	900	
Silver	100	
Advance Payment of Tax	60	
Interest accrued on Investments	125	
Interim Dividend on Share Capital	25	
Non-Banking Assets acquired in satisfaction of Claims	10	
Borrowed from Banks		140
Bills Payable		1,000
Profit and Loss Account		150
Dividend Equalisation Fund		300
	24,218	24,218

The directors decided to Reserve ₹ 1,000 more for unexpired discounts. Bonus to staff to be provided ₹ 42,000. The Directors decided to transfer Reserve for Building to Depreciation Fund Account as new premises have been completed. Out of Loans to clients, a Loan to the extent of ₹ 5,000 is considered bad. All other Loans and Debtors are considered good. You are required to prepare Profit and Loss Account and Balance Sheet as at 31st March, 2023 as required by the Banking Regulation Act.

Ans. **[Net Profit ₹ 2,02,000; Balance Sheet Total ₹ 2,36,10,000].**

MODULE 4

CHAPTER 1

Financial Statements of Life Insurance Companies

Definition of Insurance

Insurance is a form of contract or agreement under which one party agrees in return of a consideration to pay an agreed amount of money to another party to make good for a loss, damage, injury to something of value in which the insured has a pecuniary interest as a result of some uncertain event. This agreement or contract when put in writing is known as policy. The person whose risk is covered is called insured or assured and the company or corporation which insures is known as insurer, assurer or underwriter. The consideration in return for which the insurer agrees to make good the loss is known as premium.

Types of Insurance

From accounting point of view, insurance may be divided into two types, *i.e.,*

(1) Life Insurance. Life Insurance business is carried on by Life Insurance Corporation of India since 1956 when life insurance business was nationalised. Under this type of insurance the corporation guarantees to pay a certain sum of money to the policyholder on reaching a certain age or on his death, whichever is earlier. Life insurance has an element both of protection and investment.

(2) General Insurance. It includes all other types of insurance except life insurance as fire insurance, marine insurance, accident insurance, burglary, fidelity, third party, workmen compensation, consequential loss etc. Under this type of insurance the insurer undertakes to indemnify the loss suffered by the insured on happening of a certain event in consideration for a fixed premium.

The general insurance business was also taken over by the Central Government with effect from 13th May, 1971. Recently the insurance business has been opened to the private sector. The Government has allowed registration of private insurance firms under the Companies Act, 1956. Thus, private insurance firms are now-a-days allowed to engage themselves in life insurance and general insurance business.

Accounts of Life Insurance Business

Final accounts of the insurance companies are prepared according to the provisions of the Insurance Act, 1938. For maintaining accounts, two types of books are kept by such companies.

(1) Statutory Books. Following books are to be maintained by all insurance offices :

(i) Register of Policies. This register will contain the particulars in respect of each policy issued by the insurer such as the name and address of the policy holder, the date when the policy was effected and record of the assignment of the policy (if any).

(ii) Register of Claims. It contains the particulars of each claim such as the date of claim, the name and address of claimants, the date on which the claim was discharged, date and ground for rejection, in case the claim is rejected.

(iii) Register of Licensed Insurance Agents. It contains the particulars of various insurance agents, their names, addresses, particulars of business done and commission due to them.

(2) Subsidiary Books. For proper maintenance of accounts important subsidiary books are maintained according to the convenience of the concern. These are register of proposals and proposal advance cash book, first year's premium cash book, renewal premium cash book, agency and branch cash book, petty cash book, claims cash book, general cash book containing the summary of all previous books, bank cash book, commission register, lapsed and cancelled policies book, journal, agency ledger, policy loan ledger, general loan ledger, investment ledger etc.

Insurance Regulatory and Development Authority

In order to regulate the insurance business, the Government set up in 1996, the Insurance Regulatory Authority (IRA). Now, this authority is known as the Insurance Regulatory and Development Authority. In 2002, the authority came with regulations for the preparation of the financial statements of insurance companies. According to the Insurance (Amendment) Act, 2002, the First, Second and Third Schedules prescribed for Balance Sheet, Profit and Loss Account and Revenue Account respectively as given in Insurance Act, 1938 have been omitted. Now Revenue Account, Profit and Loss Account and Balance Sheet are to be prepared as per the formats prescribed by the Insurance Regulatory and Development Authority (IRDA).

THE INSURANCE REGULATORY AND DEVELOPMENT AUTHORITY (PREPARATION OF FINANCIAL STATEMENTS AND AUDITOR'S REPORT OF INSURANCE COMPANIES) REGULATIONS, 2002

A brief description of important regulations prescribed by IRDA is given below :

Preparation of Financial Statements, Management Report and Auditor's Report

(1) An insurer carrying on life insurance business, after the commencement of these Regulations, shall comply with the requirements of Form A.

(2) An insurer carrying on general insurance business, after the commencement of these Regulations, shall comply with the requirements of Form B.

(3) The report of the auditors on the financial statements of every insurer and reinsurer shall be in conformity with the requirements of Form C, or as near thereto as the circumstances permit.

General Instructions for Preparation of Financial Statements

1. The corresponding amounts for the immediately preceding financial year for all items shown in the Balance Sheet, Revenue Account, Profit and Loss Account and Receipts and Payments Accounts shall be given.
2. The figures in the financial statements may be rounded off to the nearest thousands.
3. **Interest, dividends and rentals receivable in connection with an investment should be stated at gross amount, the amount of income tax deducted at source should be included under 'advance taxes paid and taxes deducted at source.**
4. (I) For the purposes of financial statements, unless the context otherwise requires :
   (*a*) the expression 'provision' shall, subject to (II) below mean any amount written off or retained by way of providing for depreciation, renewals or diminution in value of assets, or retained by way of providing for any known liability or loss of which the amount cannot be determined with substantial accuracy;
   (*b*) the expression 'reserve' shall not, subject to as aforesaid, include any amount written off or retained by way of providing for depreciation, renewals or diminution in value of assets or retained by way of providing for any known liability or loss;
   (*c*) the expression 'capital reserve' shall not include any amount regarded as free for distribution through the profit and loss account; and the expression 'revenue reserve' shall mean any reserve other than a capital reserve;
   (*d*) The expression "liability" shall include all liabilities in respect of expenditure contracted for and all disputed or contingent liabilities.

   (II) Where :
   (*a*) any amount written off or retained by way of providing for depreciation, renewals or diminution in value of assets, or
   (*b*) any amount retained by way of providing for any known liability or loss, is in excess of the amount which in the opinion of the directors is reasonably necessary for the purpose, the excess shall be treated as a reserve and not provision.
5. The company shall make provisions for damages under lawsuits where the management is of the opinion that the award may go against the insurer.
6. Extent of risk retained and re-insured shall be separately disclosed.
7. Any debit balance of the Profit and Loss Account shall be shown as deduction from uncommitted reserves and the balance, if any, shall be shown separately.

PREPARATION OF FINANCIAL STATEMENTS

1. An insurer shall prepare the Revenue Account [Policyholders' Account], Profit and Loss Account [Shareholders' Account] and the Balance Sheet in Form A-RA, Form A-PL and Form A-BS, as prescribed in this Part, or as near thereto as the circumstances permit.

   Provided that an insurer shall prepare Revenue Account and Balance Sheet for the under mentioned businesses separately and to that extent the application of AS 17 shall stand modified :

   (*a*) Participating policies and Non-participating policies;

(b) (i) Linked business ;
(ii) Non-Linked business separately for Ordinary Life, General Annuity, Pensions and Health Insurance.
(c) Business within India and business outside India.

2. An insurer shall prepare separate Receipts and Payments Account in accordance with the Direct Method prescribed in Ind AS-7 – "Cash Flow Statement" issued by the ICAI.

FORM A-RA

Name of the Insurer:
Registration No. and Date of Registration with the IRDA

REVENUE ACCOUNT FOR THE YEAR ENDED 31ST MARCH, 20.....

Policyholders' Account (Technical Account)

No.	*Particulars*	*Schedule*	*Current Year* (₹ '000)	*Previous Year* (₹ '000)
	Premiums earned – net			
	(a) Premium	1		
	(b) Reinsurance ceded			
	(c) Reinsurance accepted			
	Income from Investments			
	(a) Interest, Dividends & Rent – Gross			
	(b) Profit on sale/redemption of investments			
	(c) (Loss on sale/redemption of investments)			
	(d) Transfer/Gain on revaluation/change in fair value*			
	Other Income (to be specified)			
	Total (A)			
	Commission	2		
	Operating Expenses related to Insurance Business	3		
	Provision for doubtful debts			
	Bad debts written off			
	Provision for Tax			
	Provisions (other than taxation)			
	(a) For diminution in the value of investments (Net)			
	(b) Others (to be specified)			
	Total (B)	4		
	Benefits Paid (Net)			
	Interim Bonuses Paid			
	Change in valuation of liability in respect of life policies			
	(a) Gross**			
	(b) Amount ceded in Reinsurance			
	(c) Amount accepted in Reinsurance			
	Total (C)			
	Surplus (Deficit) (D) = (A) – (B) – (C)			
	Appropriations			
	Transfer to Shareholders' Account			
	Transfer to Other Reserves (to be specified)			
	Balance being Funds for Future Appropriations			
	Total (D)			

Notes :

* Represents the deemed realised gain as per norms specified by the Authority.

** Represents Mathematical Reserves after allocation of bonus.

The total surplus shall be disclosed separately with the following details :

(*a*) Interim Bonuses Paid ;

(*b*) Allocation of Bonus to policyholders ;

(*c*) Surplus shown in the Revenue Account ;

(*d*) Total Surplus: [(*a*) + (*b*) + (*c*)].

See Notes appended at the end of Form A-PL

FORM A-PL

Name of the Insurer :
Registration No. and Date of Registration with the IRDA

PROFIT AND LOSS ACCOUNT FOR THE YEAR ENDED 31ST MARCH, 20...

Shareholders' Account (Non-technical Account)

No.	*Particulars*	*Schedule*	*Current Year* (₹ '000)	*Previous Year* (₹ '000)
	Amounts transferred from/to the Policyholders Account (Technical Account).			
	Income From Investments			
	(*a*) Interest, Dividends & Rent – Gross			
	(*b*) Profit on sale/redemption of investments			
	(*c*) (Loss on sale/redemption of investments)			
	Other Income (To be specified)			
	Total (*A*)			
	Expense other than those directly related to the insurance business			
	Bad debts written off			
	Provisions (Other than taxation)			
	(*a*) For diminution in the value of investments (Net)			
	(*b*) Provision for doubtful debts			
	(*c*) Others (to be specified)			
	Total (*B*)			
	Profit (Loss) before tax			
	Provision for Taxation			
	Profit/(Loss after tax			
	Appropriations			
	(*a*) Balance at the beginning of the year			
	(*b*) Interim dividends paid during the year			
	(*c*) Proposed final dividend			
	(*d*) Dividend distribution tax			
	(*e*) Transfer to reserves/other accounts (to be specified)			
	Profit carried.......................to the Balance Sheet			

Notes to Form A-RA and A-PL.

(*a*) Premium income received from business concluded in and outside India shall be separately disclosed.

(*b*) Reinsurance premiums whether on business ceded or accepted are to be brought into account gross (*i.e.*, before deducting commissions) under the head reinsurance premiums.

(*c*) Claims incurred shall comprise claims paid, specific claims settlement costs wherever applicable and change in the outstanding provisions for claims at the year-end.

(*d*) Items of expenses and income in excess of one percent of the total premiums (less reinsurance) or ₹ 5,00,000 whichever is higher, shall be shown as a separate line item.

(*e*) Fees and expenses connected with claims shall be included in claims.

(*f*) Under the sub-head "Others" shall be included items like foreign exchange gains or losses and other items.

(*g*) Interest, dividends and rentals receivable in connection with an investment should be stated at gross amount, the amount of income tax deducted at source being included under 'advance taxes paid and taxes deducted at source".

(*h*) Income from rent shall include only the realised rent. It shall not include any notional rent.

FROM A-BS

Name of the Insurer:
Registration No. and Date of Registration with the IRDA

BALANCE SHEET AS AT 31ST MARCH, 20...

No.	*Particulars*	*Schedule*	*Current Year* (₹ '000)	*Previous Year* (₹ '000)
	Sources of Funds			
	Shareholders' Funds :			
	Share Capital	**5**		
	Reserves and Surplus	**6**		
	Credit/[Debit] Fair Value Change Account			
	Sub-Total			
	Borrowings	**7**		
	Policyholders' Funds :			
	Credit/[Debit] Fair Value Change Account			
	Policy Liabilities			
	Insurance Reserves			
	Provision for Linked Liabilities			
	Sub-Total			
	Funds for Future Appropriations			
	Total			
	Application of Funds			
	Investments			
	Shareholders'	**8**		
	Policyholders'	**8A**		
	Assets held to Cover Linked Liabilities	**8B**		
	Loans	**9**		
	Fixed Assets	**10**		
	Current Assets			
	Cash and Bank Balances	**11**		

	Advances and Other Assets	12		
	Sub-Total (A)			
	Current Liabilities	13		
	Provisions	14		
	Sub-Total (B)			
	Net Current Assets $(C) = (A - B)$			
	Miscellaneous Expenditure (to the extent not written off or adjusted)			
	Debit Balance in Profit & Loss Account (Shareholders' Account)			
	Total			

CONTINGENT LIABILITIES

No.	*Particulars*	*Current Year* (₹ '000)	*Previous Year* (₹ '000)
1.	Partly paid-up investments		
2.	Claims, other than against policies, not acknowledged as debts by the company		
3.	Underwriting commitments outstanding (in respect of shares and securities)		
4.	Guarantees given by or on behalf of the Company		
5.	Statutory demands/ liabilities in dispute, not provided for		
6.	Reinsurance obligations to the extent not provided for in accounts		
7.	Others (to be specified)		
	Total		

SCHEDULES FORMING PART OF FINANCIAL STATEMENTS

SCHEDULE 1—PREMIUM

No.	*Particulars*	*Current Year* (₹ '000)	*Previous Year* (₹ '000)
1.	First year premiums		
2.	Renewal Premiums		
3.	Single Premiums		
	Total Premium		

SCHEDULE 2—COMMISSION EXPENSES

Particulars	*Current Year* (₹ '000)	*Previous Year* (₹ '000)
Commission paid		
Direct – First year premiums		
– Renewal premium		
– Single premiums		
Add: Commission on Re-insurance Accepted		
Less: Commission on Re-insurance Ceded		
Net Commission		

Note : The profit/commission, if any, are to be combined with the Re-insurance accepted or Re-insurance ceded figures.

SCHEDULE 3—OPERATING EXPENSES RELATED TO INSURANCE BUSINESS

No.	*Particulars*	*Current Year* (₹ '000)	*Previous Year* (₹ '000)
1.	Employees' remuneration & welfare benefits		
2.	Travel, conveyance and vehicle running expenses		
3.	Training expenses		
4.	Rents, rates & taxes		
5.	Repairs		
6.	Printing & stationery		
7.	Communication expenses		
8.	Legal & professional charges		
9.	Medical fees		
10.	Auditors' fees, expenses etc		
	(*a*) as auditor		
	(*b*) as adviser or in any other capacity, in respect of :		
	(*i*) Taxation matters		
	(*ii*) Insurance matters		
	(*iii*) Management services; and		
	(*c*) in any other capacity		
11.	Advertisement and publicity		
12.	Interest & bank charges		
13.	Others (to be specified)		
14.	Depreciation		
	Total		

Note : Items of expenses and income in excess of one per cent of the total premiums (less reinsurance) or ₹ 5,00,000 whichever is higher, shall be shown as a separate line item.

SCHEDULE 4—BENEFITS PAID [NET]

	Particulars	*Current Year* (₹ '000)	*Previous Year* (₹ '000)
	1. Insurance Claims :		
	(*a*) Claims by Death,		
	(*b*) Claims by Maturity,		
	(*c*) Annuities/Pension payment,		
	(*d*) Other benefits, specify.		
	2. (Amount ceded in reinsurance) :		
	(*a*) Claims by Death,		
	(*b*) Claims by Maturity,		
	(*c*) Annuities/Pension payment,		
	(*d*) Other benefits, specify.		
	3. Amount accepted in reinsurance :		
	(*a*) Claims by Death,		
	(*b*) Claims by Maturity.		
	(*c*) Annuities/Pension payment,		
	(*d*) Other benefits, specify.		
	Total		

Notes : (*a*) Claims include specific claims settlement costs, wherever applicable.

(*b*) Legal and other fees and expenses shall also form part of the claims cost, wherever applicable.

SCHEDULE 5—SHARE CAPITAL

No.	Particulars	Current Year (₹ '000)	Previous Year (₹ '000)
1.	Authorised Capital Equity Shares of Rs........each		
2.	Issued Capital Equity Shares of ₹....... each		
3.	Subscribed Capital Equity Shares of ₹........each		
4.	Called-up Capital Equity Shares of ₹........each *Less* : Calls unpaid *Add* : Shares forfeited (Amount originally paid up) *Less* : Par value of equity shares bought back *Less* : Preliminary Expenses Expenses including commission or brokerage on Underwriting or subscription of shares Total		

Notes :

(*a*) Particulars of the different classes of capital should be separately stated.
(*b*) Thc amount capitalised on account of issue of bonus shares should be disclosed.
(*c*) In case any part of the capital is held by a holding company, the same should be separately disclosed.

SCHEDULE 5A—PATTERN OF SHAREHOLDING
[As certified by the Management]

Shareholder	Current Year		Previous Year	
	Number of Shares	% of Holding	Number of Shares	% of Holding
Promoters				
• Indian				
• Foreign				
Others				
Total				

SCHEDULE 6—RESERVES AND SURPLUS

No.	Particulars	Current Year (₹ '000)	Previous Year (₹ '000)
1.	Capital Reserve		
2.	Capital Redemption Reserve		
3.	Share Premium		
4.	Revaluation Reserve		

5.	General Reserves		
	Less : Debit balance in Profit and Loss Account, if any		
	Less : Amount utilized for Buy-back		
6.	Catastrophe Reserve		
7.	Other Reserves (to be specified)		
8.	Balance of profit in Profit and Loss Account		
	Total		

Note : Additions to and deductions from the reserves shall be disclosed under each of the specified heads.

SCHEDULE 7—BORROWINGS

No.	*Particulars*	*Current Year* (₹ '000)	*Previous Year* (₹ '000)
1.	Debentures/Bonds		
2.	Banks		
3.	Financial Institutions		
4.	Others (to be specified)		
	Total		

Note :

(*a*) The extent to which the borrowings are secured shall be separately disclosed stating the nature of the security under each sub-head.

(*b*) Amounts due within 12 months from the date of Balance Sheet be shown separately.

SCHEDULE 8—INVESTMENTS-SHAREHOLDERS

No.	*Particulars*	*Current Year* (₹ '000)	*Previous Year* (₹ '000)
	Long -term Investments		
1.	Government securities and Government guaranteed bonds including Treasury Bills		
2.	Other Approved Securities		
3.	Other Investments		
	(*a*) Shares		
	(*aa*) Equity		
	(*bb*) Preference		
	(*b*) Mutual Funds		
	(*c*) Derivative Instruments		
	(*d*) Debentures/ Bonds		
	(*e*) Other Securities (to be specified)		
	(*f*) Subsidiaries		
	Investment Properties-Real Estate		
4.	Investments in Infrastructure and Social Sector		
5.	Other than Approved Investments		
	Short-term Investments		
1.	Government securities and Government guaranteed bonds including Treasury Bills		
2.	Other Approved Securities		

3.	Other Investments		
	(*a*) Shares		
	(*aa*) Equity		
	(*bb*) Preference		
	(*b*) Mutual Funds		
	(*c*) Derivative Instruments		
	(*d*) Debentures/ Bonds		
	(*e*) Other Securities (to be specified)		
	(*f*) Subsidiaries		
	Investment Properties-Real Estate		
4.	Investments in Infrastructure and Social Sector		
5.	Other than Approved Investments		
	Total		

Note : See Notes appended at the end of Schedule-8B

SCHEDULE 8A—INVESTMENTS—POLICYHOLDERS

No.	*Particulars*	*Current Year* (₹ '000)	*Previous Year* (₹ '000)
	Long -term Investments		
1.	Government Securities and Government Guaranteed Bonds including Treasury Bills		
2.	Other Approved Securities		
3.	(*a*) Shares		
	(*aa*) Equity		
	(*bb*) Preference		
	(*b*) Mutual Funds		
	(*c*) Derivative Instruments		
	(*d*) Debentures/ Bonds		
	(*e*) Other Securities (to be specified)		
	(*f*) Subsidiaries		
	(*g*) Investment Properties-Real Estate		
4.	Investments in Infrastructure and Social Sector		
5.	Other than Approved Investments		
	Short-term Investments		
1.	Government Securities and Government Guaranteed Bonds including Treasury Bills		
2.	Other Approved Securities		
3.	(*a*) Shares		
	(*aa*) Equity		
	(*bb*) Preference		
	(*b*) Mutual Funds		
	(*c*) Derivative Instruments		
	(*d*) Debentures/ Bonds		
	(*e*) Other Securities (to be specified)		
	(*f*) Subsidiaries		
	(*g*) Investment Properties-Real Estate		
4.	Investments in Infrastructure and Social Sector		
5.	Other than Approved Investments		
	Total		

Note : See Notes appended at the end of Schedule-8B.

SCHEDULE 8B—ASSETS HELD TO COVER LINKED LIABILITIES

No.	Particulars	Current Year (₹ '000)	Previous Year (₹ '000)
	Long-term Investments		
1.	Government Securities and Government Guaranteed Bonds including Treasury Bills		
2.	Other Approved Securities		
3.	(*a*) Shares		
	(*aa*) Equity		
	(*bb*) Preference		
	(*b*) Mutual Funds		
	(*c*) Derivative Instruments		
	(*d*) Debentures/ Bonds		
	(*e*) Other Securities (to be specified)		
	(*f*) Subsidiaries		
	(*g*) Investment Properties-Real Estate		
4.	Investments in Infrastructure and Social Sector		
5.	Other than Approved Investments		
	Short-term Investments		
1.	Government securities and Government guaranteed bonds including Treasury Bills		
2.	Other Approved Securities		
3.	(*a*) Shares		
	(*aa*) Equity		
	(*bb*) Preference		
	(*b*) Mutual Funds		
	(*c*) Derivative Instruments		
	(*d*) Debentures/ Bonds		
	(*e*) Other Securities (to be specified)		
	(*f*) Subsidiaries		
	(*g*) Investment Properties-Real Estate		
4.	Investments in Infrastructure and Social Sector		
5.	Other than Approved Investments		
	Total		

Notes : (applicable to Schedules 8 and 8A & 8B) :

(*a*) Investments in subsidiary/holding companies, joint ventures and associates shall be separately disclosed, at cost.

(*i*) Holding company and subsidiary shall be construed as defined in the Companies Act. 1956.

(*ii*) Joint Venture is a contractual arrangement whereby two or more parties undertake an economic activity, which is subject to joint control.

(*iii*) Joint control is the contractually agreed sharing of power to govern the financial and operating policies of an economic activity to obtain benefits from it.

(*iv*) Associate is an enterprise in which the company has significant influence and which is neither a subsidiary nor a joint venture of the company.

(*v*) Significant influence (for the purpose of this schedule) means participation in the financial and operating policy decisions of a company, but not control of those policies. Significant influence may be exercised in several ways, for example, by representation on the board of directors, participation in the policy making process, material inter-company transactions, interchange of managerial personnel or dependence on technical information. Significant influence may be gained by share ownership, statute or agreement. As regards share ownership, if an investor holds, directly or indirectly through subsidiaries, 20 per cent or more of the voting power of the investee, it is presumed that the investor does have significant influence, unless it can be clearly demonstrated that this is not the case. Conversely, if the investor holds, directly or indirectly through subsidiaries, less than 20 percent of the voting power of the investee, it is presumed that the investor does not have significant influence, unless such influence is clearly demonstrated. A substantial or majority ownership by another investor does not necessarily preclude an investor from having significant influence.

(*b*) Aggregate amount of company's investments other than listed equity securities and derivative instruments and also the market value thereof shall be disclosed.

(*c*) Investment made out of Catastrophe reserve should be shown separately.

(*d*) Debt securities will be considered as "held to maturity" securities and will be measured at historical costs subject to amortisation.

(*e*) Investment Property means a property [land or building or part of a building or both] held to earn rental income or for capital appreciation or for both, rather than for use in services or for administrative purposes.

(*f*) Investments maturing within twelve months from balance sheet date and investments made with the specific intention to dispose of within twelve months from balance sheet date shall be classified as short-term investments.

SCHEDULE 9—LOANS

No.	*Particulars*	*Current Year* (₹ '000)	*Previous Year* (₹ '000)
1.	**Security-wise Classification**		
	Secured		
	(*a*) On mortgage of property		
	(*aa*) In India		
	(*bb*) Outside India		
	(*b*) On Shares, Bonds, Govt. Securities, etc.		
	(*c*) Loans against policies		
	(*d*) Others (to be specified)		
	Unsecured		
	Total		
2.	**Borrower-wise Classification**		
	(*a*) Central and State Governments		
	(*b*) Banks and Financial Institutions		
	(*c*) Subsidiaries		
	(*d*) Companies		
	(*e*) Loans against policies		
	(*f*) Others (to be specified)		
	Total		
3.	**Performance-wise Classification**		
	(*a*) Loans classified as standard		
	(*aa*) In India		
	(*bb*) Outside India		
	(*b*) Non-standard loans less provisions		
	(*aa*) In India		
	(*bb*) Outside India		
	Total		

4.	**Maturity-wise Classification**		
	(*a*) Short Term		
	(*b*) Long Term		
	Total		

Notes :

(*a*) Short-term loans shall include those, which are repayable within 12 months from the date of balance sheet. Long term loans shall be the loans other than short-term loans.

(*b*) Provisions against non-performing loans shall be shown separately.

(*c*) The nature of the security in case of all long term secured loans shall be specified in each case. Secured loans for the purposes of this schedule, means loans secured wholly or partly against an asset of the company.

(*d*) Loans considered doubtful and the amount of provisions created against such loans shall be disclosed.

SCHEDULE 10—FIXED ASSETS

Particulars	*Cost/Gross Block*				*Depreciation*				*Net Block*	
	Opening	*Additions*	*Deductions*	*Closing*	*Upto Last Year*	*For the Year*	*On Sales/ Adjustments*	*To Date*	*As at year end*	*Previous Year*
Goodwill										
Intangibles (specify)										
Land-Freehold										
Leasehold Property										
Buildings										
Furniture & Fittings										
Information Technology Equipment										
Vehicles										
Office Equipment										
Others (Specify nature)										
Total										
Work-in-progress										
Grand Total										
Previous Year										

Note : Assets included in land, property and building above exclude Investment Properties as defined in note (e) to Schedule 8.

SCHEDULE 11—CASH AND BANK BALANCES

No.	*Particulars*	*Current Year* (₹ '000)	*Previous year* (₹ '000)
1.	Cash (including cheques, drafts and stamps)		
2.	Bank Balances		
	(*a*) Deposit Accounts		
	(*aa*) Short-term (due within 12 months of the date of Balance Sheet)		
	(*bb*) Others		
	(*b*) Current Accounts		
	(*c*) Others (to be specified)		

3.	Money at Call and Short Notice (*a*) With Banks (*b*) With other Institutions		
4.	Others (to be specified)		
	TOTAL		
	Balances with non-scheduled banks in 2 and 3 above		
	CASH & BANK BALANCES		
1.	In India		
2.	Outside India		
	Total		

Note : Bank balance may include remittances in transit. If so, the nature and amount shall be separately stated.

SCHEDULE—12 ADVANCES AND OTHER ASSETS

No.	*Particulars*	*Current Year* (₹ '000)	*Previous Year* (₹ '000)
	Advances		
1.	Reserve deposits with ceding companies		
2.	Application money for investments		
3.	Prepayments		
4.	Advances to Directors/Officers		
5.	Advance tax paid and taxes deducted at source (Net of provision for taxation)		
6.	Others (to be specified)		
	Total (A)		
	Others Assets		
1.	Income accrued on investments		
2.	Outstanding Premiums		
3.	Agents' Balances		
4.	Foreign Agencies Balances		
5.	Due from other entities carrying on insurance business (including reinsures).		
6.	Due from subsidiaries/holding company		
7.	Deposit with Reserve Bank of India [Pursuant to section 7 of Insurance Act, 1938]		
8.	Others (to be specified)		
	Total (B)		
	Total (A + B)		

Notes :

(*a*) The items under the above heads shall not be shown net of provisions for doubtful amounts. The amount of provision against each head should be shown separately.

(*b*) The term 'officer' should conform to the definition of that term as given under the Companies Act. 1956.

(*c*) Sundry debtors will be shown under item 8 (Others).

SCHEDULE—13 CURRENT LIABILITIES

No.	*Particulars*	*Current Year* (₹ '000)	*Previous Year* (₹ '000)
1.	Agents' Balances		
2.	Balances due to other insurance companies		
3.	Deposits held on re-insurance ceded		

4.	Premiums received in advance		
5.	Unallocated premium		
6.	Sundry creditors		
7.	Due to subsidiaries/holding company		
8.	Claims outstanding		
9.	Annuities due		
10.	Due to Officers/Directors		
11.	Others (to be specified)		
	Total		

SCHEDULE—14 PROVISIONS

No.	*Particulars*	*Current Year* (₹ '000)	*Previous Year* (₹ '000)
1.	For taxation (less payments and taxes deducted at source)		
2.	For proposed dividends		
3.	For divided distribution tax		
4.	Others (to be specified)		
	Total		

SCHEDULE—15 MISCELLANEOUS EXPENDITURE
(To the extent not written off or adjusted)

No.	*Particulars*	*Current Year* (₹ '000)	*Previous Year* (₹ '000)
1.	Discount allowed on issue of shares/ debentures		
2.	Others (to be specified)		
	Total		

Notes :

(*a*) No item shall be included under the head "Miscellaneous Expenditure" and carried forward unless
1. some benefit from the expenditure can reasonably be expected to be received in future, and
2. the amount of such benefit is reasonably determinable.

(*b*) The amount to be carried forward in respect of any item included under the head "Miscellaneous Expenditure" shall not exceed the expected future revenue/other benefits related to the expenditure.

EXPLANATION OF THE ITEMS IN REVENUE ACCOUNT

1. Claims. Any amount payable by the insurance company is called a claim. In life insurance business, claims may arise due to two reasons *i.e.*, by death or maturity. While calculating the figure for claims, all claims intimated and accepted or not accepted at the end of the year, expenses relating to claims are to be added and out of the total, claims outstanding at the beginning of the year and reinsurance recoveries are to be deducted. The amount of reinsurance recoveries is received under reinsurance contract and it reduces the total claims to be paid by the business.

ILLUSTRATION 1. From the following details relating to claims, you are required to calculate the net claim to be shown in Revenue Account for the year ending 31-3-2023 :

	₹
Claims paid in the year ended 31-3-2023	9,00,000
Claims intimated but not accepted and paid on 31-3-2023	50,000
Claims intimated and accepted but not paid on 31-3-2023	70,000
Legal expenses regarding claims	30,000
Medical expenses regarding claims	10,000
Reinsurance recoveries	12,000

SOLUTION

Calculation of Net Claim to be shown in Revenue Account during the year ending 31-3-2023

	₹
Claims—Paid	9,00,000
Add : Claims—Intimated but not Accepted and Paid	50,000
" Claims—Intimated, Accepted and not Paid	70,000
" Legal Expenses Regarding Claims	30,000
" Medical Expenses Regarding Claims	10,000
	10,60,000
Less : Reinsurance Recoveries	12,000
Net Claims	10,48,000

ILLUSTRATION 2. From the following, you are required to calculate the loss on account of claims to be shown in the Revenue Account for the year ending 31-3-2022.

Intimated in	*Admitted in*	*Paid in*	₹
2020-21	2020-21	2021-22	45,000
2021-22	2021-22	2022-23	30,000
2019-20	2020-21	2020-21	15,000
2019-20	2020-21	2021-22	36,000
2021-22	2022-23	2022-23	24,000
2021-22	2021-22	2021-22	3,06,000

Claim on account of reinsurance as ₹ 75,000.

SOLUTION

STATEMENT CALCULATING NET CLAIMS TO BE SHOWN IN REVENUE ACCOUNT

Particulars	₹	₹
Total claims paid in 2021-22 (₹ 45,000 + ₹ 36,000 + ₹ 3,06,000)		3,87,000
Less : Claims Outstanding at the beginning of 2021-22		
Intimated in 2020-21 and paid in 2021-22	45,000	
Intimated in 2019-20 and paid in 2021-22	36,000	
		81,000
		3,06,000
Add : Claims Outstanding at the end of 2021-22 :		
Intimated in 2021-22 and admitted in 2021-22 but paid in 2022-23	30,000	
Intimated in 2021-22 but admitted in 2022-23 and also paid in 2022-23	24,000	
		54,000
		3,60,000
Less : Reinsurance Claim		75,000
Claims paid and outstanding in 2021-22 to be shown in the Revenue A/c		2,85,000

2. Annuity. It is an annual payment which a life insurance company guarantees to pay for a lumpsum money received in the beginning. It is an expense and shown under the head Benefits Paid (Schedule 4).

3. Surrender Value. If an insured is unable to pay the further premium, he can get his policy paid from the corporation. It is the present cash value of the policy which a holder gets from the corporation on surrendering all the rights of the policy. There is no surrender value in case of general insurance policies. The amount paid as surrenders appears as an expense in Schedule 4 under the heading "Other Benefits" in the Revenue Account.

4. Bonus in Cash. If the insurer has with profit policy, he will get the bonus from the corporation. If the bonus is paid in cash, it is shown on the debit side of the revenue account as an expense.

5. Bonus in Reduction of Premium. Instead of paying bonus in cash, the insurer may deduct the bonus from the premiums due from the insured. This is known as bonus in reduction of premium. It is shown both as an expense and as an income by adding to the premium in the Revenue Account. Bonus in reduction of premium as an expense is shown as "Other Benefits Paid" in Schedule 4.

6. Premium. The premium received during the accounting period plus outstanding at the end of the period, plus bonus in reduction of premium minus outstanding premium at the beginning of the period minus reinsurance premium is to be shown under the heading "Premium Earned (Net)" (Schedule 1).

ILLUSTRATION 3. Compute the net premium to be credited to Revenue Account from the following data during the year ended 31-3-2023

	₹
Premium Received during the year ended 31-3-2023	**16,00,000**
Reinsurance Premium Paid	**5,40,000**
Reinsurance Premium Received	**6,20,000**
Bonus in Reduction of Premium (not yet adjusted)	**20,000**
Premium Outstanding on 31-3-2023	**5,00,000**
Premium Outstanding on 1-4-2022	**2,00,000**

SOLUTION

Calculation of Premium to be credited to Revenue Account during the year ended 31-3-2023

		₹
Premium received during the year		16,00,000
Add : Reinsurance Premium received	6,20,000	
Bonus in Reduction of Premium	20,000	
Premium Outstanding on 31-3-2023	5,00,000	
		11,40,000
		27,40,000
Less : Reinsurance Premium paid	5,40,000	
Premium Outstanding on 1-4-2022	2,00,000	
		7,40,000
Net Premium to be credited to Revenue Account		20,00,000

7. Consideration for Annuities Granted. Any lumpsum payment received by the insurance company in lieu of granting annuity is called as consideration for annuity granted and will be shown as an income under the heading "Other Income."

8. Interest, Dividend and Rent. If the life insurance company has received any interest, dividend and rent on its investment, income tax thereon should not be deducted. Interest accrued and outstanding is added to this item. Interest, Dividends and Rent should be shown at gross value and tax deducted at source should be shown as Advance under the head "Advances and Other Assets" (Schedule 12).

9. Registration Fees. This is an item of income and shown as other income in the revenue account.

10. Reinsurance. When a company accepts a business of more value and in order to reduce the risk, may pass on some business to the other company, it is called reinsurance.

11. Commission on Reinsurance Accepted/Ceded. The company which passes some business to the other company gets some commission which is known as Commission on Reinsurance Business Ceded and is deducted from commission paid account. The company which accepts such business is required to pay commission on reinsurance business accepted which is known as Commission on Reinsurance Accepted. Such commission will become an expense and will be added to commission paid on direct business.

Co-insurance in case of Insurance business

In case of large risk exposure, the business is showed between more than one insurer, under co-insurance arrangements at agreed percentages. The ending insurer issues the documents, collect premium and settle claims. Settlement of accounts are rendered by the main insure to the other co-insures. Such co-insurance may be either incoming or outgoing.

ILLUSTRATION 4. A Life Insurance Company disclosed a fund of ₹ 20,00,000 and the Balance Sheet total ₹ 45,00,000 on 31st March, 2023 before taking the following into consideration :

(*a*) A claim of ₹ 10,000 was intimated and admitted but not paid during the year.

(*b*) A claim of ₹ 6,000 outstanding in the books for 8 years is written back

(*c*) Interest on Securities accrued ₹ 800 but not received during the year.

(*d*) Rent of the own building occupied ₹ 2,000.

(*e*) Premium of ₹ 600 is payable under re-insurance.

(*f*) Reinsurance recoveries ₹ 26,000.

(*g*) Bonus utilised in reduction of premium ₹ 10,000.

(*h*) Agents commission to be paid ₹ 8,000.

Pass the necessary journal entries for the above omissions to recompute the fund and show the Balance Sheet total after making the above adjustments.

SOLUTION

JOURNAL ENTRIES

2023			Dr.	Cr.
March 31			₹	₹
(*a*)	Claims A/c	Dr.	10,000	
	To Outstanding Claim A/c			10,000
	(Being claim intimated and admitted but not paid recorded)			

(b)	Outstanding Claims A/c Dr. To Claims A/c (Being claim outstanding in the books for 8 years is written back)	6,000	6,000
(c)	Accrued Interest A/c Dr. To Interest A/c (Being Adjustment for accrued interest)	800	800
(d)	No Entry		
(e)	Premium A/c Dr. To Reinsurance Premium Payable A/c (Being adjustment made for premium payable under reinsurance)	600	600
(f)	Reinsurance Claims A/c Dr. To Claims A/c (Being claims covered under reinsurance not received)	26,000	26,000
(g)	Bonus in Reduction of Premiums A/c Dr. To Premiums A/c (Being adjustment of bonus utilised in reduction of premium)	10,000	10,000
	Commission A/c Dr. To Commission Payable A/c (Being adjustment of commission payable to agents)	8,000	8,000

RECOMPUTATION OF LIFE ASSURANCE FUND

		₹
Balance of Life Assurance Fund on 31-3-2023		20,00,000
Add : Outstanding claim written back		6,000
Accrued interest		800
Claims covered under reinsurance		26,000
Bonus utilised in reduction of premium		10,000
		20,42,800
	₹	
Less : Claims intimated and admitted but not paid	10,000	
Premium payable under reinsurance	600	
Commission payable to agents	8,000	
Bonus in reduction of premium	10,000	
		28,600
Correct Balance of Life Assurance Fund		20,14,200

BALANCE SHEET

as on 31-3-2023

Liabilities		₹	*Assets*	₹
B/S Total (as given)		45,00,000	B/S Total (as given)	45,00,000
Add : Increase in Life Assurance			Accrued Interest	800
Fund (₹ 20,14,200 – ₹ 20,00,000)	₹	14,200	Reinsurance Claim Receivable	26,000
Outstanding Claim	10,000			

Less : Outstanding Claim written back 6,000	4,000		
Reinsurance Premium Payable	600		
Commission Payable	8,000		
	45,26,800		45,26,800

ILLUSTRATION 5. From the figures set out below, prepare the Revenue Account of Southern India Life Insurance Company for the year ending 31st March, 2023 :

	₹ '000		₹ '000
Life Assurance Fund as on 1st April, 2022	7,50,000	Commission	16,000
		Bonus in Reduction of Premium	500
Premiums	3,72,000	Annuities Paid	18,500
Interest, Dividends and Rent	2,26,000	Surrenders	25,500
Consideration for Annuities Granted	12,500	Surplus on Revaluation of Reversions Purchased	1,500
Fines for Revival of Lapsed Policies	200		
Claims Paid	42,500	Income Tax Paid	32,000
Bad Debts	400	Bonus in Cash	18,000
Expenses of Management	35,000		

SOLUTION

Southern India Life Insurance Company
REVENUE ACCOUNT
for the year ending 31st March, 2023

Particulars	*Schedule*	*Current Year*	*Previous Year*
		₹ '000	₹ '000
Premiums Earned (Net)	1	3,72,000	
Income from Investments :			
Interest, Dividends & Rent		2,26,000	
Surplus on Revaluation of Reversions		1,500	
Other Income :			
Consideration for Annuities Granted		12,500	
Fines for Revival of Lapsed Policies		200	
Total (A)		6,12,200	
Commission	2	16,000	
Operating Expenses related to Insurance Business	3	35,000	
Bad Debts		400	
Income Tax Paid		32,000	
Total (B)		83,400	
Benefits Paid	4	1,05,000	
Total (C)		1,05,000	
Surplus (D) = (A) – (B) – (C)		4,23,800	

Schedules Forming Part of Revenue Account

SCHEDULE 1—PREMIUMS EARNED (NET)

Particulars	*Current Year*	*Previous Year*
	₹ '000	₹ '000
Premiums Earned (Net)	3,72,000	

SCHEDULE 2—COMMISSION EXPENSES

Particulars	*Current Year*	*Previous Year*
	₹ '000	₹ '000
Commission	16,000	

SCHEDULE 3—OPERATING EXPENSES RELATED TO INSURANCE BUSINESS

Particulars	*Current Year*	*Previous Year*
	₹ '000	₹ '000
Management Expenses	35,000	

SCHEDULE 4—BENEFITS PAID (NET)

Particulars	*Current Year*	*Previous Year*
	₹ '000	₹ '000
Claims Paid	42,500	
Annuities	18,500	
Surrenders	25,500	
Bonus in Cash	18,000	
Bonus in Reduction of Premium	500	
	1,05,000	

ILLUSTRATION 6. The Young India Life Assurance Limited had a paid-up capital of ₹ 2,50,000 divided into 25,000 shares of ₹ 10 each. Its net liability on all contracts in force as on 31-3-2023 was ₹ 22,50,000 and on 31-3-2022 this liability was ₹ 20,00,000. From the following figures extracted from its books for the year ended 31-3-2023 prepare Revenue Account. The company has paid an interim bonus of ₹ 1,10,000 and 20% of the surplus is to be allocated to shareholders, 10% to the Catastrophe Reserve and the balance being carried forward.

	₹		₹
Life fund	**24,50,000**	**Annuities paid**	**10,000**
Premiums less reinsurance premiums	**13,80,000**	**Commission**	**54,000**
		Surrenders	**85,000**
Interest, dividends and rents	**7,50,000**	**Surplus on revaluation of reversions**	**4,000**
Fines and fees	**4,000**	**Re-assurances irrecoverable**	**1,000**
Income tax	**1,18,000**	**Claims less reinsurance claims**	**8,90,000**
Management expenses	**1,75,000**	**Consideration for annuities granted**	**45,000**

SOLUTION

The Young India Life Assurance Company Ltd.

REVENUE ACCOUNT

for the year ending 31st March, 2023

Particulars		*Schedule*	*Current year*	*Pervious year*
			₹ '000	₹ '000
Premiums Earned (Net)		1	1,380	
Income from Investments :				
Interest, Dividends and Rents			750	
Surplus on Revaluation of Reversions			4	
Other Income :				
Consideration for Annuities Granted			45	
Fines and Fees			4	
Total (A)			2,183	
Commission		2	54	
Operating Expenses related to Insurance Business		3	175	
Re-assurances Irrecoverable			1	
Income Tax			118	
Total (B)			348	
Benefits Paid (Net)		4	985	
Interim Bonus Paid			110	
Change in Valuation of Liability in respect of Life Policies :				
Net Liability on all Contracts in force on 31-3-2023 (₹ '000)	2,250			
Less : Net Liability on all Contracts in force on 31-3-2022 (₹ '000)	2,000			
			250	
Total (C)			1,345	
Surplus (D) = (A) – (B) – (C)			490	
Appropriations				
Transfer to Shareholders' Account (20% of ₹ 490 thousands Surplus)			98	
Transfer to Catastrophe Reserve (10% of ₹ 490 thousands Surplus)			49	
Balance being Funds for Future Appropriations			343	
Total (D)			490	

Schedules Forming Part of Revenue Account

SCHEDULE 1—PREMIUMS EARNED (NET)

₹ in thousands

Particulars	*Current year*	*Previous year*
Premiums less Reinsurance Premiums	1,380	

SCHEDULE 2—COMMISSION EXPENSES

₹ in thousands

Particulars	Current year	Previous year
Commission Paid	54	

SCHEDULE 3—OPERATING EXPENSES RELATED TO INSURANCE BUSINESS

₹ in thousands

Particulars	Current year	Previous year
Management Expenses	175	

SCHEDULE 4—BENEFITS PAID

₹ in thousands

Particulars	Current year	Previous year
Claims less Reinsurance Claims	890	
Annuities	10	
Surrenders	85	
	985	

ILLUSTRATION 7. **Best Life Insurance Co. Ltd. had a paid-up capital of ₹ 10,00,000 divided into 1,00,000 shares of ₹ 10 each. Its net liability on all contracts in force as on 31st March, 2023 was ₹ 96,00,000 and on 31st March, 2022, this liability was ₹ 84,00,000. The company has paid an interim bonus of ₹ 2,60,000 and 20% of the surplus is to be allocated to shareholders, 20% to reserves and balance being carried forward. Following figures are extracted from the books of the company for the year ended 31st March, 2023 :**

	₹		₹
Premium less re-insurance premium	**57,20,000**	**Commission**	**2,20,000**
Interest, dividend and rent	**28,00,000**	**Surrenders**	**3,20,000**
Fees	**16,000**	**Surplus on revaluation of reversions**	**20,000**
Income-tax	**4,40,000**	**Re-insurance irrecoverable**	**16,000**
Management expenses	**7,00,000**	**Claims less re-insurance claims**	**34,00,000**
Annuities paid	**50,000**	**Consideration for annuities granted**	**1,60,000**

Prepare Revenue Account.

SOLUTION

Best Life Insurance Co. Ltd.
REVENUE ACCOUNT
For the year ended 31st March, 2023

Particulars	Schedule	Current Year	Previous Year
		₹	₹
Premium Earned (Net)		57,20,000	
Income from Investments :			
Interest, Dividend and Rent		28,00,000	
Surplus on Valuation of Reversions		20,000	

Other Income :				
Consideration for Annuities Granted			1,60,000	
Fees			16,000	
Total (A)			87,16,000	
Commission		2	2,20,000	
Operating Expenses relating to Insurance Business		3	7,00,000	
Re-insurance Irrecoverable			16,000	
Income Tax			4,40,000	
Total (B)			13,76,000	
Benefits Paid (Net)		4	37,70,000	
Interim Bonus Paid			2,60,000	
Change in Valuation of Liability in respect of Life Policies :				
Net Liability on all Contracts in force on 31-3-23	₹ 96,00,000			
Less : Net Liability on all Contracts in force on 31-3-2022	84,00,000			
			12,00,000	
Total (C)			52,30,000	
Surplus (D) = (A) – (B) – (C)			21,10,000	
Appropriations :				
Transfer to Shareholders A/c (20% of ₹ 21,10,000)			4,22,000	
Transfer to Reserve (20% of ₹ 21,10,000)			4,22,000	
Balance being Fund for Future Appropriations			12,66,000	
Total (D)			21,10,000	

Schedules Forming Part of Revenue Account

SCHEDULE 1—PREMIUMS EARNED (NET)

Particulars	*Current Year*	*Previous Year*
	₹	₹
Claims *less* Reinsurance Claims	57,20,000	

SCHEDULE 2—COMMISSION EXPENSES

Particulars	*Current Year*	*Previous Year*
	₹	₹
Commission Paid	2,20,000	

SCHEDULE 3—OPERATING EXPENSES RELATED TO INSURANCE BUSINESS

Particulars	*Current Year*	*Previous Year*
	₹	₹
Management Expenses	7,00,000	

SCHEDULE 4—BENEFITS PAID

Particulars	Current Year	Previous Year
	₹	₹
Claims *less* Reinsurance Claims	34,00,000	
Annuities	50,000	
Surrenders	3,20,000	
	37,70,000	

ILLUSTRATION 8. Following Trial Balance was extracted from the books of the Life Insurance Corporation as on 31st March, 2023.

	Dr. (₹ '000)	*Cr.* (₹ '000)
Paid-up Share Capital—1,00,00,000 Shares of ₹ 10 each	—	1,00,000
Life Assurance Fund as on 1st April, 2022	—	29,72,300
Bonus to Policyholders	31,500	—
Premiums received	—	1,61,500
Claims paid	1,97,000	—
Commission paid	9,300	—
Management Expenses	32,300	—
Mortgages in India	4,92,200	—
Interest and Dividends received	—	1,12,700
Agents' Balances	9,300	—
Freehold Premises	40,000	—
Investments	23,05,000	—
Loans on Company's Policies	1,73,600	—
Cash on Deposits	27,000	—
Cash in hand and Current Account	7,300	—
Surrenders	7,000	—
Dividend Paid	15,000	
	33,46,500	33,46,500

You are required to prepare the Corporation's Revenue Account for the year as on 31st March, 2023 and its Balance Sheet as on that date after taking the following matter into consideration :

(*a*) Claims admitted but not paid ₹ 90,00,000 ; (*b*) Management expenses due ₹ 2,00,000 ; (*c*) Interest accrued ₹ 1,93,00,000 ; (*d*) Premiums outstanding ₹ 1,00,00,000; (*e*) Bonus utilised in reduction of premium ₹ 20,00,000 ; (*f*) Claims covered under reinsurance ₹ 23,00,000.

SOLUTION

Life Insurance Corporation
REVENUE ACCOUNT
for the year ending 31st March, 2023

Particulars	Schedule	₹ '000
Premiums Earned – Net	1	1,73,500
Income from Investments :		
Interest, Dividends and Rent (Gross)		1,32,000
Total (A)		3,05,500

Commission	2	9,300
Operating Expenses Related to Insurance Business	3	32,500
Total (B)		41,800
Benefits Paid (Net) (C)	4	2,27,700
Surplus (D) = (A) – (B) – (C)		36,000
Allocation of Surplus :		
Bonus to Policyholders		31,500
Surplus shown in the Revenue Account		4,500
		36,000

Life Insurance Corporation
BALANCE SHEET
as at 31st March, 2023

Particulars	*Schedule*	₹ '000
Sources of Funds		
Share Capital	5	1,00,000
Reserves & Surplus	6	29,76,800
Borrowings	7	—
Total		30,76,800
Application of Funds		
Investments	8	23,05,000
Loans	9	6,65,800
Fixed Assets	10	40,000
Current Assets :		
Cash & Bank Balances	11	7,300
Advances & Other Assets	12	67,900
Sub-Total (A)		75,200
Current Liabilities (B)	13	9,200
Net Current Assets (C) = (A) – (B)		66,000
Total		30,76,800
(Total of Schedules 8, 9, 10 & Net Currents Assets)		

Schedules Forming Part of Financial Statements
SCHEDULE 1—PREMIUMS

Particulars		(₹ '000)
Premiums :		
Received	1,61,500	
Add : Outstanding	10,000	
Add : Bonus utilised in Reduction of Premium	2,000	
		1,73,500

SCHEDULE 2—COMMISSION

Particulars	(₹ '000)
Commission Paid	9,300

SCHEDULE 3—OPERATING EXPENSES RELATED TO INSURANCE BUSINESS

Particulars		(₹ '000)
Management Expenses Paid	32,300	
Add : Outstanding	200	
		32,500

SCHEDULE 4 —BENEFITS PAID (NET)

Particulars		(₹ '000)
Claims Paid	1,97,000	
Add : Outstanding Claims	9,000	
Less : Covered under Reinsurance	2,06,000	
	2,300	
		2,03,700
Bonus utilised in Reduction of Premium		2,000
Surrenders		7,000
Dividends Paid		15,000
		2,27,700

SCHEDULE 5—SHARE CAPITAL

Particulars	(₹ '000)
Paid up Share Capital	
1,00,00,000 Equity Shares of ₹ 10 each fully paid up	1,00,000

SCHEDULE 6—RESERVES & SURPLUS

Particulars		(₹ '000)
Life Assurance Fund at the beginning of the year	29,72,300	
Add : Surplus as per Revenue A/c for the Current year	4,500	
		29,76,800

SCHEDULE 8—INVESTMENTS

Particulars	(₹ '000)
Investments	23,05,000

SCHEDULE 9—LOANS

Particulars		(₹ '000)
Secured : Mortgages in India	4,92,200	
Loan on Policies	1,73,600	
		6,65,800

SCHEDULE 10—FIXED ASSETS

Particulars	(₹ '000)
Freehold Premises	40,000

SCHEDULE 11—CASH & BANK BALANCES

Particulars	(₹ '000)
Cash in hand and Current Account	7,300

SCHEDULE 12—ADVANCES AND OTHER ASSETS

Particulars	(₹ '000)
Advances	
Other Assets :	
Interest Accrued	19,300
Outstanding Premiums	10,000
Agents' Balances	9,300
Amount Recoverable from Reinsurance Companies	2,300
Cash on Deposits	27,000
	67,900

SCHEDULE 13—CURRENT LIABILITIES

Particulars	(₹ '000)
Claims Unpaid	9,000
Management Expenses Outstanding	200
	9,200

ILLUSTRATION 9. Following balances relate to New India Life Assurance Company Ltd. as on 31st March, 2023.

	₹ in thousands		*₹ in thousands*
Shareholders' capital (1,00,00,000 shares of ₹ 25 each, ₹ 10 per share paid-up)	1,00,000	Bonus in reduction of premium	2,000
Claims under policies paid and outstanding *less* received on re-assurance	22,50,000	Gain on redemption of debentures (to be carried to investment reserve fund)	10,000
Life assurance fund on 1st April, 2022	2,40,00,000	Interest, dividends and rents received	16,00,168
Investment reserve fund on 1st April, 2022	25,00,000	Interest accrued, but not yet receivable	1,58,500
Expenses of management	7,50,213	Income-tax paid	1,40,074
Investments	2,55,00,000	Transfer and other fees	3,215
Freehold and leasehold property	12,50,000	Agents' balances outstanding	72,952
Unpaid dividend	25,895	Furniture and fittings	45,250
Outstanding premiums (net)	3,01,600	Loans on the company's policies within their surrender value	24,50,000
		Cash in hand and at bank (as per Pass Book)	1,82,000

Claims admitted or intimated, but not paid	15,00,000	Stamps in hand	3,661
Outstanding interest	2,95,000	Cheques paid into bank and in course of realisation	24,500
Surrenders	1,29,475	Cheques issued but not presented for payment	33,260
Annuities	15,000		
Premiums *less* re-assurance	37,50,000	Sundry creditors	22,437
Commission paid	50,000	Premium received in advance	50,000
Consideration for annuities granted	25,250	Income tax on interest and dividends (item of adjustment)	60,000

You are required to prepare the Revenue Account for the year ended 31st March, 2023 and a Balance Sheet at that date of the New India Life Assurance Company Ltd.

SOLUTION

New India Life Assurance Company Ltd.
REVENUE ACCOUNT
for the year ending 31st March, 2023

₹ in thousands

Particulars	*Schedule year*	*Current year*	*Previous*
Premiums Earned – Net	1	37,50,000	
Income from Instruments :			
Interest, Dividends and Rent – Gross		16,60,168	
Other Income :			
Consideration for Annuities Granted		25,250	
Transfer and Other Fees		3,215	
Total (A)		54,38,633	
Commission	2	50,000	
Operating Expenses related to Insurance Business	3	7,50,213	
Total (B)		8,00,213	
Benefits Paid – Net	4	23,96,475	
Total (C)		23,96,475	
Surplus (D) = (A) – (B) – (C)		22,41,945	

New India Life Assurance Company Ltd.
BALANCE SHEET
as at 31st March, 2023

₹ in thousands

Particulars	*Schedule*	*Current year*	*Previous year*
Sources of Funds			
Share Capital	5	1,00,000	
Reserves and Surplus	6	2,87,51,945	
Borrowings	7	—	
Total		2,88,51,945	

Application of Funds			
Investments	8	2,55,00,000	
Loans	9	24,50,000	
Fixed Assets	10	12,95,250	
Current Assets :			
Cash & Bank Balances	11	1,76,901	
Advances & Other Assets	12	10,28,126	
Sub-Total (A)		12,05,027	
Current Liabilities (B)	13	15,98,332	
Net Current Assets (C) = (A) – (B)		–3,93,305	
Total		2,88,51,945	
(of Schedules 8, 9 & 10 + Net Current Assets)			

Schedules Forming Part of Financial Statements

SCHEDULE 1—PREMIUMS

₹ in thousands

Particulars	*Current year*	*Previous year*
Premiums less Reinsurance	37,50,000	

SCHEDULE 2—COMMISSION

₹ in thousands

Particulars	*Current year*	*Previous year*
Commission Paid	50,000	

SCHEDULE 3—OPERATING EXPENSES RELATED TO INSURANCE BUSINESS

₹ in thousands

Particulars	*Current year*	*Previous year*
Expenses of Management	7,50,213	

SCHEDULE 4 —BENEFITS PAID (NET)

₹ in thousands

Particulars	*Current year*	*Previous year*
Claims Paid and Outstanding		
Less : Received on Reinsurance	22,50,000	
Annuities	15,000	
Surrenders	1,29,475	
Bonus in Reduction of Premium	2,000	
	23,96,475	

SCHEDULE 5—SHARE CAPITAL

₹ in thousands

Particulars	*Current year*	*Previous year*
Authorised Capital		
Equity shares of ₹ 25 each		
Issued Capital		
Equity shares of ₹ 25 each		

		Current year	Previous year
Subscribed Capital			
Equity shares of ₹ 25 each			
Called-up Capital			
1,00,00,000 Equity Shares of ₹ 25 each, ₹ 10 per share paid up		1,00,000	

SCHEDULE 6—RESERVES AND SURPLUS

₹ in thousands

Particulars		Current year	Previous year
Life Assurance Fund at the beginning of the year	2,40,00,000		
Add : Surplus during the year	22,41,945	2,62,41,945	
Investment Reserve Fund	25,00,000		
Add : Gain on Redemption of Debentures	10,000	25,10,000	
		2,87,51,945	

SCHEDULE 8—INVESTMENTS

₹ in thousands

Particulars	Current year	Previous year
Investments	2,55,00,000	

SCHEDULE 9—LOANS

₹ in thousands

Particulars	Current year	Previous year
Secured		
Loans on Policies	24,50,000	

SCHEDULE 10—FIXED ASSETS

₹ in thousands

Particulars	Current year	Previous year
Freehold & Leasehold Property	12,50,000	
Furniture & Fittings	45,250	
	12,95,250	

SCHEDULE 11—CASH AND BANK BALANCES

₹ in thousands

Particulars	Current year	Previous year
Cash (including cheques, drafts and stamps) :		
Balance	1,82,000	
Add : Cheques paid into bank for realisation	24,500	
	2,06,500	
Less : Cheques issued but not presented for payment	33,260	
	1,73,240	
Add : Stamps in hand	3,661	
	1,76,901	

SCHEDULE 12—ADVANCES AND OTHER ASSETS

₹ in thousands

Particulars	Current year	Previous year
Advances :		
Income Tax (Treated as advance)	1,40,074	
Tax deducted at source on income from interest, dividends and rent	60,000	
Other Assets :		
Accrued Interest	1,58,500	
Outstanding Interest	2,95,000	
Outstanding Premiums	3,01,600	
Agents' Balances	72,952	
	10,28,126	

SCHEDULE 13—CURRENT LIABILITIES

₹ in thousands

Particulars	Current year	Previous year
Premiums Received in Advance	50,000	
Sundry Creditors	22,437	
Claims Outstanding	15,00,000	
Unpaid Dividend	25,895	
	15,98,332	

ILLUSTRATION 10. From the following Trial Balance of Long Life Assurance Company, prepare the Revenue Account and the Balance Sheet. The statements need to be in the prescribed formats.

	Amount ₹ in lakhs		Amount ₹ in lakhs
Debit Balances :		*Credit Balances :*	
Income Tax on Interest, Dividend and Rents	30	Life Assurance Fund— Opening Balance	5,500
Income Tax paid	25	Premium less Reinsurances	2,000
Claims paid (net of Reinsurances)		Outstanding Claims (net of reinsurances)	
By death	250	Opening Balances	
By maturity	170	By death	110
Property at cost (additions of ₹ 80 lakhs)	600	By maturity	75
Furniture & Office Equipment at cost	50	Consideration for Annuities Granted	100
Annuities	150	Registration Fees	5
Stationery	8	Interest, Dividend & Rents	250
Cash at Bank	396	Contingencies Reserve	200
Cash in hand	4	Provision for Taxation	50
Surrenders (net of reinsurances)	5	Property Depreciation	35

Commission	80	Furniture & Office Equipment	
Expenses of Management	400	Depreciation	5
Sundry Debtors	12	Sundry Creditors	30
Loans on Policies	350		
Deposits with R.B.I.	30		
Investment in Equity Shares of Companies	5,800		
	8,360		8,360

Other informations :

(1) Premium less reinsurances include ₹ 8 crores first year's premium, ₹ 11 crores renewal premium and ₹ 1 crore single premium.

(2) Premium outstanding at the end of the year ₹ 250 lakhs.

(3) Commission on outstanding premium ₹ 7.5 lakhs.

(4) Claims less reinsurances outstanding at the end of the year are ₹ 50 lakhs (by death) and ₹ 30 lakhs (by maturity).

(5) Depreciation to be provided ₹ 10 lakhs on property and ₹ 1.6 lakhs on furniture and office equipment.

(6) Income tax provision to be made for ₹ 20 lakhs.

(7) Expenses of ₹ 3 lakhs and ₹ 10 lakhs are prepaid and outstanding respectively, at the end of the year.

(8) Accrued interest, dividend and rent are ₹ 25 lakhs.

SOLUTION

Long Life Assurance Company
REVENUE ACCOUNT

Particulars	*Schedule*	*₹ in lakhs*
Premium Earned—Net	1	2,250.0
Income from Investments :		
Interest, Dividends and Rent—Gross		275.0
Other Income :		
Consideration for Annuities Granted		100.0
Registration Fees		5.0
Total (A)		2,630.0
Commission	2	87.5
Operating Expenses related to Insurance Business	3	426.6
Income Tax on Interest, Dividends and Rent		30.0
Provision for Income Tax		20.0
Total (B)		564.1
Benefits Paid (Net)	4	470.0
Total (C)		470.0
Surplus (D) = (A) – (B) – (C)		1,595.9

Appropriations		
Transfer to Shareholders' Account		–
Transfer to Other Reserves		–
Balance being Funds for Future Appropriations		1,595.9
Total (D)		1,595.9

Long Life Assurance Company
BALANCE SHEET
as at ....

Particulars	*Schedule*	*₹ in lakhs*
Sources of Funds		
Share Capital	5	–
Reserves & Surplus	6	7,295.9
Borrowings	7	–
Total		7,295.9
Application of Funds		
Investments	8	5,800.0
Loans	9	350.0
Fixed Assets	10	598.4
Current Assets :		
Cash and Bank Balances	11	400.0
Advances and Other Assets	12	320.0
Sub-Total (A)		720.0
Current Liabilities	13	127.5
Provisions	14	45.0
Sub-Total (B)		172.5
Net Current Assets (C) = (A) – (B)		547.5
Total (Total of Schedules 8, 9, 10 and Net Current Assets)		7,295.9

Schedules Forming Part of Financial Statements
SCHEDULE 1—PREMIUMS

Particulars	*₹ in lakhs*
First Year's Premiums	800
Renewal Premiums	1,100
Single Premiums	100
Outstanding Premiums	250
	2,250

SCHEDULE 2—COMMISSION

Particulars	*₹ in lakhs*
Commission Paid	80.0
Add : Outstanding	7.5
	87.5

SCHEDULE 3—OPERATING EXPENSES RELATED TO BUSINESS

Particulars		*₹ in lakhs*
Management Expenses	400	
Add : Outstanding at the end of the year	10	
	410	
Less : Prepaid	3	
		407.0
Stationery		8.0
Depreciation		11.6
		426.6

SCHEDULE 4—BENEFITS PAID (NET)

Insurance Claims		₹ in lakhs
(*a*) Claims by Death	250	
Add : Outstanding at the end of the year	50	
	300	
Less : Outstanding at the beginning of the year	110	
		190
(*b*) Claims by Maturity	170	
Add : Outstanding at the end of the year	30	
	200	
Less : Outstanding at the beginning of the year	75	
		125
(*c*) Annuities		150
(*d*) Surrenders		5
		470

SCHEDULE 6—RESERVES AND SURPLUS

		₹ in lakhs
Contingency Reserve		200
Life Assurance Fund at the beginning of the year	5,500	
Add : Surplus as per Revenue A/c this year	1,595.9	
		7,095.9
		7,295.9

SCHEDULE 8—INVESTMENTS

	₹ in lakhs
Investment in Equity Shares of Companies	5,800

SCHEDULE 9—LOANS

	₹ in lakhs
Loans on Policies	350

SCHEDULE 10—FIXED ASSETS

				₹ in lakhs
Property at Cost : Opening			520	
Addition			80	
			600	
Less : Depreciation : Upto last year		35		
For the year		10	45	555.0
Furniture & Office Equipment at Cost :	Opening		50	
	Addition		Nil	
			50	
Less : Depreciation : Upto last year		5.0		
For the year		1.6	6.6	43.4
				598.4

SCHEDULE 11—CASH AND BANK BALANCES

	₹ in lakhs
Cash in hand	4
Cash at Bank	396
	400

SCHEDULE 12—ADVANCES AND OTHER ASSETS

	₹ in lakhs
Advances	
Prepaid Expenses	3
Other Assets	
Interest, Dividend & Rent Receivable	25
Outstanding Premium	250
Deposits with Reserve Bank of India	30
Sundry Debtors	12
	320

SCHEDULE 13—CURRENT LIABILITIES

	₹ in lakhs
Sundry Creditors	30.0
Claims Outstanding	80.0
Outstanding Commission	7.5
Outstanding Expenses	10.0
	127.5

SCHEDULE 14—PROVISIONS

		₹ in lakhs
Provision for taxation : Opening	50	
This year	20	
	70	
Less : Income Tax Paid	25	45

ILLUSTRATION 11. **Following balances appeared in the books of the Happy Mutual Life Assurance Society Ltd. as on 31st March, 2023 :**

(*₹ in Lakhs*)

Dr.	₹		*Cr.* ₹
Claims less reassurances paid during the year :		Life assurance fund at the beginning of the year	50,000
By death	2,200	Premiums less reassurances	15,000
By maturity	1,500	Claims less reassurances outstanding at the beginning of the year :	
Annuities	6	By death	900
Furniture and office equipment at cost (including ₹ 40 lakh bought during the year)	250	By maturity	600
		Credit balances pending adjustment	60
Printing and stationery	77	Consideration for annuities granted	2
Cash with bank in current account	1,350	Interest, dividends and rents	1,800
Cash and stamps in hand	30	Registration and other fees	2
Surrenders less reassurances	40	Sundry deposits	100
Commission	250	Taxation provision	300
Expenses of management	3,100	Premium deposits	1,150
Sundry deposits with electricity companies, etc.	1	Sundry creditors	350
		Contingency reserve	150
Advance payment of income-tax	50	Furniture and office equipment depreciation account	40
Sundry debtors	50		
Agents' balances	100	Building depreciation account	300
Income-tax	450		
Income-tax on interest, dividends and rents.	500		
Loans and mortgages	150		
Loans on policies	3,250		
Investments (₹ 250 lakh deposited with the Reserve Bank of India)	52,000		
House property at cost (including ₹ 85 lakh added during the year)	5,400		
	70,754		70,754

From the foregoing balances and the following information, prepare the Balance Sheet of the Happy Mutual Life Assurance Society Ltd. as on 31st March, 2023 and its Revenue Account for the year ended on that date :

(*i*) Claims less reassurances outstanding at the end of the year :
By death: ₹ 600 lakh; By maturity : ₹ 400 lakh.

(*ii*) Expenses outstanding ₹ 60 lakh and prepaid ₹ 15 lakh.

(*iii*) Provide ₹ 45 lakh for depreciation on buildings; ₹ 15 lakh for depreciation on furniture and office equipment; and ₹ 110 lakh for taxation.

(*iv*) **Premiums outstanding ₹ 2,028 lakh; commission thereon ₹ 65 lakh.**

(*v*) **Interests, dividends and rents outstanding (net) ₹ 30 lakh and interest and rent accrued (net) ₹ 350 lakh.**

SOLUTION

Happy Mutual Life Assurance Society Ltd.
REVENUE ACCOUNT
for the year ended 31-3-2023

₹ in lakhs

Particulars	*Schedule Year*	*Current Year*	*Previous*
Premiums Earned—Net	1	17,028	
Income from Investments :			
Interest, Dividends and Rent-Gross		2,180	
Other Income :			
Annuities Granted		2	
Registration and Other Fees		2	
Total (A)		19,212	
Commission	2	315	
Operating Expenses related to Insurance Business	3	3,282	
Provision for Tax		(I) 760	
Total (B)		4,357	
Benefits Paid (Net)	4	3,246	
Total (C)		3,246	
Surplus (D) = (A) – (B) – (C)		11,609	

(I) Figure of *provision for taxation* has been calculated as shown below :

	₹ in lakhs
Income tax paid	450
Income tax on interest, dividend and rent	500
Provision for taxation to be made	110
	1,060
Less : Existing taxation provision	300
	760

Happy Mutual Life Assurance Society Ltd.
BALANCE SHEET
as on 31-3-2023

₹ in lakhs

Particulars	*Schedule Year*	*Current Year*	*Previous*
Sources of Funds			
Share Capital	5	–	
Reserves & Surplus	6	61,759	
Borrowings	7	1,250	
Total		63,009	

Application of Funds			
Investments	8	56,805	
Loans	9	3,400	
Fixed Assets	10	195	
Current Assets :			
Cash & Bank Balance	11	1,380	
Advances and Other Assets	12	2,874	
Sub-Total (A)		4,254	
Current Liabilities	13	1,535	
Provisions	14	110	
Sub-Total (B)		1,645	
Net Current Assets (C) = (A) – (B)		2,609	
Total of Schedules 8, 9, 10 & Net Current Assets		63,009	

Schedules Forming Part of Financial Statements

SCHEDULE 1—PREMIUMS

₹ in lakhs

Particulars	*Current Year*	*Previous Year*
Premiums	15,000	
Add : Outstanding	2,028	
	17,028	

SCHEDULE 2—COMMISSION

₹ in lakhs

Particulars	*Current Year*	*Previous Year*
Commission Paid	250	
Add : Commission on Reinsurance Accepted	65	
	315	

SCHEDULE 3—OPERATING EXPENSES RELATED TO INSURANCE BUSINESS

₹ in lakhs

Particulars		*Current Year*	*Previous Year*
Expenses of Management—Paid		3,100	
Add : Outstanding		60	
		3,160	
Less : Prepaid		15	
		3,145	
Printing and Stationery		77	
Depreciation :			
Building	45		
Machinery	15	60	
		3,282	

SCHEDULE 4—BENEFITS PAID (NET)

₹ in lakhs

Particulars		Current Year	Previous Year
Insurance Claims :			
(*a*) Claims by Death			
Paid	2,200		
Add : Outstanding at the end of the year	600		
	2,800		
Less : Outstanding at the beginning of the year	900	1,900	
(*b*) Claims by Maturity			
Paid	1,500		
Add : Outstanding at the end of the year	400		
	1,900		
Less : Outstanding at the beginning of the year	600	1,300	
(*c*) Annuities		6	
(*d*) Other Benefits :			
Surrenders		40	
		3,246	

SCHEDULE 6—RESERVES & SURPLUS

₹ in lakhs

Particulars		Current Year	Previous Year
Contingency Reserve		150	
Other Reserves :			
Life Assurance Fund :			
At the beginning of the year	50,000		
Add : Surplus as per Revenue A/c	11,609	61,609	
		61,759	

SCHEDULE 7—BORROWINGS

₹ in lakhs

Particulars	Current Year	Previous Year
Premium Deposits	1,150	
Sundry Deposits	100	
	1,250	

SCHEDULE 8—INVESTMENTS

₹ in lakhs

Particulars		Current Year	Previous Year
Sundry Other Investments (52,000 – 250 deposited with Reserve Bank of India)		51,750	
Investment in House Property at Cost	5,315		
Add : Addition during the year	85		
	5,400		
Less : Depreciation	345	5,055	
		56,805	

SCHEDULE 9—LOANS

₹ in lakhs

Particulars	Current Year	Previous Year
Secured		
On Mortgages	150	
On Policies	3,250	
	3,400	

SCHEDULE 10—FIXED ASSETS

₹ in lakhs

Particulars		Current Year	Previous Year
Furniture & Office Equipment at Cost	210		
Addition during the year	40		
	250		
Less : Depreciation to date	55	195	
		195	

SCHEDULE 11—CASH AND BANK BALANCES

₹ in lakhs

Particulars	Current Year	Previous Year
Cash and Stamps in hand	30	
Cash with Banks in Current Account	1,350	
	1,380	

SCHEDULE 12—ADVANCES AND OTHER ASSETS

₹ in lakhs

Particulars	Current Year	Previous Year
Prepaid Expenses	15	
Advance Payment of Income Tax	50	
Interest, Dividend and Rent Outstanding	30	
Interest, Dividend and Rent Accrued	350	
Outstanding Premiums	2,028	
Agents' Balances	100	
Deposit with Reserve Bank of India	250	
Deposit with Electricity Companies	1	
Sundry Debtors	50	
	2,874	

SCHEDULE 13—CURRENT LIABILITIES

₹ in lakhs

Particulars	Current Year	Previous Year
Sundry Creditors	350	
Claims Outstanding	1,000	

Expenses Outstanding	60	
Credit Balances Pending Adjustment	60	
Commission due but not yet paid	65	
	1,535	

SCHEDULE 14—PROVISIONS

₹ in lakhs

Particulars	*Current Year*	*Previous Year*
Provision for Tax	110	

Determination of Profit in Life Insurance Business

A life policy is generally taken for a number of years. The premium received for such long-term contracts cannot be treated as income for ascertaining the profits for that year. For example, under a contract of annuity only one premium as initial payment is received whereas the annuitant is required to be paid annuity till he dies. In case of life insurance, the claim must arise either on death or expiry of the period of the policy whichever is earlier. That the future premium may or may not be received depends on the existence of the insured. Thus on a particular date a liability of the corporation is to be calculated as the premiums to be received in future will generally be less than the amount payable as claims. There is a gap between claims which are expected to arise and premiums which are expected to be received. This gap is known as net liability. Thus it becomes desirable to create a reserve equal to its net liability in order to ascertain the profit made by the corporation. The Life Insurance Corporation of India makes the valuation of its net liability every year in order to ascertain its profit. This is done by a person known as actuary *i.e.* mathematician well versed in the intricacies of life insurance. The process by which net liability is ascertained by an actuary, is known as actuarial valuation. This is necessary to determine the profit in case of life insurance business.

Procedure for Ascertaining Profit or Loss

Net liability is compared with life assurance fund on a particular date in order to calculate the surplus or deficiency. This comparison is made by preparing a Valuation Balance Sheet, a specimen form of which is given as follows :

VALUATION BALANCE SHEET

as on......,

	₹		₹
To Net Liability as per Actuary's Valuation		By Life Assurance Fund as per Balance Sheet	
To Surplus		By Deficiency	

Only surplus (and not deficiency) will be shown in the Balance Sheet. With profit policyholders have a right to participate in the profits of life insurance business to the extent of 95% of true profit. For calculation of true profit, surplus as disclosed by Valuation Balance Sheet must be adjusted by :

(*i*) Adding interim bonus (if any) as it is really advance payment of bonus.

(*ii*) Deducting any expenses still to be incurred.

Out of 95% of true profit, interim bonus already paid should be deducted to calculate the amount due to the policyholders.

ILLUSTRATION 12. A life insurance company gets its valuation made once in every two years. Its Life Assurance Fund on 31st March, 2023, amounted to ₹ 41,40,000 before providing ₹ 30,000 for the shareholders dividend for the year 2022-23. Its actuarial valuation due on 31st March, 2023 disclosed a net liability of ₹ 40,40,000 under assurance annuity contracts.

An interim bonus of ₹ 60,000 was paid to the policyholders during the year ending 31st March, 2023.

Prepare a statement showing the amount now available as bonus to policyholders.

SOLUTION

VALUATION BALANCE SHEET

as on 31st March, 2023

	₹		₹
To Net Liability as per Actuary's Valuation	40,40,000	By Life Assurance Fund as per	
" Surplus	1,00,000	Balance Sheet	41,40,000
	41,40,000		41,40,000

STATEMENT SHOWING THE AMOUNT DUE TO POLICY HOLDERS

	₹
Surplus as per Valuation Balance Sheet	1,00,000
Add : Interim bonus paid to policyholders	60,000
	1,60,000
Less : Dividend for 2022-23 due to Shareholders	30,000
Profit	1,30,000
Policyholders will get 95% of ₹ 1,30,000	1,23,500
Less : Already paid as interim bonus	60,000
Amount now due to the policyholders	63,500

ILLUSTRATION 13. The life fund of a Life Assurance Company was ₹ 86,48,000 as on 31st March, 2023. The interim bonus paid during the intervaluation period was ₹ 1,48,000. The periodical actuarial valuation determined the net liability at ₹ 74,25,000. Surplus brought forward from the previous valuation was ₹ 8,50,000. The Directors of the company proposed to carry forward ₹ 9,31,000 and to divide the balance between the shareholders and the policyholders in the ratio of 1 : 10.

Show (*a*) the Valuation Balance Sheet ;

(*b*) the net profit for the valuation period ; and

(*c*) the distribution of the surplus.

SOLUTION

VALUATION BALANCE SHEET

as on 31st March, 2023

	₹		₹
To Net Liability as per Actuarial Valuation	74,25,000	By Life Fund as per Balance Sheet	86,48,000
" Surplus	12,23,000		
	86,48,000		86,48,000

(*b*) **Calculation of net profit for the valuation period**

	₹
Surplus as per Valuation Balance Sheet	12,23,000
Add : Interim Bonus paid	1,48,000
	13,71,000
Less : Surplus at the beginning of the period	8,50,000
Net Profit for the Valuation Period	5,21,000

(*c*) **Distribution of Surplus**

		₹
Total Surplus		13,71,000
Less : Surplus to be carried forward		9,31,000
		4,40,000
Distribution :	₹	
To Shareholders		40,000
Policyholders	4,00,000	
Less : Interim bonus already paid	1,48,000	
Amount payable to policyholders		2,52,000
This is equal to [₹ 4,40,000 – ₹ 1,48,000]		2,92,000

Entries for Dealing with Profits

There are two methods to deal with the profits in the books.

Under the *first method*, the following entries are passed :

(*i*) *For transferring the whole of Profits to Profit & Loss A/c*

Life Assurance Fund A/c Dr.

To Profit & Loss A/c

(*ii*) Profit & Loss A/c (and not to Revenue A/c)

To Dividend (to Shareholders) A/c

To Income Tax (on profits)

To Bonus paid to Policyholders in Cash

To Bonus Utilised in Reduction of Premiums

To General/Contingency Reserve

(*iii*) *For transferring reversionary bonus declared out of surplus to Life Assurance Fund*

Profit & Loss A/c

To Life Assurance Fund

The balance in P. & L. A/c is shown in the Balance Sheet.

Under the *Second* (*or Alternative*) *Method* to deal with the profits the amount due to various parties is determined and entries are passed through Life Assurance Fund or Revenue Account. All items *i.e.,* dividend to shareholders, income tax on profits, bonus payable in Cash etc. all are debited to Revenue Account provided the amounts do not exceed those warranted by profits. No separate entry is required to be passed for declaring the reversionary bonus as full profit has not been debited to the Life Assurance Fund in the first instance. This will be more clear from the following illustration :

ILLUSTRATION 14. After the valuation on March 31, 2023 in the books of Life Assurance Company Ltd. the actuary's certificate disclosed the net liability on policies and annuities at ₹ 50,40,000.

From the following information prepare the Revenue Account and ascertain profit and loss made by the company. It was further decided by the directors to transfer a sum of ₹ 1,00,000 to the Investment Fluctuation Fund which stood at ₹ 2,00,000 on that date to write down investments from ₹ 49,00,000 to ₹ 46,00,000 if the valuation revealed a surplus :

	₹		₹
Bonus in Cash	**1,00,000**	**Expenses of Management**	**2,50,000**
Bonus in Reduction of Premiums	**10,000**	**Commission**	**1,00,000**
Surrenders	**2,00,000**	**Annuities**	**8,00,000**
Premiums	**35,00,000**	**Consideration for Annuities Granted**	**12,00,000**
Interests, Dividends and Rents (net)	**12,00,000**	**Life Assurance Fund on 1-4-2022**	**40,00,000**
Claims	**22,00,000**	**Interim Bonus paid for the valuation period**	**1,50,000**

As a result of valuation it was decided that a reversionary bonus of ₹ 150 per ₹ 10,000 be granted and the company gave the policyholders the option to get bonus in cash @ ₹ 60 per ₹ 10,000. The total business in force was ₹ 9 crores. One third of the policy holders in value decided to get the bonus in cash. Draft the journal entries for the above decisions, giving effect to utilisation of the surplus ; show how much the policyholders can get by way of share in profit (Ignore taxation).

SOLUTION

Life Assurance Company Ltd.
REVENUE ACCOUNT
for the year ending 31st March, 2023

	₹	₹
Premiums Earned (Net)		35,00,000
Income from Investments :		
Interest, Dividends and Rent	12,00,000	
Less : Loss on Revaluation of Investments	1,00,000	11,00,000
Other Income : Consideration for Annuities Granted		12,00,000
Total (A)		58,00,000
Commission		1,00,000
Operating Expenses related to Insurance Business—Expenses of Management		2,50,000
Total (B)		3,50,000

		₹	
Benefits Paid (Net) :	Claims	22,00,000	
	Annuities	8,00,000	
	Surrenders	2,00,000	32,00,000
Bonus in Cash		1,00,000	
Bonus in Reduction of Premiums		10,000	1,10,000
	Total (C)		33,10,000
Surplus (D) = (A) – (B) – (C)			21,40,000

	₹
Balance in Life Assurance at the beginning of the year	40,00,000
Add : Surplus as per Revenue A/c this year	21,40,000
Total Life Assurance Fund	61,40,000

VALUATION BALANCE SHEET

as on 31st March, 2023

	₹		₹
To Net Liability as per Actuarial Valuation	50,40,000	By Life Assurance Fund	61,40,000
To Surplus	11,00,000		
	61,40,000		61,40,000

	₹
Surplus as revealed by Valuation Balance Sheet	11,00,000
Add : Interim Bonus Paid	1,50,000
True Surplus Subject to Taxation	12,50,000
Policyholders will get 95%	11,87,500
Less : Interim bonus paid to policyholders	1,50,000
Amount due to policyholders	10,37,500

JOURNAL

2023			₹	₹
Mar. 31	Life Assurance Fund A/c Dr.		11,00,000	
	To Profit & Loss A/c			11,00,000
	(Being profit revealed by valuation balance sheet transferred to P/L A/c)			
	Profit & Loss A/c Dr.		1,80,000	
	To Bonus in Cash			1,80,000
	(Being the immediate bonus payable @ ₹ 60 per ₹ 10,000 on ₹ 3 crores)			
	Profit & Loss A/c Dr.		3,60,000	
	To Life Assurance Fund A/c			3,60,000
	(Being the transfer of the amount to Life Assurance Fund of net liability at present value in respect of reversionary bonus @ ₹ 60 per ₹ 10,000 on ₹ 6 crores)			

As a result of the above mentioned entries the Life Assurance Fund would stand at ₹ 54,00,000 (*i.e.*, 61,40,000 + 3,60,000 – 11,00,000) and Profit & Loss A/c would show a balance of ₹ 5,60,000 (*i.e.*, ₹ 11,00,000 – ₹ 1,80,000 – ₹ 3,60,000).

Alternative Method3

			₹	₹
	Life Assurance Fund A/c	Dr.	1,80,000	
	To Bonus in Cash (Payable)			1,80,000

QUESTIONS

SHORT ANSWER TYPE

1. What is the meaning of surrender value ? Is there a surrender value of general insurance policy also ?
2. What is the difference between Annuities and Consideration for Annuities Granted ?
3. How is Bonus in Reduction of Premium treated in the Revenue Account ?
4. What is the difference between Commission on Reinsurance Accepted and Commission on Reinsurance Ceded ?
5. What is life assurance fund ?
6. What is the basic difference between life insurance and general insurance ?
7. What is the difference between life policy and endowment policy ?
8. How does Valuation Balance Sheet differ from normal Balance Sheet ?
9. Distinguish between cash bonus and reversionary bonus.
10. How does a life insurance company ascertain its profit ?
11. What is meant by reinsurance ? How is it helpful to insurance companies ?
12. Distinguish between claims by death and claims by maturity in life insurance business.
13. Draw a proforma of Revenue Account of Life Insurance Company with imaginary figures.
14. Calculate the net claim to be shown in Revenue Account of an Assurance Company :

	₹
Claims paid during year ended 31-3-2023	5,60,000
Claims outstanding on 1-4-2022	52,000
Claims outstanding on 31-3-2023	92,000
Claims covered under reinsurance	25,000

Ans. [₹ 5,75,000].

15. Calculate the amount of benefit paid (Net) to be derived in schedule 4 of a life insurance company :

	₹
Claims paid	5,91,000
Claims Outstanding at the end of the year	30,000
Claims Outstanding at the beginning of the year	21,000
Reinsurance Recoveries	2,40,000
Annuities paid	30,000
Surrenders paid	21,000

Ans. [Benefits paid (Net) : ₹ 4,11,000]

16. From the following, you are required to calculate the amount on account of claim to be shown in the revenue account for the year ending 31st March 2022.

Intimated in	*Admitted in*	*Paid in*	₹
2020-21	2020-21	2021-22	15,000
2021-22	2021-22	2022-23	10,000
2019-20	2020-21	2020-21	5,000
2019-20	2020-21	2021-22	12,000
2021-22	2022-23	2022-23	8,000
2021-22	2021-22	2021-22	1,02,000

Claim on account of reinsurance in 2021-22 was ₹ 25,000.

Ans. [Net Claims to be shown in Revenue Account ₹ 95,000 (₹ 1,29,000 + ₹ 18,000 – ₹ 27,000 – ₹ 25,000)]

17. From the following particulars of an insurance company, ascertain the amount of claims chargeable to Revenue account and claims outstanding for the year ended 31-3-2022 :

Intimated in	*Admitted in*	*Paid in*	₹
2020-21	2020-21	2021-22	1,36,000
2020-21	2021-22	2022-23	1,20,000
2020-21	2022-23	2022-23	80,000
2021-22	2021-22	2021-22	4,00,000
2021-22	2021-22	2022-23	2,20,000
2021-22	2022-23	2022-23	1,44,000

Ans. [Claims chargeable to Revenue A/c—₹ 7,64,000 (*i.e.* 5,36,000 + 5,64,000 – 3,36,000); Claims outstanding for the year 2021-22—₹ 3,64,000; Claims outstanding on 31-3-22—₹ 5,64,000; Claims outstanding on 1-4-21—₹ 3,36,000]

TRUE FUND

18. A life assurance fund of ₹ 25,00,000 was ascertained without taking into account the following :

(*a*) Claims Covered under re-insurance ₹ 18,000

(*b*) Reinsurance Premium ₹ 15,000.

Calculate the correct life assurance fund.

Ans. [Correct Life Fund : ₹ 25,03,000]

19. A Life Insurance Company prepared its Revenue A/c for the year ended 31-3-2023 and ascertained its life assurance fund to be ₹ 22,34,400. It has found later that the following had been omitted from the accounts :

	₹
(*a*) Interest Accrued on Investments	32,000
Income Tax Liable to be deducted estimated to be ₹ 10,000	
(*b*) Outstanding Premiums	31,400
(*c*) Bonus utilised for reduction of Premium	6,600
(*d*) Claim intimated but not admitted	15,200
(*e*) Claims covered under Reinsurance	5,300

What is the true life assurance fund ?

Ans. [₹ 22,77,900]

ASCERTAINMENT OF PROFIT

20. The Life Assurance Fund of Company stood at ₹ 5,25,00,000 on 31st March, 2023 and the valuation of its net liability in respect of policies in fire on that date revealed at figure of ₹ 4,86,00,000. How much do the policyholders stand to get by way of bonus ?

Ans. [₹ 37,05,000].

21. The net liability in respect of life policies annuity contracts of Long Life Insurance Co. Ltd. on 31st March, 2023 was ₹ 1,08,60,000; its life fund on that date was ₹ 1,22,50,000. During the valuation period, it had paid interim bonus amounting to ₹ 60,000. The dividend for 2022-23 amounting to ₹ 40,000 was still unpaid. Ascertain the share of profits that the policy holders can get as a result of the valuation.

Ans. [Surplus ₹ 13,90,000; Amount due to policyholders ₹ 12,79,500]

22. The life fund of Well-Life Assurance Co. was ₹ 90,00,000 as on 31st December, 2023. The interim bonus paid during the valuation period was ₹ 1,50,000. The periodical actuarial valuation determined the net liability at ₹ 75,00,000. Surplus brought forward from the *previous valuation* was ₹ 9,00,000. The directors of the company proposed to carry forward ₹ 10,00,000 and to divide the balance between the shareholders and the policy holders. You are required to show :
   (*i*) The Valuation Balance Sheet.
   (*ii*) The Net Profit for the valuation period.
   (*iii*) The distribution of the surplus.

Ans. [(*i*) Surplus ₹ 15,00,000; (*ii*) ₹ 7,50,000; (*iii*) Distribution of Surplus ₹ 6,50,000 (*i.e.* to Shareholders and ₹ 32,500 to Policy holders ₹ 4,67,500 (*i.e.* ₹ 6,17,500 – 1,50,000)]

LONG ANSWER TYPE

1. Explain the method followed for arriving at profit in the life insurance business.
2. Explain what do you understand by Life Fund. Where does it appear in the Final Accounts ?
3. How is profit or loss determined in Fire Insurance Business ?
4. Write short notes on the following :
   (*a*) Reinsurance ; (*b*) Premium Deposits ; (*c*) Annuities ; (*d*) Actuarial Valuation ; (*e*) Endowment Policy ; (*f*) Reversionary Bonus ; and (*g*) Surrender Value.
5. Prepare (with imaginary figures) Revenue Account of Life Insurance Company.
6. Prepare (with imaginary figures) the Balance Sheet of a Life Insurance Company.
7. Give entries necessary to bring the following into account, at the end of each period :
   (*i*) Outstanding premiums, (*ii*) Outstanding claims (*iii*) Outstanding interest, (*iv*) Bonus in reduction of premium, (*v*) Claims covered under reinsurance.
8. Prepare (with imaginary figures) Revenue Accounts of Fire and Marine Departments of a General Insurance Company.
9. Prepare (with imaginary figures) the Balance Sheet of an insurance company carrying on fire, marine and miscellaneous insurance business.
10. What important points should be kept in mind in preparing the annual accounts of general Insurance companies?
11. Point out the main features of Accounts of 'General Insurance Companies'. What statutory books are required to be maintained by a General Insurance Company under the Insurance Act?
12. What provision should be made by a Fire Insurance Company in regard to Unexpired Risks at the end of each financial period ?

13. Explain how the profit or loss from general insurance business is ascertained and prepare a fire Revenue Account with imaginary figures.

14. Explain the following items in the annual accounts of a General Insurance Co. :
(*i*) Reinsurance Recoveries, (*ii*) Estimated Liability in respect of Outstanding Claims, (*iii*) Profit on Sale of Investments, (*iv*) Deposits with Reserve Bank of India, (*v*) Interest and Dividend Outstanding, (*vi*) Unclaimed Dividends, (*vii*) Agent's Balance.

PRACTICAL PROBLEMS

1. From the following Trial Balance as on 31-3-2023, prepare Revenue Account and Balance Sheet of the Life Assurance business :

	₹ '000	₹ '000
Mortgages on Properties within India	4,00,000	
Mortgages on Property out of India	50,000	
Loans on Life Interest	1,00,000	
Loans on Reversions	2,00,000	
Loans on Policies within their Surrender Values	6,00,000	
Investments :		
Municipal Securities	5,00,000	
Indian and Foreign Government Securities	10,00,000	
Freehold Ground Rents	8,00,000	
Reversions	5,00,000	
Outstanding Premiums	50,000	
Outstanding Interests, Dividends and Rent	10,000	
Surrenders on business outside India	1,000	
Surrenders on business within India	20,000	
Cash in hand	50,000	
Claims admitted but not paid		10,000
Claims on business within India	2,00,000	
Claims on business outside India	10,000	
Sundry Creditors		15,000
Amount of Life Insurance Fund at the beginning of the year		40,00,000
Expenses of Management	20,000	
Premiums on business within India		4,80,000
Premiums on business outside India		6,000
	45,11,000	45,11,000

Ans. [Surplus (₹ '000) 2,35,000; Life Assurance Fund (₹ '000) 42,35,000 ; B/S Total (₹ '000) 42,35,000].

2. Following were the balances extracted from the Trial Balance of the Indian Life Assurance Society at 31st March, 2023 :

	₹ '000		₹ '000
Balance of account at the beginning of the year	20,00,000	Premiums (other than single)	2,00,000
		Claims admitted but not paid	6,000
Govt. securities	10,00,000	Surrenders 20,000	
Profit on realisation of assets	2,000	Single premiums	80,000

Investment Fluctuation A/c	10,000	Consideration for annuities granted	50,000
Claims under policies by death	60,000	Interest, dividends and rent received	70,000
Claims under policies by maturity	1,00,000	Depreciation of furniture	3,000
Loans on mortgages	5,60,000	Administrative expenses	36,000
Loans on policies	3,00,000	Salaries	3,000
Freehold property and furniture	1,03,000	Auditor's fees	1,500
Agent's balances owing	3,600	Director's fees	300
Sundry creditors	2,000	Legal expenses	1,000
Outstanding premiums	24,000	Advertising	1,400
Commission paid	24,000	Printing, stationery and others	10,800
Interest accrued not due	3,000	Cash at Bank	1,68,400
		Provision for depreciation	3,000

Prepare a Revenue Account and Balance Sheet.

Ans. [Surplus (₹ '000) 1,41,000 ; B/S Total (₹ '000) 21,51,000].

3. The Life Assurance Fund of an Insurance Company on 31st March, 2023 showed a balance of ₹ 87,76,500. It was later found that the following were not taken into account :

(*i*) Dividend from Investment ₹ 4,80,000. (*ii*) Income-tax on above ₹ 48,000. (*iii*) Bonus in reduction of premium ₹ 8,77,500. (not taken as expense) (*iv*) Claims covered under Re-Insurance ₹ 4,23,000. (*v*) Claims intimated, but not accepted by the company ₹ 7,62,000.

Ascertain correct balance of the Fund.

Ans. [Correct Balance ₹ 79,92,000].

4. Following balances form part of the books of Bharat Assurance Company as on 31st March, 2023.

Life fund on 1st April, 2022 ₹ 15,70,562 ; Claims by death ₹ 1,16,980. Claims by maturity ₹ 96,420 ; Premiums ₹ 2,70,572 ; Management expenses ₹ 29,890 ; Commission ₹ 36,541 ; Consideration for annuities granted ₹ 10,620 ; Interest, dividend and rent ₹ 52,461 ; Income tax on profit ₹ 3,060 ; Surrenders ₹ 21,768 ; Annuities ₹ 29,420 ; Bonus paid in cash ₹ 9,450 ; Bonus paid in reduction of premium ₹ 3,500. Preliminary expenses ₹ 600 ; Claims admitted but not paid at the end of the year, ₹ 80,034 ; Annuities due but not paid ₹ 22,380 ; Capital paid up ₹ 6,00,000 ; Govt. Securities ₹ 16,90,890 ; Sundry Assets 5,68,110.

Additional relevant data ; Claims covered under reinsurance ₹ 10,000. Further claims intimated ₹ 8,000. Further bonus utilised in reduction of premiums ₹ 1,500. Interest accrued ₹ 15,400. Premiums outstanding ₹ 7,400. Prepare a Revenue Account and the Balance Sheet.

Ans. [Surplus (₹ '000) 14,484; Life Assurance Fund (₹ '000) 15,81,986 ; B/S Total (₹ '000) 21,81,386].

Note : Tax on profit is deducted from Surplus as per Revenue A/c under Reserves and Surplus in Schedule 6. Income tax on profit can be taken in Revenue A/c, then Surplus taken to Balance Sheet will reduce. Answer will remain same.

5. Following figures are extracted from the books of Mutual Life Assurance Co. Limited for the year ended 31st March, 2023.

	₹		₹
Premium *less* Reinsurance Premium	42,90,000	Commission	1,65,000
Claims *less* Reinsurance Claims	25,50,000	Surplus on Revaluation of Reversions	15,000
Re-insurance Irrecoverable	12,000	Interest, Dividends and Rents	21,00,000
Consideration for Annuities Granted	1,32,500	Income Tax	3,30,000
Annuities Paid	37,500	Management Expenses	5,25,000
Surrenders	2,40,000		

Net Liability on all contracts in force as on 31-3-2023 was ₹ 72,00,000 and on 31-3-2022 the liability was ₹ 63,00,000.

You are required to prepare Revenue Account according to the IRDA Regulations, 2020.

(**Note :** Schedules need not be prepared)

Ans. [Surplus ₹ 17,77,500].

6. The Life Assurance Fund of Moon Light Life Assurance Company had a balance of ₹ 3.80 crores on 31-3-2023. The actuarial valuation carried out on the same date revealed a net liability of ₹ 2.60 crores. During the previous three years an interim bonus of ₹ 30 lakhs was paid to the policy holders.

   The Company now proposes to carry forward ₹ 50 lakhs the balance being divided between the policy holders (95%) and shareholders (5%).

   You are required to show the following :

   (*i*) Valuation Balance Sheet (*ii*) Net Profit for the three years period and (*iii*) Distribution of Profit.

Ans. [(*i*) ₹ 1.20 crores (*ii*) ₹ 1.50 crores (*iii*) Provisionary Bonus to be declared ₹ 0.65 crore, Shareholders' Share ₹ 0.05 crore]

7. The Life Assurance Fund of a company on 31st March, 2023 was ₹ 4,00,00,000. Its net liability on that date was estimated to be ₹ 3,80,00,000 by the company actuary. The investment held by the company amounted to ₹ 3,20,00,000 against which the Investment Reserve stood at ₹ 5,00,000. The investments have to be written down be ₹ 8,00,000.

   The company declared a reversionary bonus of ₹ 40 per 1,000 with the option to policyholders of the bonus in cash at the rate of ₹ 16 per ₹ 1,000. Total value of policies in force was ₹ 8 crore. One fourth of the policyholders (in value) decided to receive the bonus in cash. The company estimated that its liability for income tax would be ₹ 3,20,000.

   Pass the Journal Entries to record the above.

MODULE 5

CHAPTER 1

Financial Statements of General Insurance Companies

General Insurance

General insurance means insurance other than life insurance. Section 2(6B) of the Insurance Act, 1938 defines general insurance business as fire, marine and miscellaneous insurance business whether carried on singly or in combination with one or more of them. Miscellaneous insurance can be for any type of risk which an insurance company agrees to bear other than risks which are covered by life insurance, fire insurance and marine insurance. Some of the examples of general insurance are : accident insurance, motor vehicle insurance, burglary insurance, workmen's compensation insurance, cash in transit insurance, fidelity insurance, loss of profit insurance etc.

In general insurance, the policy is taken usually for a year at a time and can be renewed yearly or a fresh policy can be taken with some other insurance company.

Distinction Between Life Insurance and General Insurance

1. *Timing of Payment of Claim.* In case of life insurance, insurable amount is payable either on happening of the event (death) or at the maturity. But in case of general insurance reimbursement of loss or liability insured will be paid at the happening of the uncertain event only.
2. *Value of Policy.* In case of life insurance policy can be taken for any amount depending upon the premium due insured is willing to pay but in case of general insurance, the sum payable is limited to the amount of loss suffered or liability incurred, notwithstanding the amount of policy.
3. *Duration of Contract.* Life insurance contract is a long-term contract in which premiums have to be paid for a number of years till the maturity of the policy period whereas general insurance contract is for a short *period* usually a year.
4. *Assurance.* Life insurance is also known as life *assurance* because the insured gets an assured sum on the maturity of the policy or on the death of the insured, whichever is earlier. Thus,

life insurance is a saving device and also covers risk whereas general insurance only covers risk in case of loss.

5. *Determination of Liability*. In case of life insurance business, *profit is determined* by estimating the liability under existing policies by an actuary. In case of general insurance, business profit is determined after making provision for unexpired risks and the balance of Revenue Account is taken as profit or loss.

6. In case of life insurance, policyholders are entitled to get bonus whereas in general insurance there is no provision of bonus.

Important Points in Final Accounts of General Insurance Companies

Following are the important points which should be kept in mind while preparing the final accounts of general insurance companies :

1. General insurance company may be doing more than one business, *e.g.*, fire, marine, accidental etc. For each type of business a separate Revenue Account is to be prepared in the prescribed form B-RA.

2. **Reserve for Unexpired Risks.** The need for unexpired risks reserve arises from the fact that all policies are renewed annually except in specific cases where short period policies are issued. Since the insurers close their accounts on a particular date, not all risks under policies expire on that date. Many policies normally extend beyond this date into the following year during which risks continue. In other words, at the closing date, there is unexpired liability under various policies, which may occur during the remaining term of the policy beyond the year end.

According to the requirements of the Insurance Act, it is sufficient if the provision is made for unexpired risks at 50 per cent for Fire, Marine Cargo and Miscellaneous business except for Marine Hull which has to be 100 per cent. **Some prudent companies may make additional reserve also in case of fire and accidental insurance in order to cover the full liability as and when it arises.**

The Executive Committee of the General Insurance Council, set up under the Insurance Act for the supervision of general insurance companies, has provided that in case of marine insurance, the provision against unexpired risk should be 100% of net premium and in case of other general insurance business such as fire, accident, theft, etc. reserve against unexpired risk should be 40% of the net premium income. **However, the Income Tax Authorities allow a provision of 50% of net premium income in respect of fire and miscellaneous business and 100% of net premium in case of marine insurance. Therefore, the practice with the general insurance companies is to maintain 50% of net premium income as reserve against unexpired risk in case of fire, accident, theft, etc. and 100% in case of marine insurance. An insurance company can also make additional reserve in addition to usual reserve if it feels necessary.**

3. A combined Balance Sheet is also prepared in the prescribed form for all businesses on the closing date of the year.

4. Commission on policies effected through insurance agents cannot exceed 5% of the premium in respect of fire and marine business and 10% in case of miscellaneous business. In case policies are effected through a principal agent, the maximum limits are 20% for fire and marine policies and 15% in case of miscellaneous insurance less any commission payable to an insurance agent in respect of the policy concerned.

5. Claims paid must include all expenses directly incurred in settling claims such as legal expenses, medical expenses, surveyor's expanses etc.

6. No claim of ₹ 20,000 or more can be paid, except as the Controller of Insurance may otherwise direct, unless there is a report in respect thereof from an approved surveyor or loss assessor (licensed under the Insurance Act).

7. An insurer carrying on general insurance business, after the commencement of Regulations given by the Insurance Regulatory and Development Authority on 30th March, 2003, shall comply with the requirements of Schedule B for the preparation of financial statements, management report and auditor's report. Schedule B as given by IRDA is reproduced below :

SCHEDULE B

(*See Regulation 3*)

Part-I

ACCOUNTING PRINCIPLES FOR PREPARATION OF FINANCIAL STATEMENTS

1. Applicability of Accounting Standards

Every Balance Sheet, Receipts and Payments Account [Cash Flow Statement] and Profit and Loss Account [Shareholders' Account] of the insurer shall be in conformity with the Accounting Standards (AS) issued by the ICAI, to the extent applicable to the insurers carrying on general insurance business, except that :

(*i*) Ind AS 7 – Cash Flow Statements Cash Flow Statement shall be prepared only under the Direct Method.

(*ii*) Ind AS 40 – Accounting for investment property shall not be applicable.

(*iii*) Ind AS 108 – Operating segments Reporting – shall apply to all insurers irrespective of the requirements regarding listing and turnover mentioned therein.

2. Premium

Premium shall be recognised as income over the contract period of risk, whichever is appropriate. Premium received in advance, which represents premium income not relating to the current accounting period, shall be disclosed separately in the financial statements.

A reserve for unexpired risks shall be created as the amount representing that part of the premium written which is attributable to, and to be allocated to the succeeding accounting periods and shall not be less than as required under section 64 V(I) (ii) (b) of the Act.

Premium Received in Advance, which represents premium received prior to commencement of the risk, shall be shown separately under the head '*Current Liabilities*' in the financial statements.

3. Premium Deficiency

Premium deficiency shall be recognised if the sum of expected claim costs, related expenses and maintenance costs exceeds related reserve for unexpired risks.

4. Acquisition Costs

Acquisition costs, if any, shall be expended in the period in which they are incurred. Acquisition costs are those costs that vary with, and are primarily related to, the acquisition of new and renewal insurance contracts. The most essential test is the obligatory relationship between costs and the execution of insurance contracts (*i.e.*, commencement of risk).

5. Claims

The components of the ultimate cost of claims to an insurer comprise the claims under policies and specific claims settlement costs. Claims under policies comprise the claims made for losses incurred, and those estimated or anticipated under the policies following a loss occurrence.

A liability for outstanding claims shall be brought to account in respect of both direct business and inward reinsurance business.

The liability shall include :

(*a*) Future payments in relation to unpaid reported claims;

(*b*) Claims Incurred But Not Reported (IBNR) including inadequate reserves [sometimes referred to as Claims Incurred But Not Enough Reported (IBNER)]

which will result in future cash/asset outgo for settling liabilities against those claims. Change in estimated liability represents the difference between the estimated liability for outstanding claims at the beginning and the end of the financial period.

The accounting estimate shall also include claims cost adjusted for estimated salvage value if there is sufficient degree of certainty of its realisation.

Claims made in respect of contracts where the claims payment period exceeds four years shall be recognised on an actuarial basis, subject to regulations that may be prescribed by the Authority. In such cases, certificate from a recognised actuary as to the fairness of liability assessment must be obtained. Actuarial assumptions shall be suitably disclosed by way of notes to the account.

6. Procedure to determine the value of investments

An insurer shall determine the values of investments in the following manner :

(*a*) Real Estate—Investment Property. Investment Property shall be measured at historical cost less accumulated depreciation and impairment loss, residual value being considered zero and no revaluation being permissible.

The insurer shall assess at each balance sheet date whether any impairment of the investment property has occurred.

An impairment loss shall be recognised as an expense in the Revenue/Profit and Loss Account immediately.

Fair value as at the balance sheet date and the basis of its determination shall be disclosed in the financial statements as additional information.

(*b*) Debt Securities. Debt securities including government securities and redeemable preference shares, shall be considered as "held to maturity" securities and shall be measured at historical cost subject to amortisation.

(*c*) **Equity Securities and Derivative Instruments that are traded in active markets.** Listed equity securities and derivative instruments that are traded in active markets shall be measured at fair value as at the balance sheet date. For the purpose of calculation of fair value, the lowest of the last quoted closing price of the stock exchanges where the securities are listed shall be taken.

The insurer shall assess on each balance sheet date whether any impairment of listed equity security(ies)/derivative(s) instruments has occurred.

An active market shall mean a market, where the securities traded are homogeneous, availability of willing buyers and willing sellers is normal and the prices are publicly available.

Unrealised gains/losses arising due to changes in the fair value of listed equity shares and derivative instruments shall be taken to equity under the head 'Fair Value Change Account'. The 'Profit on sale of investments' or 'Loss on sale of investments', as the case may be, shall include accumulated changes in the fair value previously recognised in equity under the heading Fair Value Change Account in respect of a particular security and being recycled to Profit and Loss Account on actual sale of that listed security.

For the removal of doubt, it is clarified that balance or any part thereof shall not be available for distribution as dividends. Also, any debit balance in said Fair Value Change Account shall be reduced from the profits/free reserves while declaring dividends.

The insurer shall assess, at each balance sheet date, whether any impairment has occurred. An impairment loss shall be recognised as an expense in Revenue/Profit and Loss Account to the extent of the difference between the re-measured fair value of the security/investment and its acquisition cost as reduced by any previous impairment loss recognised as expense in Revenue/Profit and Loss Account. any reversal of impairment loss, earlier recognised in Revenue/Profit and Loss Account shall be recognised in Revenue/Profit and Loss Account.

(*d*) **Unlisted and other than actively traded Equity Securities and Derivative Instruments.** Unlisted equity securities and derivative instruments and listed equity securities and derivative instruments that are not regularly traded in active market will be measured at historical cost. Provision shall be made for diminution in value of such investments. The provision so made shall be reversed in subsequent periods if estimates based on external evidence show an increase in the value of the investment over its carrying amount. The increased carrying amount of the investment due to the reversal of the provision shall not exceed the historical cost.

For the purposes of this regulation, a security shall be considered as being not actively traded, if as per guidelines governing mutual funds laid down from time to time by SEBI, such a security is classified as "thinly traded".

7. Loans

Loans shall be measured at historical cost subject to impairment provisions. The insurer shall assess the quality of its loan assets and shall provide for impairment. The impairment provision shall not be lower than the amounts derived on the basis of guidelines prescribed from time to time by the Reserve Bank of India that apply to companies and financial institutions.

8. Catastrophe Reserve

Catastrophe reserve shall be created in accordance with norms, if any, prescribed by the Authority. Investment of funds of catastrophe reserve shall be made in accordance with prescription of the Authority.

DISCLOSURES FORMING PART OF FINANCIAL STATEMENTS

A. Following shall be disclosed by way of notes to the Balance Sheet

1. Contingent Liabilities :
   (*a*) Partly-paid up investments;
   (*b*) Underwriting commitments outstanding;
   (*c*) Claims, other than those under policies, not acknowledged as debts;
   (*d*) Guarantees given by or on behalf of the company;
   (*e*) Statutory demands/liabilities in dispute, not provided for;
   (*f*) Reinsurance obligations to the extent not provided for in accounts;
   (*g*) Others (to be specified).
2. Encumbrances to assets of the company in and outside India.
3. Commitments made and outstanding for Loans, Investments and Fixed Assets.
4. Claims, less reinsurance, paid to claimants in/outside India.
5. Actuarial assumptions for determination of claim liabilities in the case of claims where the claims payment period exceed four years.
6. Ageing of claims—distinguishing between claims outstanding for more than six months and other claims.
7. Premiums, less reinsurance, written from business in/outside India.
8. Extent of premium income recognised, based on varying risk pattern, category wise, with basis and justification therefor, including whether reliance has been placed on external evidence.
9. Value of contracts in relation to investments, for
   (*a*) Purchases where deliveries are pending;
   (*b*) Sales where payments are overdue.
10. Operating expenses relating to insurance business: basis of allocation of expenditure to various classes of business.
11. Historical costs of those investments valued on fair value basis.
12. Computational of managerial remuneration.
13. Basis of amortisation of debt securities.
14. (*a*) Unrealised gain/losses arising due to changes in the fair value of listed equity shares and derivative instruments are to be taken to equity under the head 'Fair Value Change Account' and on realisation reported in Profit and Loss Account.

(*b*) Pending realisation, the credit balance in the 'Fair Value Change Account' is not available for distribution.

15. Fair value of investment property and the basis therefor.
16. Claims settled and remaining unpaid for a period of more than six months as on the balance sheet date.

B. Following accounting policies shall form an integral part of the financial statements

1. All significant accounting policies in terms of the accounting standards issued by the ICAI, and significant principles and policies given in Part I of Accounting Principles. Any other accounting policies, followed by the insurer, shall be stated in the manner required under Ind AS 1 issued by the ICAI.
2. Any departure from the accounting policies as aforesaid shall be separately disclosed with reasons for such departure.

C. Following information shall also be disclosed

1. Investments made in accordance with any statutory requirement should be disclosed separately together with its amount, nature, security and any special rights in and outside India.
2. Segregation into performing/non performing investments for purpose of income recognition as per the directions, if any, issued by the Authority.
3. Percentage of business sector-wise.
4. A summary of financial statements for the last five years, in the manner as may be prescribed by the Authority.
5. Accounting Ratios as may be prescribed by the Authority.
6. Basis of allocation of Interest, Dividends and Rent between Revenue Account and Profit and Loss Account.

GENERAL INSTRUCTIONS FOR PREPARATION OF FINANCIAL STATEMENTS

1. The corresponding amounts for the immediately preceding financial year for all items shown in the Balance Sheet, Revenue Account, Profit and Loss Account shall be given.
2. The figures in the financial statements may be rounded off to the nearest thousands.
3. Interest, dividends and rentals receivable in connection with an investment should be stated at gross value ; the amount of income tax deducted at source being included under 'advance taxes paid'.
4. Income from rent shall not include any notional rent.
5. (I) For the purposes of financial statements, unless the context otherwise requires :
   (*a*) the expression 'provision' shall, subject to note (II) below mean any amount written off or retained by way of providing for depreciation, renewals or diminution in value of assets, or retained by way of providing for any known liability or loss of which the amount cannot be determined with substantial accuracy.
6. The company should make provisions for damages under lawsuits where the management is of the opinion that the award may go against the insurer.

7. Extent of risk retained and reinsured shall be separately disclosed.
8. Any debit balance of the Profit and Loss Account shall be shown as deduction from uncommitted reserves and the balance, if any, shall be shown separately.

PREPARATION OF FINANCIAL STATEMENTS

1. An insurer shall prepare the Revenue Account, Profit and Loss Account [Shareholders' Account] and the Balance Sheet in Form B-RA, Form B-PL and Form B-BS, or as near thereto as the circumstances permit.
   Provided that an insurer shall prepare Revenue Account and Balance Sheet for fire, marine and miscellaneous insurance business and separate schedules shall be prepared for Marine Cargo, Marine—other than Marine Cargo and the following classes of miscellaneous insurance business under miscellaneous insurance and accordingly application of Ind AS 108–Operating Segments—shall stand modified.

   1. Motor 2. Workmen's Compensation/Employers' Liability 3. Public/Product Liability 4. Engineering 5. Aviation 6. Personal Accident 7. Health Insurance 8. Others.

2. An insurer shall prepare separate Receipts and Payments Account in accordance with the Direct Method prescribed in Ind AS 7—"Cash Flow Statement" issued by the ICAI.

FORM B-RA

Name of the Insurer :

Registration No. and Date of Registration with the IRDA

REVENUE ACCOUNT FOR THE YEAR ENDED 31ST MARCH, 20...

Policyholders' Account (Technical Account)

No.	*Particulars*	*Schedule*	*Current Year*	*Previous Year*
			(₹ '000)	(₹ '000)
1.	Premiums Earned (Net)	1		
2.	Profit/Loss on Sale /Redemption of Investments			
3.	Others (to be specified)			
4.	Interest, Dividend & Rent—Gross			
	Total (A)			
1.	Claims Incurred (Net)	2		
2.	Commission	3		
3.	Operating Expenses related to Insurance Business	4		
	Total (B)			
	Operating Profit/(Loss) from Fire/Marine / Miscellaneous Business C = (A–B)			
	APPROPRIATIONS			

	Particulars			
	Transfer to Shareholders' Account Transfer to Catastrophe Reserve Transfer to Other Reserves (to be specified) Total (C)			

Note : See Notes appended at the end of Form B-PL

FORM B-PL

Name of the Insurer:
Registration No. and Date of Registration with the IRDA

PROFIT AND LOSS ACCOUNT FOR THE YEAR ENDED 31ST MARCH, 20...

Shareholders' Account (Non-technical Account)

No.	*Particulars*	*Schedule*	*Current Year* (₹ '000)	*Previous Year* (₹ '000)
1.	**Operating Profit / (Loss)**			
	(*a*) Fire Insurance			
	(*b*) Marine Insurance			
	(*c*) Miscellaneous Insurance			
2.	Income from Investments			
	(*a*) Interest, Dividend & Rent – Gross			
	(*b*) Profit on sale of investments			
	Less : Less on Sale of Investments			
3.	**Other Income** (To be specified)			
	TOTAL (A)			
4.	**Provisions (Other than taxation)**			
	(*a*) For Diminution in the Value of Investments			
	(*b*) For Doubtful Debts			
	(*c*) Others (to be specified)			
5.	Other Expenses			
	(*a*) Expenses other than those related to Insurance Business			
	(*b*) Bad Debts written off			
	(*c*) Others (to be specified)			
	Total (B)			
	Profit before Tax			
	Provision for Taxation			
	Profit after Tax			
	Appropriations			
	(*a*) Interim Dividends paid during the year			
	(*b*) Proposed Final Dividend			
	(*c*) Dividend distribution tax			
	(*d*) Transfer to Reserves or other Accounts (to be specified)			
	Balance of Profit/Loss brought forward from last year			
	Balance carried forward to Balance Sheet			

Notes : To Form B-RA and B-PL.

(*a*) Premium income received from business concluded in and outside India shall be separately disclosed.

(*b*) Reinsurance premiums whether on business ceded or accepted are to be brought into account gross (*i.e.*, before deducting commissions) under the head reinsurance premiums.

(*c*) Claims incurred shall comprise claims paid, specific claims settlement costs wherever applicable and change in the outstanding provisions for claims at the year-end.

(*d*) Items of expenses and income in excess of one per cent of the total premiums (less reinsurance) or ₹ 5,00,000 whichever is higher, shall be shown as a separate line item.

(*e*) Fees and expenses connected with claims shall be included in claims.

(*f*) Under the sub-head "Others" shall be included items like foreign exchange gains or losses and other items.

(*g*) Interest, dividends and rentals receivable in connection with an investment should be stated at gross amount, the amount of income tax deducted at source being included under 'advance taxes paid and taxes deducted at source".

(*h*) Income from rent shall include only the realised rent. It shall not include any notional rent.

FROM B-BS

Name of the Insurer :

Registration No. and Date of Registration with the IRDA

BALANCE SHEET AS AT 31ST MARCH, 20...

No.	*Particulars*	*Schedule*	*Current Year*	*Previous Year*
	Sources of Funds		(₹ '000)	(₹ '000)
	Share Capital	5		
	Reserves and Surplus	6		
	Fair Value Change Account			
	Borrowings	7		
	Total			
	Application of Funds			
	Investments	8		
	Loans	9		
	Fixed Assets	10		
	Current Assets			
	Cash and Bank Balances	11		
	Advances and Other Assets	12		
	Sub-total (A)			
	Current Liabilities	13		
	Provisions	14		
	Sub-Total (B)			
	Net Current Assets (C) = (A – B)			
	Miscellaneous Expenditure (to the extent not written off or adjusted)	15		
	Debit Balance in Profit & Loss Account			
	Total			

CONTINGENT LIABILITIES

No.	Particulars	Current Year (₹ '000)	Previous Year (₹ '000)
1.	Partly paid-up investments		
2.	Claims, other than against policies, not acknowledged as debts by the company		
3.	Underwriting commitments outstanding (in respect of shares and securities)		
4.	Guarantees given by or on behalf of the Company		
5.	Statutory demands/ liabilities in dispute, not provided for		
6.	Reinsurance obligations to the extent not provided for in accounts		
7.	Others (to be specified)		
	Total		

SCHEDULES FORMING PART OF FINANCIAL STATEMENTS

SCHEDULE 1—PREMIUM EARNED [NET]

No.	Particulars	Current Year (₹ '000)	Previous Year (₹ '000)
	Premium from direct business written		
	Add : Premium on reinsurance accepted		
	Less : Premium on reinsurance ceded		
	Net Premium		
	Adjustment for change in reserve for unexpired risks		
	Total Premium Earned (Net)		

Note : Reinsurance premiums whether on business ceded or accepted are to be brought into account, before deducting commission under the head of reinsurance premiums.

SCHEDULE 2—CLAIMS INCURRED [NET]

Particulars	Current Year (₹ '000)	Previous Year (₹ '000)
Claims paid		
Direct		
Add : Re-insurance accepted		
Less : Re insurance ceded		
Net Claims paid		
Add Claims outstanding at the end of the year		
Less Claims outstanding at the beginning		
Total Claims Incurred		

Notes :

(a) *Incurred But Not Reported (IBNR). Incurred but not enough reported (IBNER) claims should be included in the amount for outstanding claims.*

(b) *Claims include specific claims settlement cost but not expenses of management.*

(c) *The surveyor fees, legal and other expenses shall also form part of claims cost.*

(d) *Claims cost should be adjusted for estimated salvage value if there is a sufficient certainty of its realisation.*

SCHEDULE 3—COMMISSION

Particulars	*Current Year (₹ '000)*	*Previous Year (₹ '000)*
Commission paid		
Direct		
Add : Re-insurance Accepted		
Less : Commission on Re-insurance Ceded		
Net Commission		

Note : The profit / commission, if any, are to be combined with the Re-insurance accepted or Re-insurance ceded figures

SCHEDULE 4—OPERATING EXPENSES RELATED TO INSURANCE BUSINESS

No.	*Particulars*	*Current Year (₹ '000)*	*Previous Year (₹ '000)*
1.	Employees' remuneration & welfare benefits		
2.	Travel, conveyance and vehicle running expenses		
3.	Training expenses		
4.	Rents, rates & taxes		
5.	Repairs		
6.	Printing & stationery		
7.	Communication		
8.	Legal & professional charges		
9.	Auditors' fees, expenses etc.		
	(*a*) as auditor		
	(*b*) as adviser or in any other capacity, in respect of :		
	(*i*) Taxation matters		
	(*ii*) Insurance matters		
	(*iii*) Management services; and		
	(*c*) in any other capacity		
10.	Advertisement and publicity		
11.	Interest & Bank Charges		
12.	Others (to be specified)		
13.	Depreciation		
	Total		

Note : Items of expenses and income in excess of one per cent of the total premiums (less reinsurance) or ₹ 5,00,000 whichever is higher, shall be shown as a separate line item.

SCHEDULE 5—SHARE CAPITAL

No.	Particulars	Current Year (₹ '000)	Previous Year (₹ '000)
1.	Authorised Capital Equity Shares of Rs.........each		
2.	Issued Capital Equity Shares of ₹....... each		
3.	Subscribed Capital Equity Shares of ₹........each		
4.	Called-up Capital Equity Shares of ₹........each *Less* : Calls unpaid *Add* : Equity Shares forfeited (Amount originally paid up) *Less* : Par Value of Equity Shares bought back *Less* : Preliminary Expenses Expenses including commission or brokerage on underwriting or subscription of shares		
	Total		

Notes :

(*a*) Particulars of the different classes of capital should be separately stated.

(*b*) The amount capitalised on account of issue of bonus shares should be disclosed.

(*c*) In case any part of the capital is held by a holding company, the same should be separately disclosed.

SCHEDULE 5A— SHARE CAPITAL PATTERN OF SHAREHOLDING
[As certified by the Management]

Shareholder	Current Year		Previous Year	
	Number of Shares	% of Holding	Number of Shares	% of Holding
Promoters • Indian • Foreign Others				
Total				

SCHEDULE 6—RESERVES AND SURPLUS

No.	Particulars	Current Year (₹ '000)	Previous Year (₹ '000)
1.	Capital Reserve		
2.	Capital Redemption Reserve		
3.	Securities Premium		
4.	General Reserves *Less* : Debit balance in Profit and Loss Account *Less* : Amount utilized for Buy-back		
5.	Catastrophe Reserve		
6.	Other Reserves (to be specified)		
7.	Balance of Profit in Profit and Loss Account		
	Total		

Note : Additions to and deductions from the reserves should be disclosed under each of the specified heads.

SCHEDULE 7—BORROWINGS

No.	Particulars	Current Year (₹ '000)	Previous Year (₹ '000)
1.	Debentures/Bonds		
2.	Banks		
3.	Financial Institutions		
4.	Others (to be specified)		
	Total		

Note :

(a) The extent to which the borrowings are secured shall be separately disclosed stating the nature of the security under each sub-head.

(b) Amounts due within 12 months from the date of Balance Sheet be shown separately.

SCHEDULE 8—INVESTMENTS

No.	Particulars	Current Year (₹ '000)	Previous Year (₹ '000)
	LONG TERM INVESTMENTS		
1.	Government securities and Government guaranteed bonds including Treasury Bills		
2.	Other Approved Securities		
3.	Other Investments		
	(a) Shares		
	(aa) Equity		
	(bb) Preference		
	(b) Mutual Funds		
	(c) Derivative Instruments		
	(d) Debentures/ Bonds		
	(e) Other Securities (to be specified)		
	(f) Subsidiaries		
	(g) Investment Properties-Real Estate		
4.	Investments in Infrastructure and Social Sector		
5.	Other than Approved Investments		
	SHORT TERM INVESTMENTS		
1.	Government securities and Government guaranteed bonds including Treasury Bills		
2.	Other Approved Securities		
3.	Other Investments		
	(a) Shares		
	(aa) Equity		
	(bb) Preference		
	(b) Mutual Funds		
	(c) Derivative Instruments		
	(d) Debentures/ Bonds		
	(e) Other Securities (to be specified)		
	(f) Subsidiaries		
	(g) Investment Properties-Real Estate		
4.	Investments in Infrastructure and Social Sector		
5.	Other than Approved Investments		
	Total		

Notes:

(*a*) Investments in subsidiary/holding companies, joint ventures and associates shall be separately disclosed, at cost.

(*i*) Holding company and subsidiary shall be construed as defined in the Companies Act. 2013.

(*ii*) Joint Venture is a contractual arrangement whereby two or more parties undertake an economic activity, which is subject to joint control.

(*iii*) Joint control —is the contractually agreed sharing of power to govern the financial and operating policies of an economic activity to obtain benefits from it.

(*iv*) Associate—is an enterprise in which the company has significant influence and which is neither a subsidiary nor a joint venture of the company.

(*v*) Significant influence (for the purpose of this schedule)—means participation in the financial and operating policy decisions of a company, but not control of those policies. Significant influence may be exercised in several ways, for example, by representation on the board of directors, participation in the policy making process, material inter-company transactions, interchange of managerial personnel or dependence on technical information. Significant influence may be gained by share ownership, statute or agreement. As regards share ownership, if an investor holds, directly or indirectly through subsidiaries, 20 per cent or more of the voting power of the investee, it is presumed that the investor does have significant influence, unless it can be clearly demonstrated that this is not the case. Conversely, if the investor holds, directly or indirectly through subsidiaries less than 20 per cent of the voting power of the investee,. it is presumed that the investor does not have significant influence, unless such influence is clearly demonstrated . A substantial or majority ownership by another investor does not necessarily preclude an investor from having significant influence.

(*b*) Aggregate amount of company's investments other than listed equity securities and derivative instruments and also the market value thereof shall be disclosed.

(*c*) Investment made out of Catastrophe reserve should be shown separately.

(*d*) Debt securities will be considered as "held to maturity" securities and will be measured at historical costs subject to amortisation.

(*e*) Investment property means a property [land or building or part of a building or both] held to earn rental income or for capital appreciation or for both, rather than for use in services or for administrative purposes.

(*f*) Investments maturing within twelve months from balance sheet date and investments made with the specific intention to dispose of within twelve months from balance sheet date shall be classified as short-term investments.

SCHEDULE 9—LOANS

No.	*Particulars*	*Current Year* (₹ '000)	*Previous Year* (₹ '000)
1.	**Security-wise Classification**		
	Secured		
	(*a*) On Mortgage of Property		
	(*aa*) In India		
	(*bb*) Outside India		
	(*b*) On Shares, Bonds, Govt. Securities, etc.		
	(*c*) Others (to be specified)		
	Unsecured		
	Total		

2.	**Borrower-wise Classification**		
	(*a*) Central and State Governments		
	(*b*) Banks and Financial Institutions		
	(*c*) Subsidiaries		
	(*d*) Industrial Undertakings		
	(*e*) Others (to be specified)		
	Total		
3.	**Performance-wise Classification**		
	(*a*) Loans Classified as Standard		
	(*aa*) In India		
	(*bb*) Outside India		
	(*b*) Non-performing Loans less Provisions		
	(*aa*) In India		
	(*bb*) Outside India		
	Total		
4.	**Maturity-wise Classification**		
	(*a*) Short Term		
	(*b*) Long Term		
	Total		

Notes:

(*a*) Short-term loans shall include those, which are repayable within 12 months from the date of balance short. Long term loans shall be the loans other than short-term loans.

(*b*) Provisions against non-performing loans shall be shown separately.

(*c*) The nature of the security in case of all long term secured loans shall be specified in each case. Secured loans for the purposes of this schedule, means loans secured wholly or partly against an asset of the company.

(*d*) Loans considered doubtful and the amount of provision created against such loans shall be disclosed.

SCHEDULE 10—FIXED ASSETS

Particulars	*Cost/Gross Block*				*Depreciation*				*Net Block*	
	Open -ing	Addit -ions	Deduct- ions	Closing	Upto Last Year	For the Year	On Sales/ Adjust ments	To Date	As at year end	Previous Year
Goodwill										
Intangibles (specify)										
Land-Freehold										
Leasehold Property										
Buildings										
Furniture & Fittings										
Information Technology Equipment										
Vehicles										
Office Equipment										

Others (Specify nature)										
Total										
Work in progress										
Grand Total										
Previous Year										

Note : Assets included in land, building and property above exclude Investment Properties as defined in note (e) to Schedule 8.

SCHEDULE 11—CASH AND BANK BALANCES

No.	*Particulars*	*Current Year* (₹ '000)	*Previous year* (₹ '000)
1.	Cash (including cheques, drafts and stamps)		
2.	Bank Balances		
	(*a*) Deposit Accounts		
	(*aa*) Short-term (due within 12 months)		
	(*bb*) Others		
	(*b*) Current Accounts		
	(*c*) Others (to be specified)		
3.	Money at Call and Short Notice		
	(*a*) With Banks		
	(*b*) With Other Institutions		
4.	Others (to be specified)		
	Total		
	Balances with non-scheduled banks in 2 and 3 above		

Note : Bank balance may include remittances in transit. If so, the nature and amount shall be separately stated.

SCHEDULE—12 ADVANCES AND OTHER ASSETS

No.	*Particulars*	*Current Year* (₹ '000)	*Previous year* (₹ '000)
	Advances		
1.	Reserve deposits with ceding companies		
2.	Application money for investments		
3.	Prepayments		
4.	Advances to Directors/Officers		
5.	Advance tax paid and taxes deducted at source (Net of provision for taxation)		
6.	Others (to be specified)		
	Total (A)		
	Others Assets		
1.	Income Accrued on Investments		
2.	Outstanding Premiums		
3.	Agents' Balances		
4.	Foreign Agencies Balances		

5.	Due from other entities carrying on insurance business (including reinsurers).		
6.	Due from subsidiaries/holding		
7.	Deposit with Reserve Bank of India [Pursuant to section 7 of Insurance Act, 1938]		
8.	Others (to be specified)		
	Total (B)		
	Total (A + B)		

Notes :

(*a*) The items under the above heads shall not be shown net of provisions for doubtful amounts. The amount of provision against each head should be shown separately.

(*b*) The term 'officer' should conform to the definition of that term as given under the Companies Act, 2013.

(*c*) Sundry debtors will be shown under item 8 (Others).

SCHEDULE—13 CURRENT LIABILITIES

No.	*Particulars*	*Current Year* (₹ '000)	*Previous Year* (₹ '000)
1.	Agents' Balances		
2.	Balances due to other insurance companies		
3.	Deposits held on re-insurance ceded		
4.	Premiums received in advance		
5.	Unallocated premium		
6.	Sundry creditors		
7.	Due to subsidiaries/holding company		
8.	Claims outstanding		
9.	Due to officers/directors		
10.	Others (to be specified)		
	Total		

SCHEDULE—14 PROVISIONS

No.	*Particulars*	*Current Year* (₹ '000)	*Previous year* (₹ '000)
1.	Reserve for Unexpired Risk		
2.	For taxation (less advance tax paid and taxes deducted at source)		
3.	For proposed dividends		
4.	For dividend distribution tax		
5.	Others (to be specified)		
	Total		

SCHEDULE—15
MISCELLANEOUS EXPENDITURE
(To the extent not written off or adjusted)

No.	Particulars	Current Year (₹ '000)	Previous year (₹ '000)
1.	Discount Allowed on issue of shares/debentures		
2.	Others (to be specified)		
	TOTAL		

Notes :

(*a*) No item shall be included under the head "Miscellaneous Expenditure" and carried forward unless :

1. some benefit from the expenditure can reasonably be expected to be received in future, and
2. the amount of such benefit is reasonably determinable.

(*b*) The amount to be carried forward in respect of any item included under the head "Miscellaneous Expenditure" shall not exceed the expected future revenue/other benefits related to the expenditure.

ILLUSTRATION 1. Prepare Fire Insurance Revenue A/c as per IRDA regulations for the year ended 31st March, 2023 from the following details :

	₹		₹
Claims Paid	4,90,000	Expenses of Management	2,00,000
Legal Expenses Regarding Claims	10,000	Provision against Unexpired Risk	
Premiums Received	13,00,000	on 1st April, 2022	5,50,000
Re-insurance Premium Paid	1,00,000	Claims Unpaid on 1st April, 2022	50,000
Commission	3,00,000	Claims Unpaid on 31st March, 2023	80,000

SOLUTION

Form B—RA

Name of the Insurer :

Registration No. and Date of Registration with the IRDA :

FIRE INSURANCE REVENUE ACCOUNT

for the year ended 31st March, 2023

Particulars	Schedule	Amount (₹)
(1) Premium Earned (Net)	1	11,50,000
(2) Other Income		–
(3) Interest, Dividend and Rent		–
Total (A)		11,50,000
(4) Claims Incurred	2	5,30,000
(5) Commission	3	3,00,000
(6) Operating Expenses related to Fire Insurance Business	4	2,00,000
Total (B)		10,30,000
Operating Profit (C) = (A) – (B)		1,20,000

Schedule 1 : *Premium Earned (Net)*

	₹
Premium Received	13,00,000
Less : Re-insurance Premium	1,00,000
Net Premium	12,00,000
Adjustment for Change in Reserve for Unexpired Risk (1)	50,000
	11,50,000

Schedule 2 : *Claims Incurred*

	₹
Claims paid including Legal Expenses (₹ 4,90,0000 + ₹ 10,000)	5,00,000
Add : Claims Outstanding at the end of the year	80,000
Less : Claims Outstanding at the beginning of the year	(50,000)
Total Claims Incurred	5,30,000

Schedule 3 : *Commission*

	₹
Commission paid	3,00,000
	3,00,000

Schedule 4 : *Operating Expenses*

	₹
Expenses of Management	2,00,000
	2,00,000

Working Note (1) :

	₹
Change in the Provision for Unexpired Risk	
Unexpired Risk Reserve on 31st March, 2023 = 50% of Net Premium *i.e.* 50% of ₹ 12,00,000 (See Schedule 1)	6,00,000
Less : Unexpired Risk Reserve as on 1st April, 2022	5,50,000
Change in the Provision for Unexpired Risk	50,000

ILLUSTRATION 2. **From the following information of M/s Bigfish Marine Insurance Co. Ltd. prepare Revenue Account as per regulations of IRDA for the year ended 31st March, 2023 :**

	₹
Premiums received	**18,75,000**
Premiums outstanding on March 31, 2023	**1,25,000**
Premium paid on reinsurance ceded	**2,28,000**
Claims paid	**10,54,000**
Estimated liability in respect of outstanding claims :	
On April 1, 2022	**1,89,000**
On March 31, 2023	**2,25,000**

Expenses of management (include ₹ 45,000 surveyor's fee and ₹ 65,000 legal expenses paid for settlement of claims)	4,85,000
Interest and Dividend (Gross)	1,65,250
Income tax on the above	49,575
Profit on sale of investments	46,000
Commission paid	1,94,000

Balance of fund on 1st April, 2022 was ₹ 18,50,000 including additional reserve of ₹ 1,80,000. Additional reserve has to be maintained at 10% of net premium for the year.

SOLUTION

Form B—RA

M/s Bigfish Marine Insurance Co. Ltd.

MARINE REVENUE ACCOUNT

for the year ending 31st March, 2023

Particulars	*Schedule*	*Amount* ₹
1. Premiums Earned (Net)	1	16,72,800
2. Profit on Sale of Investments		46,000
3. Interest and Dividend (Gross)		1,65,250
Total (A)		18,84,050
1. Claims Incurred (Net)	2	12,00,000
2. Commission	3	1,94,000
3. Operating Expenses related to Insurance Business	4	3,75,000
Total (B)		17,69,000
Operating Profit from Marine Insurance Business (C) = (A) – (B)		1,15,050

SCHEDULE 1—PREMIUMS EARNED (NET)

	₹
Premiums Received	18,75,000
Add : Outstanding Premiums as on 31-3-2023	1,25,000
	20,00,000
Less : Premiums on Reinsurance ceded	2,28,000
Net Premiums	17,72,000
Less : Adjustment for Change in Reserve for the Unexpired Risk (1)	99,200
	16,72,800

SCHEDULE 2—CLAIMS INCURRED (NET)

	₹
Claims Paid	10,54,000
Add : Surveyor's Fee and Legal Expenses Paid for Settlement of Claims (₹ 45,000 + ₹ 65,000)	1,10,000
Add : Outstanding Claims on 31-3-2023	2,25,000
	13,89,000
Less : Outstanding claims as on 1-4-2022	1,89,000
Claims Incurred (Net)	12,00,000

SCHEDULE 3—COMMISSION

	₹
Commission Paid	1,94,000

SCHEDULE 4—OPERATING EXPENSES RELATED TO INSURANCE BUSINESS

	₹
Expenses Management	4,85,000
Less : Surveyor's Fee and Legal Expenses	1,10,000
	3,75,000

Working Notes

(1) Calculation for Change in Reserve for Unexpired Risks

		₹
Reserve for Unexpired Risk as on 1-4-2022 including Additional Reserve ₹ 1,80,000)		18,50,000
Less : Reserve for Unexpired Risk as on 31-3-2023	₹	
[100% of ₹ 17,72,000(1)]	17,72,000	
Add : Additional Reserve (10% of ₹ 17,72,000)	1,77,200	
		19,49,200
Change in Reserve for Unexpired Risk		99,200

(2) Income tax on interest and dividend ₹ 49,575 is part of Profit and Loss A/c Therefore, it has not been taken in Revenue Account.

ILLUSTRATION 3. **Prepare Revenue Account of M/s Ishan Insurance Co. engaged in marine insurance business :**

Particulars			*Direct Business*	*Pre-insurance*
I. **Premium :**				
	Received		3,60,000	38,000
	Receivable :	**1st April, 2022**	10,000	1,600
		31st March, 2023	16,000	1,800
	Paid		—	24,000
	Payable :	**1st April, 2022**		1,000
		31st March, 2023		2,200
II.	**Claims :**			
	Paid		1,54,000	14,000
	Payable :	**1st April, 2022**	78,000	1,500
		31st March, 2023	16,000	4,200
	Received			17,000
	Receivable :	**1st April, 2022**		1,400
		31st March, 2023		1,900
III. **Commission :**				
	On Insurance Accepted		96,000	5,600
	On Insurance Ceded		—	8,000

Details of Other Expenses and Income is as below :	₹
Establishment Expenses	30,000
Rent, Rates and Taxes	14,000
Printing and Stationery	1,800
Income Tax paid	10,000
Income from Dividend	18,000
Legal Expenses (Inclusive of ₹ 1,200 in Connection with Settlement of Claims)	2,000
Double Income Tax Refund	24,000
Bad Debts	1,300
Profit on Sale of Furniture	700

Balance of fund as on 1st April, 2022 was ₹ 7,65,000 including additional reserve of ₹ 33,000.

Additional reserve is to be created @ 5% of the net premium of the year.

SOLUTION

(*a*)

Form B—RA

Name of Insurer : M/s Ishan Co.

REVENUE ACCOUNT

for the year ended 31st March, 2023

	Schedule	*Current Year*
		₹
1. Premium Earned (Net)	1	7,46,050
2. Other Income		—
3. Interest, Dividends and Rent—Assumed Gross		18,000
Total (A)		7,64,050
1. Claims Incurred (Net)	2	92,400
2. Commission	3	93,600
3. Operating Expenses related to Insurance Business	4	46,600
Total (B)		2,32,600
Operating Profit from Marine Insurance Business (C) = (A – B)		5,31,450

Schedules Forming Part of Revenue Account

SCHEDULE 1 : PREMIUM EARNED (NET)

		Current Year
		₹
Premium Earned (Net)		
Total Premium Earned	(1)	4,04,200
Less : Premium on Reinsurance Ceded	(2)	25,200
Total Premium Earned (Net)		3,79,000
Adjustment for Change in Reserve for Unexpired Risk [(Opening) ₹ 7,65,000 – (Closing) ₹ 3,97,950 (*i.e.* ₹ 3,79,000 + ₹ 18,950 Additional Reserve @ 5%)]		3,67,050
Net Premium Earned		7,46,050

SCHEDULE 2 : CLAIMS INCURRED (NET)

Claims Incurred (Net)	(3)	92,400

SCHEDULE 3 : COMMISSION

	Current Year
Commission paid	₹
Direct	96,000
Add : Re-insurance accepted	5,600
	1,01,600
Less : Re-insurance Ceded	8,000
Net Commission	93,600

SCHEDULE 4 : OPERATING EXPENSES

	Current Year
Operating Expenses related to Insurance Business	₹
Establishment Expenses	30,000
Rent, Rates and Taxes	14,000
Printing and Stationary	1,800
Legal and Professional Charges ₹ (2,000 – 1,200)	800
	46,600

Note : Profit on sale of furniture, double income tax refund, bad debts and Income tax paid have not been shown in the above Revenue Account assuming that these items are not related specifically with marine business. Thus, they will be shown in the Profit and Loss Account of M/s Ishan Co.

Working Notes :

	Direct	Re-insurance
(1) Total Premium Income	₹	₹
Received	3,60,000	38,000
Add : Receivable on 31st March, 2023	16,000	1,800
	3,76,000	39,800
Less : Receivable on 1st April, 2022	(10,000)	(1,600)
	3,66,000	38,200

Total premium income ₹ 3,66,000 + ₹ 38,200 = ₹ 4,04,200

(2) Premium Expenses on Reinsurance Ceded	₹
Premium paid during the year	24,000
Add : Payable on 31st March, 2023	2,200
	26,200
Less : Payable on 1st April, 2022	1,000
	25,200
(3) Claims Paid	₹
Direct Business	1,54,000
Re-insurance	14,000

Legal Expenses		1,200
		1,69,200
Less : Re-insurance claims received		(17,000)
		1,52,200
Add : Claims Outstanding as on 31st March, 2023 :	₹	
Direct	16,000	
Re-insurance	4,200	
	20,200	
Less : Recoverable from Re-insurers on 31st March, 2023	1,900	18,300
		1,70,500
Less : Claims Outstanding as on 1st April, 2022 :	₹	
Direct	78,000	
Re-insurance	1,500	
	79,500	
Less : Recoverable from Re-insurers on 1st April, 2022	(1,400)	78,100
Claims incurred during the year		92,400

ILLUSTRATION 4. Following balances are extracted from the books of Moonshine Insurance Co. Ltd. for the year ended 31st March, 2023 :

	₹
Commission on Re-insurance Accepted	1,86,458
Commission on Direct Business	1,95,172
Depreciation on Furniture	650
Depreciation on Library	148
Depreciation on Motor Cars	6,240
Loss on Sale of Motor Cars	12,074
General Manager's Salary	24,000
Telephone	5,100
Postage and Telegrams	5,150
Rent	62,500
Travelling Expenses	45,600
Motor Car Expenses	45,500
Establishment	1,45,500
Bonus	24,000
Stationery	35,550
Newspaper and Periodicals	14,062
Legal Expenses	23,400
Electricity Charges	16,100
Provident Fund Contribution	11,875
Audit Fees	2,500
Professional Taxes	250
Miscellaneous Expenses	2,875

Bad Debts written off	**2,206**
Claims under policies less re-insurance paid during the year	**1,52,930**
Total estimated liability in respect of outstanding claims as at 31st March, 2022 whether due or intimated	**6,264**
Total estimated liability in respect of outstanding claims as at 31st March, 2023 whether due or intimated	**1,198**
Reserve for unexpired risks as at 31-3-2022	**3,66,594**
Additional Reserve for unexpired risks as at 31-3-2022	**45,824**
Premiums received less Re-insurance	**9,89,980**
Commission on Re-insurance ceded	**2,41,208**

You are required to make 40% of the net premium received as reserve for unexpired risks 31-3-2023 and 10% of the net premiums as additional reserve for the same.

Prepare Revenue Account in accordance with the format prescribed by the Insurance Regulatory and Development Authority. Assume that all items of management expenses were incurred for the fire insurance business.

SOLUTION **FIRE REVENUE A/C OF MOONSHINE INSURANCE COMPANY**

for the year ended 31st March, 2023

Particulars	*Schedule No.* (₹ '000)	*Current Yr.* (₹ '000)	*Previous Yr.*
1. Premiums Earned (Net)	1	907.408	
2. Profit/Loss on Sale of Investments		—	
3. Others		—	
4. Interest, Dividend & Rent (Gross)		—	
Total (A)		907.408	
1. Claims Incurred (Net)	2	157.996	
2. Commission	3	140.422	
3. Operating Expenses related to Insurance Business	4	463.962	
Depreciation, Loss on Sale of Assets and Bad Debts		21.318	
Total (B)		783.698	
Operating Profit from Fire Business (C) = (A) – (B)		123.710	
Schedule 1 : Premium Earned (Net)			
Premium from direct business written *less*		₹	
Reinsurance Premium		9,89,980	
Less : Increase in Provision for Unexpired Risks (1)		82,572	
Total Premiums Earned (Net)		9,07,408	
Schedule 2 : Claims Incurred (Net)			
Claims under policies less reinsurance		1,52,930	
Add : Total estimated liability for outstanding claims at the end of the year		6,264	
		1,59,194	
Less : Claims outstanding at the end of the previous year		1,198	
		1,57,996	

Schedule 3 : Commission			
Commission paid—Direct		1,95,172	
Add : Commission paid—Reinsurance accepted		1,86,458	
		3,81,630	
Less : Commission on reinsurance ceded		2,41,208	
		1,40,422	
Schedule 4 : Operating Expenses Relating to Insurance Business		₹	
Establishment		1,45,500	
Bonus		24,000	
Provident fund contributions		11,875	
General Manager's salary		24,000	
Travelling Expenses		45,600	
Motor car expenses		45,500	
Rent		62,500	
Stationery		35,550	
Newspapers and periodicals		14,062	
Electricity charges		16,100	
Legal expenses (assumed not connected with claim)		23,400	
Telephone		5,100	
Postage and Telegram		5,150	
Audit Fees		2,500	
Professional Tax		250	
Misc. Expenses		2,875	
		4,63,962	

Working Note (1) :

Change in Provision for Unexpired Risks :	₹
Reserve for unexpired risks at the beginning of the year	3,66,594
Additional reserve at the beginning of the year	45,824
(A)	4,12,418
Reserve for unexpired risk at the end of the year :	₹
40% of ₹ 9,89,980	3,95,992
Additional reserve 10% of ₹ 9,89,980	98,998
(B)	4,94,990
Increase (B) – (A)	82,572

ILLUSTRATION 5. From the following particulars you are required to prepare Fire Revenue Account for the year ended on 31st March, 2023.

	(₹ '000)		(₹ '000)
Claims paid	4,80,000	Additional reserve for unexpired risk	20,000
Claims outstanding on 1st April, 2022	40,000	Reinsurance recoveries of claims	8,000
Claims intimated but not accepted on 31st March, 2023	10,000	Sundry expenses regarding claims	5,000
		Loss on sale of Motor Car	5,000

Claims intimated and accepted but not paid on 31st March, 2023	60,000	Bad Debts	3,000
Premium Received	12,12,000	Refund of Double Taxation	5,000
Reinsurance premium paid	1,20,000	Interest and Dividends	6,000
Commission	2,00,000	Income Tax deducted thereon	1,000
Commission on reinsurance ceded	10,000	Legal expenses regarding claims	3,000
Commission on reinsurance accepted	5,000	Profit on sale of investments	2,000
Expenses of management	3,17,000	Rent of staff quarters deducted from salaries	2,000
Reserve for unexpired risk on 1st April, 2022	4,00,000	Depreciation on furniture	6,000

You are required to provide for additional reserve for unexpired risks at 1% of the net premium in addition to the opening balance.

SOLUTION

REVENUE ACCOUNT

for the year ended on 31st March, 2023

in respect of Fire Business

(₹ '000)

Particulars	*Schedule*	*Current Year*	*Previous Year*
Premiums Earned (Net)	1	9,35,080	
Profit on Sale of Investments		2,000	
Refund of Double Taxation		5,000	
Rent of Staff Quarters		2,000	
Interest, Dividends & Rent (Gross)		6,000	
Total (A)		9,50,080	
Claims Incurred (Net)	2	5,10,000	
Commission	3	1,95,000	
Operating Expense related to Insurance Business	4	3,31,000	
Total (B)		10,36,000	
Operating Loss from Fire Business (C) = (A) – (B)		85,920	

Schedules Forming Part of Financial Statements

SCHEDULE 1—PREMIUMS EARNED (NET)

		Current Year	*Previous Year*
		(₹ '000)	*(₹ '000)*
Premium from direct business written		12,12,000	
Less : Premium on reinsurance ceded		1,20,000	
		10,92,000	
Less : Adjustment for Change in Reserve for Unexpired Risk :			
Reserve for Unexpired Risk at the end of the year	₹		
50% of Net Premium ₹ 10,92,000	5,46,000		
Additional Reserve (₹ 20,000 old to be continued + 1% of ₹ 10,92,000 net premium)	30,920		
	5,76,920		
Less : Reserve for Unexpired Risks at the beginning of the year	4,20,000		
		1,56,920	
		9,35,080	

SCHEDULE 2—CLAIMS INCURRED (NET)

	₹	Current Year (₹ '000)	Previous Year (₹ '000)
Claims paid	4,80,000		
Less : Reinsurance recoveries of claims	8,000		
	4,72,000		
Claims intimated but not accepted at the end of the year	10,000		
Claims intimated and accepted at the end of the year	60,000		
Sundry expenses regarding claims	5,000		
Legal expenses regarding claims	3,000		
	5,50,000		
Less : Claims outstanding at the beginning of the year	40,000		
		5,10,000	

SCHEDULE 3—COMMISSION

	₹	Current Year (₹ '000)	Previous Year (₹ '000)
Commission paid	2,00,000		
Add : Commission on reinsurance accepted	5,000		
	2,05,000		
Less : Commission on reinsurance ceded	10,000		
		1,95,000	

SCHEDULE 4—OPERATING EXPENSES RELATED TO REINSURANCE BUSINESS

	Current Year (₹ '000)	Previous Year (₹ '000)
Expenses of Management	3,17,000	
Bad Debts	3,000	
Loss on Sale of Motor Car	5,000	
Depreciation on Furniture	6,000	
	3,31,000	

ILLUSTRATION 6. From the following balances extracted from the books of REAL General Insurance Company Ltd. as on 31st March, 2023, you are required to prepare Revenue Accounts in respect of Fire and Marine Insurance Business for the year ended 31st March, 2023.

Particulars	*Fire* ₹	*Marine* ₹
Outstanding Claims as on 1st April, 2022	**28,000**	**7,000**
Claims Paid	**1,00,000**	**80,000**

Reserve for Unexpired Risk as on 1st April, 2022	2,00,000	1,40,000
Premium Received	4,50,000	3,30,000
Agent's Commission	40,000	20,000
Expenses of Management	60,000	45,000
Re-insurance Premium—Dr.	25,000	15,000

The following additional points are also to be taken into consideration :

1. Claims outstanding as on 31st March, 2023 were as follows :
   (*a*) Fire Insurance—₹ 10,000
   (*b*) Marine Insurance—₹ 15,000
2. Premiums Outstanding as on 31t March, 2023 were as follows :
   (*a*) Fire Insurance—₹ 30,000
   (B) Marine Insurance—₹ 20,000
3. Reserve for unexpired risk to be maintained at 50% and 100% of net premiums in respect of Fire and Marine Insurance respectively.
4. Expenses of management due on 31st March, 2023 were ₹ 10,000 for Fire Insurance and ₹ 5,000 in respect of Marine Insurance.

SOLUTION

Form B-RA
Real General Insurance Company Ltd.
REVENUE ACCOUNT
for the year ending 31st March, 2023

Particulars	*Schedule*	Amount (₹) *Fire*	*Marine*
1. Premiums Earned (Net)	1	4,27,500	1,40,000
Total (A)		4,27,500	1,40,000
1. Claims Incurred (Net)	2	82,000	88,000
2. Commission		40,000	20,000
3. Operating Expenses related to Insurance Business	3	70,000	50,000
Total (B)		1,92,000	1,58,000
Operating Profit/(Loss) from Fire & Marine Insurance Business (C) = (A) – (B)		2,35,500	(18,000)

SCHEDULE 1—PREMIUMS EARNED (NET)

		Fire	*Marine*
		₹	₹
Premiums Received		4,50,000	3,30,000
Add : Outstanding Premiums		30,000	20,000
		4,80,000	3,50,000
Less : Reinsurance Premium		25,000	15,000
		4,55,000	3,35,000
Less : Adjustment for Change in Reserve for Unexpired Risks	(1)	27,500	1,95,000
Premiums		4,27,500	1,40,000

SCHEDULE 2—CLAIMS INCURRED (NET)

	Fire	Marine
	₹	₹
Claims paid	1,00,000	80,000
Add : Claims Outstanding at the end of the year	10,000	15,000
	1,10,000	95,000
Less : Claims Outstanding at the beginning of the year	28,000	7,000
Claims Incurred (Net)	82,000	88,000

SCHEDULE 3—OPERATING EXPENSES RELATED TO INSURANCE BUSINESS

	Fire	Marine
	₹	₹
Expenses of Management	60,000	45,000
Add : Expenses Due at the end of the year	10,000	5,000
total	70,000	50,000

Working Note

(1) CALCULATION OF CHANGE IN RESERVE FOR UNEXPIRED RISKS

	Fire	Marine
	₹	₹
Closing Reserve for Unexpired Risks Required	2,27,500 (50% of 4,55,000)	3,35,000 (100% of 3,35,000)
Less : Opening Balance of Reserve for Unexpired Risks	2,00,000	1,40,000
	27,500	1,95,000

ILLUSTRATION 7. From the following information of Reliable Marine Insurance Ltd. for the year ending 31st March, 2023 find out the

(*i*) Net premiums earned (*ii*) Net claims incurred.

	₹ *Direct Business*	₹ *Re-insurance*
Premium :		
Received	88,00,000	7,52,000
Receivable—1-4-2022	4,39,000	36,000
Receivable—31-3-2023	3,77,000	32,000
Paid	6,09,000	
Payable—1-4-2022		27,000
Payable 31-3-2023		18,000
Claims :		
Paid	69,00,000	5,54,000
Payable—1-4-2022	89,000	15,000

Payable—31-3-2023	95,000	12,000
Received		2,01,000
Receivable—1-4-2022		40,000
Receivable—31-3-2023		38,000

SOLUTION

(i) Net Premium Earned

		₹	₹
Premium from Direct Business Received	₹	88,00,000	
Add : Receivable as 31-3-2023	3,77,000		
Less : Receivable as on 1-4-2022	4,39,000	–62,000	
			87,38,000
Add : Premium on Re-insurance accepted		7,52,000	
Add : Receivable as on 31-3-2023	32,000		
Less : Receivable as on 1-4-2022	36,000	–4,000	
			7,48,000
			94,86,000
Less : Premium on Re-insurance ceded		6,09,000	
Add : Payable as on 31-3-2023	18,000		
Less : Payable as on 1-4-2022	27,000	–9,000	
			6,00,000
Net Premium earned			88,86,000

(ii) Net Claims Incurred

		₹	₹
Claims paid on Direct Business			69,00,000
Add : Re-insurance	₹	5,54,000	
Add : Outstanding as on 31-3-2023	12,000		
Less : Outstanding as on 1-4-2022	15,000	–3,000	
			5,51,000
			74,51,000
Less : Claims received from Re-insurance		2,01,000	
Add : Outstanding as on 31-3-2023	38,000		
Less : Outstanding as on 1-4-2022	40,000	–2,000	
			1,99,000
			72,52,000
Add : Outstanding direct claims at the end of the year			95,000
			73,47,000
Less : Outstanding Claims at the beginning of the year			89,000
Net Claims incurred			72,58,000

ILLUSTRATION 8. Ayushman General Insurance Company submits the following information for the year ended 31st March, 2023 :

Particulars	*Direct Business* (₹)	*Reinsurance* (₹)
Premiums received	52,67,500	5,77,500
Premiums paid	—	3,43,000

Claims paid during the year	34,79,000	3,57,000
Claims payable :		
1st April, 2022	4,79,500	66,500
31st March, 2023	5,16,600	49,000
Claims received	—	2,76,500
Claims receivable :		
1st April, 2022	—	52,500
31st March, 2023	—	87,500
Commission :		
On Insurance accepted	1,12,000	10,500
On Insurance ceded	—	12,600

Other Expenses and Income are as under :

(1) Expenses :

(*a*) Rent, Rates & Taxes—₹ 12,000

(*b*) Establishment Expenses—₹ 30,000

(*c*) Legal Expense (inclusive of ₹ 20,000 in connection with settlement of claims)—₹ 50,000

(2) Income :

(*a*) Interest, dividend, rentals (net)—₹ 11,000

(*b*) Income tax deducted on above source—₹ 2,400

(3) Reserve for unexpired risks is to be maintained @ 40%.

Balance of Reserve for unexpired risk as on 1st April, 2022 was ₹ 19,88,000.

You are required to make the Revenue Account for the year ended 31st March, 2023.

SOLUTION

Ayushman General Insurance Company

REVENUE ACCOUNT

for the year ended 31st March, 2023

Particulars	*Schedule*	*Amount (₹)*
Premiums Earned (Net)	1	52,89,200
Profit/Loss on Sale/Redemption of Investments		
Others		
Interest, Dividend and Rent (Gross)		13,400
Total (A)		53,02,600
Claims Incurred (Net)	2	35,64,100
Commission	3	1,09,900
Operating Expenses related to Insurance Business	4	72,000
Total (B)		37,46,000
Operating Profit from General Insurance Business (A – B)		15,56,600

Schedules Forming Part of Revenue Account

SCHEDULE 1 : PREMIUMS EARNED (NET)

Particulars	₹
Premiums from Direct Business	52,67,500
Add : Premiums on Reinsurance Accepted	5,77,500
	58,45,000
Less : Premiums on Reinsurance Ceded	3,43,000
Net Premiums	55,02,000
Less : Adjustment for Change in Reserve for Unexpired Risks (2)	2,12,800
Net Premiums Earned (Net)	52,89,200

SCHEDULE 2 : CLAIMS INCURRED (NET)

Particulars	₹
Claims paid on Direct Business (1)	35,36,100
Add : Re-insurance Accepted (1)	3,39,500
	38,75,600
Less : Re-insurance Ceded (1)	3,11,500
Net Claims Paid	35,64,100

SCHEDULE 3 : COMMISSION

Particulars	₹
Commission Paid on Direct Business	1,12,000
Add : Commission on Reinsurance Accepted	10,500
	1,22,500
Less : Commission on Reinsurance Ceded	12,600
	1,09,900

SCHEDULE 4 : OPERATING EXPENSES RELATED TO INSURANCE BUSINESS

Particulars	₹
Rent, Rates and Taxes	12,000
Establishment Expenses	30,000
Legal Expenses (₹ 50,000 – ₹ 20,000)	30,000
	72,000

Working Notes :

(1) Claims Incurred

Particulars	*Direct business (₹)*	*Re-insurance accepted (₹)*	*Re-insurance ceded (₹)*
Paid/Received	34,79,000	3,57,000	2,76,500
Add : Outstanding at the end of year	5,16,600	49,000	87,500

Expenses in Connection with Settlement of Claim	20,000		
Less : Outstanding at the beginning of the year	(4,79,500)	(66,500)	(52,500)
	35,36,100	3,39,500	3,11,500

(2) Change in Reserve for Unexpired Risks

	₹
Opening Reserve for Unexpired Risks as on 31st March, 2022	19,88,000
Less : Closing Reserve for Unexpired Risks as on 31st March, 2023 (₹ 55,02,000 × 40%)	22,00,800
Additional Provision required	2,12,800

Note : Interest and dividends are shown at gross value in Revenue Account. Income tax on it will not be included in the Revenue Account as it is the part of Profit and Loss Account in case of an insurance company.

ILLUSTRATION 9. Indian Insurance Co. Ltd. furnishes you with the following information:

(*i*) On 31-12-2022 it had reserve for unexpired risks to the tune of ₹ 40 crores. It comprised of ₹ 15 crores in respect of marine insurance business, ₹ 20 crores in respect of fire insurance business and ₹ 5 crores in respect of miscellaneous insurance business.

(*ii*) It is the practice of Indian Insurance Company Ltd. to create reserves at 100% of net premium income in respect of marine insurance policies and at 50% of net premium income in respect of fire and miscellaneous income policies.

(*iii*) During 2023, the following business was conducted :

₹ in crores	*Marine*	*Fire*	*Miscellaneous*
Premia collected from :			
(*a*) Insureds in respect of policies issued	18	43	12
(*b*) Other insurance companies in respect of risks undertaken	7	5	4
Premiums paid/payable to other insurance companies on business ceded	6.7	4.3	7

Indian Insurance Co. Ltd. asks you to :

(*a*) Pass journal entries relating to "Unexpired Risks Reserve."

(*b*) Show in columnar form "Unexpired Risks Reserve A/c for 2023.

SOLUTION

Indian Insurance Co. Ltd.
JOURNAL ENTRIES

(₹ in Crores)

2023 Dec. 31	Unexpired Risks Reserve A/c Dr.		40	
	To Marine Revenue A/c			15
	To Fire Revenue A/c			20
	To Miscellaneous Revenue A/c			5
	(Being unexpired risks reserve as on 1-1-2023 transferred to Revenue A/c)			

Dec. 31	Marine Revenue A/c	Dr.	18·30	
	Fire Revenue A/c	Dr.	21·85	
	Miscellaneous Revenue A/c	Dr.	4·50	
	To Unexpired Risks Reserve A/c			44·65
	(Being reserve required at the end of the year for unexpired risks @ 100% of net premium in case of marine (*i.e.* 18 + 7 – 6.7) and 50% of net premium in case of fire (*i.e.* 43 + 5 – 4.3) and miscellaneous (*i.e.* 12 + 4 – 7)]			

UNEXPIRED RISKS RESERVE ACCOUNT (₹ in Crores)

2023		*Marine*	*Fire*	*Misc.*	2023		*Marine*	*Fire*	*Misc.*
Dec. 31	To Revenue A/c (Transfer)	15.00	20.00	5.00	Jan. 1	By Balance b/d	15.00	20.00	5.00
" 31	To Balance c/d	18.30	21.85	4.50	Dec. 31	By Revenue A/c	18.30	21.85	4.50
		33.30	41.85	9.50			33.30	41.85	9.50
					2024				
					Jan. 1	By Balance b/d	18.30	21.85	4.50

ILLUSTRATION 10. From the following balances of Prudential General Insurance Co. prepare—*(i)* Fire Revenue Account ; *(ii)* Marine Revenue Account ; and *(iii)* Profit and Loss Account for the year ending on 31st March, 2023 :

	Fire	*Marine*	*Not related to any business*
	₹ '000	₹ '000	₹ '000
Claims Paid and Outstanding	3,60,000	7,60,000	
Additional Reserve on 1-4-2022	1,00,000	—	—
Sundry Expenses regarding Claims	20,000		
Bad Debts	10,000	24,000	
Auditors' Fees			2,400
Directors' Fees			10,000
Share Transfer Fees			1,600
Bad Debts Recovered		—	2,400
Fund on 1-4-2022	5,00,000	16,40,000	—
Commission @ 5% of premiums earned on reinsurance ceded	20,000	40,000	
Depreciation			70,000
Interest, Dividends etc. received			28,000
Difference in Exchange (Cr.)			600
Miscellaneous Receipts			10,000
Profit on Sale of Land			1,20,000
Insurance Premiums less Reinsurance	12,00,000	21,60,000	—
Management Expenses	2,90,000	8,00,000	—

Additional reserve in case of fire insurance is to be raised by 5% of net premiums in addition to usual reserve. Reinsurance premiums received amounted to ₹ 30,00,00,000 for fire business and ₹ 64,00,00,000 for marine business. Management expenses are exclusive of commission. Rate of commission on direct business, reinsurance accepted and reinsurance ceded is 5%.

SOLUTION

Prudential General Insurance Company
REVENUE ACCOUNT (IN RESPECT OF FIRE BUSINESS)
for the year ending 31st March, 2023

Particulars	*Schedule*	(₹ '000)
Premiums Earned (Net)	1	10,40,000
Total (A)		10,40,000
Claims Incurred (Net)	2	3,80,000
Commission	3	60,000
Operating Expenses related to Insurance Business	4	3,00,000
Total (B)		7,40,000
Operating Profit from Fire Insurance Business (C) = (A) – (B)		3,00,000

REVENUE ACCOUNT IN RESPECT OF MARINE BUSINESS
for the year ending 31st March, 2023

Particulars	*Schedule*	*(₹ '000)*
Premiums Earned (Net)	1	16,40,000
Total (A)		16,40,000
Claims Incurred (Net)	2	7,60,000
Commission	3	1,08,000
Operating Expenses related to Insurance Business	4	8,24,000
Total (B)		16,92,000
Operating Loss from Marine Business (C) = (A) – (B)		52,000

Prudential General Insurance Company
PROFIT AND LOSS ACCOUNT
for the year ending 31st March, 2023

	(₹ '000)
Operating Profit from Fire Insurance	3,00,000
Operating Loss from Marine Insurance	(52,000)
Income from Investments : Interest & Dividend	28,000
Other Income :	
Share Transfer Fees	1,600
Bad Debts Recovered	2,400
Difference in Exchange	600
Profit on Sale of Land	1,20,000
Miscellaneous Receipts	10,000
Total (A)	4,10,600

	(₹ '000)
Other Expenses :	
Auditors' Fees	2,400
Directors' Fees	10,000
Depreciation	70,000
Total (B)	82,400
Profit before Tax (C) = (A) – (B)	3,28,200

Schedules Relating to Fire Revenue Account

SCHEDULE 1—PREMIUMS EARNED (NET)

Particulars		(₹ '000)
Premiums from direct business written [See Working Note (1)]		13,00,000
Less : Reinsurance premiums paid		4,00,000
		9,00,000
Add : Reinsurance Premiums received		3,00,000
Net Premiums		12,00,000
Less : Adjustment for increase in reserve for unexpired risks :		
Reserve for unexpired risks (including additional reserve ₹ 1,60,000) at the end of the year	(₹ '000) 7,60,000	
Less : Reserve for unexpired risks (including additional reserve of ₹ 1,00,000) at the beginning of the year	6,00,000	
		1,60,000
		10,40,000

SCHEDULE 2—CLAIMS INCURRED (NET)

Particulars	(₹ '000)
Claims paid and outstanding	3,60,000
Add : Sundry expenses regarding claims	20,000
	3,80,000

SCHEDULE 3—COMMISSION

	(₹ '000)
Commission paid on direct business (1)	65,000
Add : Commission on reinsurance accepted (2)	15,000
	80,000
Less : Commission on reinsurance ceded	20,000
	60,000

SCHEDULE 4—OPERATING EXPENSES RELATED TO FIRE INSURANCE

	(₹ '000)
Management Expenses	2,90,000
Bad Debts	10,000
	3,00,000

Schedules Relating to Marine Revenue Account

SCHEDULE 1—PREMIUMS EARNED (NET)

	(₹ '000)
Premiums from direct business written [see working note (1)]	23,20,000
Less : Reinsurance premium paid	8,00,000
	15,20,000
Add : Reinsurance premium received	6,40,000
	21,60,000
Less : Adjustment for increase in unexpired risks at the end of the year ((₹ '000) 21,60,000 – (₹ '000) 16,40,000)	5,20,000
	16,40,000

SCHEDULE 2—CLAIMS INCURRED (NET)

	(₹ '000)
Claims paid and outstanding	7,60,000

SCHEDULE 3—COMMISSION

	(₹ '000)
Commission paid on direct business (1)	1,16,000
Add : Commission on reinsurance accepted (2)	32,000
	1,48,000
Less : Commission on reinsurance ceded	40,000
	1,08,000

SCHEDULE 4—OPERATING EXPENSES RELATED TO MARINE INSURANCE

	(₹ '000)
Management Expenses	8,00,000
Bad Debts	24,000
	8,24,000

Working Notes :

(1) ***Calculation of commission on direct business*** :

	Fire ₹ '000	*Marine* ₹ '000
Premiums as given	12,00,000	21,60,000
Add : Reinsurance premiums paid (20 times of commission earned)		
$\left((₹\ '000)\ 20{,}000 \times \frac{100}{5}\right)$	4,00,000	
$\left((₹\ '000)\ 40{,}000 \times \frac{100}{5}\right)$		8,00,000
	16,00,000	29,60,000
Less : Reinsurance premiums received	3,00,000	6,40,000
Gross Premiums	13,00,000	23,20,000
Commission 5% thereof	65,000	1,16,000

(2) Commission on reinsurance accepted

5% of ₹ 3,00,000 thousands	15,000	
5% of ₹ 6,40,000 thousands		32,000

ILLUSTRATION 11. Sunlife General Insurance Company submits the following information for the year ended 31st March 2023 :

		Direct Business ₹	*Re-insurance* ₹
Premiums received		65,75,000	9,50,000
Premiums paid		—	4,75,000
Claims paid during the year		42,50,000	5,00,000
Claims Payable	1st April, 2022	6,25,000	87,000
	31st March, 2023	7,18,000	60,000
Claims received		—	3,25,000
Claims receivable	1st April, 2022		65,000
	31st March, 2023		1,10,000
Expenses of Management		2,30,000	
Commission			
On Insurance accepted		1,50,000	11,000
On Insurance ceded			14,000

The following additional information is also available :

1. Expenses of management include ₹ 35,000 surveyor's fee and ₹ 45,000 legal expenses for settlement of claims.
2. Reserve for unexpired risk is to be maintained @ 40%. The balance of reserve for unexpired risk as on 1-4-2022 was ₹ 24,50,000.

You are required to prepare the Revenue Account for the year ended 31st March, 2023.

SOLUTION

Form B-RA (Prescribed by IRDA)
Sunlife General Insurance Company
REVENUE ACCOUNT
for the year ended 31st March, 2023

Particulars	*Schedule*	*Amount (₹)*
Premiums Earned (Net)	1	66,80,000
Interest, Dividend and Rent		—
Other Income		—
Total (A)		66,80,000
Claims Incurred (Net)	2	45,26,000
Commission	3	1,47,000
Operating Expenses Related to Insurance Business	4	1,50,000
Bad Debts		—
Total (B)		48,23,000
Operating Profit from Insurance Business (C) = (A – B)		18,57,000

Schedules forming part of Revenue Account

SCHEDULE 1 : PREMIUMS EARNED (NET)

Particulars		₹
Premiums from Direct Business	₹	65,75,000
Add : Premiums on Reinsurance accepted	9,50,000	
Less : Premiums on Reinsurance ceded	4,75,000	4,75,000
Net Premiums		70,50,000
Adjustment for Change in Reserve for Unexpired Risks (2)		3,70,000
Total Premiums Earned (Net)		66,80,000

SCHEDULE 2 : CLAIMS INCURRED (NET)

Particulars	₹	₹
Claims paid on Direct Business (1)		43,30,000
Add : Re-insurance accepted (1)	4,73,000	
Less : Re-insurance ceded (1)	3,70,000	1,03,000
Net Claims paid		44,33,000
Add : Claims Outstanding at the end of the year	7,18,000	
Less : Claims Outstanding at the beginning of the year	6,25,000	93,000
Total Claims Incurred		45,26,000

SCHEDULE 3 : COMMISSION

Particulars	₹	₹
Commission paid on Direct Business		1,50,000
Add : Commission on Reinsurance accepted	11,000	
Less : Commission in Reinsurance ceded	14,000	–3,000
		1,47,000

SCHEDULE 4 : OPERATING EXPENSES RELATED TO INSURANCE BUSINESS

Particulars	₹
Expenses of Management (2,30,000 – 35,000 – 45,000)	1,50,000
	1,50,000

Working Notes :

(1) CLAIMS INCURRED

Particulars	*Direct Business (₹)*	*Re-insurance Accepted (₹)*	*Re-insurance Ceded (₹)*
Paid/Received	42,50,000	5,00,000	3,25,000
Add : Outstanding at the end of the year		60,000	1,10,000

Expenses in connection with Settlement of Claims (35,000 + 45,000)	80,000		
Less : Outstanding at the Beginning of the year		(87,000)	(65,000)
	43,30,000	4,73,000	3,70,000

(2) CHANGE IN RESERVE FOR UNEXPIRED RISKS

Particulars	₹
Opening Reserve as on 31st March, 2022	24,50,000
Less : Closing Reserve as on 31st March, 2023 (₹ 70,50,000 × 40%)	(28,20,000)
	(3,70,000)

ILLUSTRATION 12. **From the following figures taken from the books of New Asia Insurance Co. Ltd. doing fire underwriting business, prepare Revenue Account and Profit and Loss Account for the year 2022-23.**

	₹ '000		₹ '000
Fire Fund (as on 1-4-2022)	9,30,000	Commission on Direct Business	2,99,777
General Reserve	4,50,000	Commission on Reinsurance	
Investments	36,00,000	Accepted	60,038
Premiums	27,01,533	Outstanding Premiums	22,300
Claims Paid	6,02,815	Claims Intimated but not Paid	
Share Capital—Divided into		(1-4-2022)	60,000
Equity Shares of ₹ 100 each	9,00,000	Expenses on Management	4,31,947
Additional Reserve 1-4-2022	3,30,000	Audit Fees (General)	36,000
Profit and Loss A/c (Cr.)	75,000	Rent & Taxes (")	5,804
Reinsurance Premiums	1,12,525	Rents (General)	67,500
Claims Recovered from Reinsurers	21,119	Income from Investments	1,53,000
Commission on Reinsurance Ceded	48,016	Sundry Creditors	22,500
Advance Income-tax Paid	2,50,000	Cash on Hand and Bank	
Agents' Balances (Dr.)	20,000	Balances	1,82,462

Following further information may also be noted :

(*a*) Expenses of management include survey fees and legal expenses of ₹ 36,000 thousands and ₹ 20,000 thousands relating to claims ;

(*b*) Claims intimated but not paid on 31st March, 2023, ₹ 1,04,000 thousands.

(*c*) Income-tax to be provided at 25% ;

(*d*) Transfer to General Reserve, ₹ 2,00,000 thousands.

(*e*) Proposed dividend 8%.

(*f*) Reserve for unexpired risks to be kept at 40% of net premium.

SOLUTION

New Asia Insurance Co.
FIRE REVENUE ACCOUNT
for the year ending 31st March, 2023

Particulars	*Schedule*	*(₹ '000)*
1. Premiums Earned (Net)	1	24,83,405
2. Profit/Loss on Sale /Redemption of Investments		–
3. Other Income		–
4. Interest, Dividend & Rent (Gross)		–
Total (A)		24,83,405
1. Claims Incurred (Net)	2	6,81,696
2. Commission	3	3,11,799
3. Operating Expenses related to Insurance Business	4	3,75,947
Total (B)		13,69,442
Operating Profit from Fire Business (C) = (A) – (B)		11,13,963

New Asia Insurance Co.
PROFIT AND LOSS ACCOUNT
for the year ending 31st March, 2023

Particulars		*(₹ '000)*
1. Operating Profit from Fire Insurance		11,13,963
2. Income from Investments		1,53,000
3. Other Income		–
Total (A)		12,66,963
4. Provisions (other than Taxation)		–
5. Other Expenses	*(₹ '000)*	
Rents	67,500	
Rates & Taxes	5,804	
Audit Fees	36,000	
		1,09,304
Total (B)		1,09,304
Profit before Tax (C) = (A) – (B)		11,57,659
Less : Provision for Taxation @ 25% of ₹ 11,57,659		2,89,415
		8,68,244
Appropriations :		
Proposed Dividend 8% of ₹ 9,00,000 Share Capital		72,000
Transfer to General Reserve		2,00,000
Balance carried forward to Balance Sheet		5,96,244
		8,68,244

Schedules Forming Part of Revenue Account

SCHEDULE 1—PREMIUMS EARNED (NET)

Particulars			(₹ '000)
Premiums from direct business			27,01,533
Less : Reinsurance Premiums			1,12,525
Net Premiums			25,89,008
Less : Adjustment for Increase in Reserve for Unexpired Risks			
Reserve for Unexpired Risks at the end of the year :	(₹ '000)		
40% of ₹ 25,89,008 Net Premiums	10,35,603		
Additional Reserve (opening) to be continued	3,30,000	(₹ '000)	
		13,65,603	
Less : Reserve for Unexpired Risks at the beginning of the year		12,60,000	
			1,05,603
			24,83,405

SCHEDULE 2—CLAIMS INCURRED (NET)

	(₹ '000)
Claims Paid	
Direct	6,02,815
Add : Survey Fees relating to Claims	36,000
Legal Expenses relating to Claims	20,000
	6,58,815
Less : Claims Recovered from Reinsurers	21,119
Net Claims Paid	6,37,696
Add : Claims outstanding at the end of the year	1,04,000
	7,41,696
Less : Claims outstanding at the beginning of the year	60,000
	6,81,696

SCHEDULE 3—COMMISSION

	(₹ '000)
Commission paid on direct business	2,99,777
Add : Commission on Reinsurance Accepted	60,038
	3,59,815
Less : Commission on Reinsurance Ceded	48,016
	3,11,799

SCHEDULE 4—OPERATING EXPENSES RELATED TO INSURANCE BUSINESS

	(₹ '000)
Expenses of Management (excluding survey fees and legal expenses)	3,75,947

ILLUSTRATION **13. Following is the Trial Balance of Everbright Insurance Company Ltd. as on 31st March, 2023. You are required to prepare the Balance Sheet, Revenue Account and Profit and Loss Account :**

		₹ '000
Capital		30,000
Provision for bad debts		2,000
Funds as on 1st April, 2022 :		
Fire insurance account		65,410
Marine insurance account		85,000
Accidents insurance account		6,455
Unclaimed dividends		850
Due to re-insurance companies		3,450
Sundry creditors		7,250
Deposit and suspense account (credit)		2,280
Profit and loss account (credit)		8,040
Agents' balances (debit)		13,500
Interest accrued but not due		2,250
Due from insurance companies		6,450
Cash in hand		350
Cash at bank		7,480
Furniture and fixtures (cost ₹ 8,400)		3,800
Stationery stock		140
Advance payment of tax		3,000
Expenses of management :	₹ '000	
Fire insurance	48,000	
Marine insurance	36,000	
Accidents insurance	8,000	
General	3,000	
		95,000
Foreign taxes (marine)		800
Outstanding premiums		8,200
Claims unpaid on 31st March, 2023 :		
Fire		20,000
Marine		5,000
Accidents		3,250
Transfer fees		100
Tax on profit paid		12,000
Sundry debtors		4,500
Mortgage loans		7,500
Govt. securities deposited with RBI		3,700
Indian government securities		1,02,000
Debentures of public bodies		40,500
Equity shares of joint-stock companies		22,500
Claims less re-insurance :		
Fire insurance		60,000

		₹ '000
Marine insurance		39,390
Accidents insurance		9,300
Premiums less re-insurance :		
Fire		1,76,250
Marine		1,02,250
Accidents		26,225
Land and buildings		50,050
Interest and dividend received (tax deducted at source @ 25%) :	₹ '000	
Fire	2,340	
Marine	750	
Accidents	360	
General	2,400	
		5,850
Commission :		
Fire		30,000
Marine		15,000
Accidents		4,500
Provision for depreciation of furniture for 2022-23		2,000
Outstanding claims on 31st March, 2022 were :		
Fire		15,000
Marine		4,500
Accidents		3,000

Fire insurance premiums ₹ 1,76,250 thousands are after receipt of ₹ 20,000 thousands and payment of ₹ 30,000 thousands as re-insurance premiums. An adjustment in respect of commission @ 15% on such premiums is still to be made.

There is an uncalled liability of ₹ 7,500 thousands in respect of partly paid shares of joint stock companies held by the company.

SOLUTION

Everbright Insurance Company Ltd.
REVENUE ACCOUNT
for the year ending 31st March, 2023

Particulars	Schedule	Fire ₹ '000	Marine ₹ '000	Accident ₹ '000
Premiums Earned (Net)	1	1,53,535	85,000	19,567
Interest and Dividend (Gross)		3,120	1,000	480
		$\left(2,340 \times \frac{100}{75}\right)$	$\left(750 \times \frac{100}{75}\right)$	$\left(360 \times \frac{100}{75}\right)$
Total (A)		1,56,655	86,000	20,047
Claims Incurred (Net)	2	65,000	39,890	9,550
Commission	3	28,500	15,000	4,500
Operating Expenses related to Insurance Business	4	48,000	36,800	8,000
		1,41,500	91,690	22,050
Operating Profit/(Loss) (A) – (B)		15,155	(5,690)	(2,003)

PROFIT AND LOSS ACCOUNT

for the year ending 31st March, 2023

	₹ '000	₹ '000
Operating Profit from Fire Insurance Business		15,155
Less : Operating Loss : Marine Insurance Business	5,690	
Accident Insurance Business	2,003	
		7,693
		7,462
Interest and Dividends (Gross) $\left(2{,}400 \times \frac{100}{75}\right)$		3,200
Other Income : Transfer Fees		100
Total (A)		10,762
Expenses of Management (General)		3,000
Depreciation on Furniture		2,000
Total (B)		5,000
Profit before Tax (A) – (B)		5,762
Less : Tax on Profit		12,000
Net Loss		6,238
Balance of Profit b/d from Last Year		8,040
Balance of Profit carried forward to Balance Sheet		1,802

BALANCE SHEET OF EVERBRIGHT INSURANCE COMPANY LTD.

as at 31st March, 2023

		Schedule	*₹ '000*
Sources of Funds :			
Share Capital		5	30,000
Reserves and Surplus		6	1,802
Total			31,802
Application of Funds			
Investments		8	1,68,700
Loans		9	7,500
Fixed Assets		10	53,850
Current Assets :	₹ '000		
Cash and Bank Balances	7,830	11	
Advances & Others Assets	42,490	12	
Sub-Total (A)	50,320		
Current Liabilities	45,080	13	
Provisions	2,03,488	14	
Sub-Total (B)	2,48,568		
Net Current Assets (C) = (A) – (B)			– 1,98,248
Total			31,802
Contingent Liabilities :			
Uncalled Amount on Partly Paid Shares			7,500

Schedules Forming Part of Financial Statements

SCHEDULE 1—PREMIUMS EARNED (NET)

₹ in thousands

Particulars	*Fire*	*Marine*	*Accident*
Premiums less Reinsurance Premium	1,76,250	1,02,250	26,225
Adjustment for Increase in Reserve for Unexpired Risks :			
Add : Reserve for Unexpired Risks (Beginning)	65,410	85,000	6,455
	2,41,660	1,87,250	32,680
Less : Reserve for Unexpired Risks at the end of the year (50% of Net Premiums in case of Fire and Accident and 100% of Net Premiums in case of Marine)	1,88,125	1,02,250	13,113
	1,53,535	85,000	19,567

SCHEDULE 2—CLAIMS INCURRED (NET)

₹ in thousands

Particulars	*Fire*	*Marine*	*Accident*
Claims less Reinsurance Claims	60,000	39,390	9,300
Add : Outstanding Claims on 31-3-2023	20,000	5,000	3,250
	80,000	44,390	12,550
Less : Claims Outstanding on 1-4-2022	15,000	4,500	3,000
	65,000	39,890	9,550

SCHEDULE 3—COMMISSION

₹ in thousands

Particulars	*Fire*	*Marine*	*Accident*
Commission paid	30,000	15,000	4,500
Add : Commission on Reinsurance Accepted (15% of ₹ 20,000 Reinsurance Premium received)	3,000	—	—
	33,000	15,000	4,500
Less : Commission on Reinsurance Ceded (15% of ₹ 30,000 Reinsurance Premium paid)	4,500	—	—
	28,500	15,000	4,500

SCHEDULE 4— OPERATING EXPENSES RELATED TO INSURANCE BUSINESS

₹ in thousands

Particulars	*Fire*	*Marine*	*Accident*
Expenses of Management	48,000	36,000	8,000
Foreign Taxes		800	
	48,000	36,800	8,000

SCHEDULE 5— SHARE CAPITAL

₹ in thousands

Paid-up Capital	30,000

SCHEDULE 6— RESERVES AND SURPLUS

	₹ '000
Balance of Profit in Profit and Loss Account	1,802

SCHEDULE 8—INVESTMENTS

	₹ '000
Government Securities with RBI	3,700
India Government Securities	1,02,000
Equity Shares of Joint Stock Companies	22,500
Debentures of Public Bodies	40,500
	1,68,700

SCHEDULE 9—LOANS

	₹ '000
Mortgage Loans	7,500

SCHEDULE 10—FIXED ASSETS

₹ *in thousands*

Land and Buildings at Cost			50,050
Furniture & Fixtures at Cost		8,400	
Less : Depreciation upto last year	2,600		
Depreciation for the Current year	2,000		
		4,600	
			3,800
			53,850

SCHEDULE 11—CASH & BANK BALANCES

	₹ '000
Cash in Hand	350
Cash at Bank	7,480
	7,830

SCHEDULE 12—ADVANCES AND OTHER ASSETS

		₹ '000
Advances :		
Advance Payment of Tax		3,000
Tax Deducted at Source from Interest and Dividends Received	₹ '000	
Fire $\left(2,340 \times \frac{25}{75}\right)$	780	
Marine $\left(750 \times \frac{25}{75}\right)$	250	
Accidents $\left(360 \times \frac{25}{75}\right)$	120	
General $\left(2,400 \times \frac{25}{75}\right)$	800	
		1,950
Total (A)		4,950
Other Assets :		
Interest accrued but not due		2,250
Outstanding Premiums		8,200

Agents' Balances		13,500
Amount due from other Insurers		6,450
Commission Receivables		4,500
Sundry Debtors	4,500	
Less : Provision for Bad Debts	2,000	
		2,500
Stock of Stationery		140
Total (B)		37,540
Total (A) + (B)		42,490

SCHEDULE 13—CURRENT LIABILITIES

	₹ '000
Amount due to Other Insurers	3,450
Sundry Creditors	7,250
Claims Outstanding	28,250
Unclaimed Dividends	850
Commission Payable	3,000
Deposit and Suspense A/c	2,280
	45,080

SCHEDULE 14—PROVISIONS

		₹ '000
Reserve for Unexpired Risks :	₹ '000	
Fire (50% of 1,76,250 Net Premiums)	88,125	
Marine (100% of 1,02,250 Net Premiums)	1,02,250	
Accidents (50% of 26,225 Net Premiums)	13,113	
		2,03,488

QUESTIONS

SHORT ANSWER TYPE

1. What is the meaning of surrender value ? Is there a surrender value of general insurance policy also ?
2. What do you understand by Reserve for Unexpired Risks ?
3. What is the basic difference between life insurance and general (or other form of) insurance ?
4. Explain the given terms : (*a*) Additional Reserve for Unexpired Risks. (*b*) Bonus in Reduction of Premium.
5. Draw a proforma of Revenue A/c of a general insurance company.
6. Prepare **Fire Insurance Revenue** A/c for 2022-23 :

	₹		₹
Claims paid	2,40,000	Provision against Unexpired	
Premiums received	6,00,000	Risk on 1-4-2022	2,60,000

Re-insurance Premium	60,000	Unpaid Claims on 1-4-2022	20,000
Commission	1,50,000	Unpaid Claims on 31-3-2023	35,000
Expenses of Management	1,00,000		

Ans. [Operating Profit ₹ 25,000]

7. X Fire Insurance Co. Ltd. commenced its business on 1.4.2022. It submits you the following information for the year ended 31-3-2023.

	₹		₹
Premiums Received	15,00,000	Expenses of Management	3,00,000
Re-insurance Premiums paid	1,00,000	Commission paid	50,000
Claims paid	7,00,000	Claims Outstanding on 31-3-2023	1,00,000

Create Reserve for Unexpired Risk @ 40%

Prepare Revenue Account for the year ended 31-3-2023

Ans. [Operating Loss ₹ 3,10,000]

8. You are required to prepare Revenue Account of the Fire Insurance Company from the following figures for the year ended 31-3-2023 :

	₹		₹
Reserve for unexpired risk (1-4-2022)	1,65,000	Contribution to fire brigades	2,800
Fire insurance premiums	4,00,000	Additional fire insurance reserve	1,55,000
Fire insurance claims paid	2,10,000	Dividend to shareholders	8,000
Fire insurance commission	24,730	Transfer fee (general)	30
Fire insurance expenses	85,000	Interest and Dividend (fire fund)	10,000

Make provision for unexpired risk on the basis of 44% of Fire Insurance Premiums.

Ans. [Revenue Profit ₹ 76,470]

9. Following balances appeared in the books of South Indian General Insurance Company in respect of **fire insurance business** as on 31st Dec., 2023 :

Reinsurance Premiums paid ₹ 50,000 ; Reserve for Unexpired Risks on 1-1-23 ₹ 8,24,800 ; Expenses of Management ₹ 1,25,600 ; Premiums Received ₹ 7,89,000 ; Commission ₹ 1,52,000 ; Claims Paid ₹ 2,21,000 ; Claims Outstanding on 1-1-23 ₹ 2,81,000

Prepare Revenue Account for the year ending 31st Dec., 2023 after considering the following :

(*a*) Provide for Unexpired Risk at 50% of the premiums. (*b*) Create Additional Reserve of ₹ 75,000. (*c*) Premium outstanding at the end of the year ₹ 1,50,000. (*d*) On 31st Dec. 2023, the claims outstanding were ₹ 3,37,000.

Ans. [Operating Profit ₹ 6,39,700]

10. From the following particulars prepare the Fire Revenue Account for 2022-2023.

Claims paid ₹ 325 lakhs ; Legal expenses regarding claims ₹ 8 lakhs ; Premiums Received ₹ 950 lakhs ; Reinsurance Premiums ₹ 70 lakhs ; Commission ₹ 200 lakhs ; Expenses of Management ₹ 125 lakhs ; Provision for Unexpired Risks on April 1, 2022 ₹ 280 lakhs ; Claims unpaid on April 1, 2022 ₹ 30 lakhs ; Claims unpaid on March 31, 2023 ₹ 55 lakhs.

Ans. [Revenue Profit ₹ 37 lakhs]

LONG ANSWER TYPE

1. How is profit or loss determined in Fire Insurance Business ?
2. Prepare (with imaginary figures) Revenue Accounts of Fire and Marine Departments of a General Insurance Company.

3. Prepare (with imaginary figures) the Balance Sheet of an insurance company carrying on fire, marine and miscellaneous insurance business.
4. What important points should be kept in mind in preparing the annual accounts of general Insurance companies?
5. Give treatment of reserve for enexpired risk in case of marine insurance.
6. Point out the main features of Accounts of 'General Insurance Companies'. What statutory books are required to be maintained by a General Insurance Company under the Insurance Act ?
7. What provision should be made by a Fire Insurance Company in regard to Unexpired Risks at the end of each financial period ?

PRACTICAL PROBLEMS

1. Prepare the Fire Insurance **Revenue A/c** of Jasmine Fire Insurance Co. Ltd. as per IRDA regulations for the year ended 31st March, 2023 from the following details :

	(Amount ₹)		*(Amount ₹)*
Claims Paid	5,00,000	Expenses of Management	2,00,000
Legal Expenses regarding Claims	10,000	Provision against Unexpired Risk as on 1st April, 2022	5,75,000
Premiums received	12,50,000		
Re-insurance Premium paid	50,000	Claims unpaid on 1st April, 2022	50,000
Commission	3,00,000	Claims unpaid on 31st March, 2023	80,000

Provide for unexpired risk @ 50% less reinsurance.

Ans. [Operating Profit ₹ 1,35,000]

2. From the following information as on 31st March, 2023 of Bachao Insurance Co. Ltd. engaged in fire insurance business, prepare Revenue Account, reserving 40% of the net premiums for unexpired risks and an additional reserve of ₹ 3,50,000 :

Particulars	*Amount*	*Particulars*	*Amount*
Reserve for Unexpired Risk on 31st March, 2022	7,50,000	Expenses of Management (including ₹ 45,000 in connection with claims)	4,20,000
Additional Reserve on 31st March, 2022	1,50,000	Re-insurance premium paid	1,12,500
Claims paid	9,60,000	Re-insurance Recoveries	30,000
Estimated Liability in respect of Outstanding Claims on 31st March, 2022	97,500	Premiums	16,80,000
		Interest and Dividend (Gross)	75,000
		Profit on Sale of Investments	15,000
Estimated Liability in respect of Outstanding Claim on 31st March, 2023	1,35,000	Commission	1,75,000

Ans. [Operating Profit ₹ 18,000]

3. From the following particulars you are required to prepare Fire Revenue Account for the year ending 31st March, 2023 :

	₹		₹
Claims paid	4,80,000	Commission	2,00,000
Claims Outstanding as on 1-4-2022	40,000	Commission on Re-insurance Ceded	10,000

Claims Intimated but not accepted on 31-3-2023	10,000	Commission on Re-insurance Accepted	5,000
Claims Intimated and accepted but not paid on 31-3-2023	60,000	Expenses of Management	3,05,000
Premiums Received	12,00,000	Provision for Unexpired Risks on 1-4-2022	4,00,000
Re-insurance Premiums	1,20,000	Additional Provision for Unexpired Risks as on 1-4-2022	20,000
		Bonus in Reduction of Premiums	12,000

You are required to provide for additional reserve for unexpired risks @ 1% of net premium in addition to the opening balance.

Ans. [Operating Loss ₹ 78,920]

4. Prepare a **Revenue Account** in respect of Fire Business from the following details for the year 2022-23.

		₹		₹
Reserve for Unexpired Risk on 1-4-2022 @ 50%		1,80,000	Premium recovered	4,86,000
Additional Reserve		36,000	Premium on Re-Insurance Accepted	32,000
Estimated Liability for Claims Intimated on :	1-4-2022	31,000	Premium on Re-Insurance Ceded	43,000
	31-3-2023	42,000	Commission on Direct Business	48,600
Claims paid		3,65,000	Commission on Re-Insurance Accepted	1,600
Legal Expenses		6,000	Commission on Re-Insurance Ceded	2,150
Medical Expenses		4,000	Expenses of Management	90,000
Re-insurance Recoveries		32,000	Interest, Dividend and Rent	24,000
Bad Debts		800	Profit on Sale of Investments	3,000

Create Reserve on 31st March, 2023 to the same extent as on 1st April, 2022.

Ans. **[Loss ₹ 59,850].**

5. Following information are provided by the Rashtriya Beema Company for the year ended 31st March, 2023 :

(*i*) On 1st April, 2022, the unexpired risks reserve was in respect of marine insurance business ₹ 52.50 crores; in respect of fire insurance business ₹ 55 crores and in respect of miscellaneous insurance business ₹ 12.50 crores.

(*ii*) It is the practice of the company to create reserve at 100% of net premium income in respect of marine insurance policies and at 50% of net premium in respect of fire and miscellaneous insurance policies.

(*iii*) During the year 2022-23 the following business was conducted :

(₹ in crores)

Particulars	*Marine*	*Fire*	*Miscellaneous*
Premium collected from :			
1. Insured in respect of policies issued	57	125	30
2. Other insurance companies in respect of risks undertaken	17.5	12.5	10
Premiums paid/payable to other insurance companies on business ceded	21.50	16.50	8.50

You are required :

(i) pass necessary Journal Entries relating to **unexpired risk reserve.**

(i) Show Unexpired Risks Reserve Account (in columnar form) for the year ended 31st March, 2023.

Ans. [Net Premium : Marine ₹ 53 crores; Fire ₹ 121 crores; Misc. ₹ 31.5 crores. Additional Reserve to be made : Marine ₹ 0.50 crore; Fire ₹ 5.50 crores; Misc. ₹ 3.75 crores]

6. Credential General Insurance Co. supplies you the following information. You are asked to show the amount of claim as it would appear in the Revenue Account for the year ended 31-3-2023.

		Direct Business	*Indirect Business*
		₹	₹
Claims Paid during the year		90,10,000	12,40,000
Claims Payable :	1-4-2022	15,08,500	1,55,000
	31-3-2023	17,25,000	65,500
Claims Received			3,60,000
Claims Receivable	1-4-2022	—	95,000
	31-3-2023	—	1,90,500
Expenses of the Management (included ₹ 61,500 as Surveyor's Fees and ₹ 78,300 as legal expenses for settlement of claims)		4,10,000	

Ans. [Amount of Claims ₹ 1,00,55,300]

Hint. Claims paid during the year ₹ 1,00,23,800; Claims outstanding on 31-3-2023 ₹ 16,00,000; Claims outstanding on 1-4-2022 to 15,68,500]

7. From the following information of XYZ Marine Insurance Ltd,. for the year ending 31st March, 2023, find out the

(i) Net Premiums Earned

(ii) Net Claims Incurred

Particulars	*Direct Business (₹)*	*Re-insurance (₹)*
Premiums Received	92,00,000	7,86,000
Premiums Receivable as on 1-4-2022	4,59,000	37,000
Premiums Receivable as on 31-3-2023	3,94,000	33,000
Premiums paid		6,36,000
Premiums Payable as on 1-4-2022		28,000
Premiums Payable as on 31-3-2023		20,000
Claims Paid	73,00,000	5,80,000
Claims Payable as on 1-4-2022	94,000	16,000
Claims Payable as on 31-3-2023	1,01,000	12,000
Claims Received		2,10,000
Claims Receivable as on 1-4-2022		42,000
Claims Receivable as on 31-3-2023		39,000

Ans. [*(i)* ₹ 92,89,000; *(ii)* ₹ 76,76,000]

8. From the following balances as at March 31, 2023 in the books of General Insurance Co. Ltd., prepare a **Revenue Account** in respect of Fire Insurance business carried on by them :

	₹ '000		₹ '000
Claims paid	4,80,000	Commission on reinsurance accepted	4,000
Claims outstanding on 1-4-2022	40,000	Expenses of Management	3,14,000
Claims intimated and accepted but not paid on 31-3-2023	70,000	Reinsurance recoveries of claims	8,000
		Survey expenses regarding claims	5,000
Premium received	12,12,000	Loss on sale of motor car	3,500
Reinsurance Premium paid	1,20,000	Bad Debts	2,500
Commission	2,00,000	Refund of Double Taxation	4,500
Commission on reinsurance ceded	8,000	Interest and Dividends	8,000
Reserve for unexpired risks on 1-4-2022	4,00,000	Income-tax deducted thereon	1,500
		Legal expenses regarding claims	4,000
Additional Reserve for unexpired risks on 1-4-2022	20,000	Profit on sale of investments	3,500
		Rent of staff quarters deducted from salaries	2,400
		Depreciation on Furniture	4,600

You are required to provide for additional reserve for unexpired risk at 1 per cent of the net premium in addition to the opening balance of Additional Reserve.

Ans. [Operating Loss (₹ '000) 78,120].

9. Prepare **Revenue Account** of Sunlight General Insurance Ltd. engaged in Marine Insurance business for the year ended 31st March, 2023 from the following details available :

		Direct Business	*Reinsurance Business*
		₹	₹
I Premium :			
Received		1,44,00,000	21,60,000
Receivable	— 1st April, 2022	7,20,000	1,26,000
	— 31st March, 2023	10,80,000	1,68,000
Premiums Paid		—	14,40,000
Payable	— 1st April, 2022		1,20,000
	— 31st March, 2023		2,56,000
II Claims :			
Paid		99,00,000	7,50,000
Payable :	— 1st April, 2022	5,70,000	75,000
	— 31st March, 2023	10,50,000	1,32,000
Received			6,00,000
Receivable	— 1st April, 2022		54,000
	— 31st March, 2023		72,000
III Commission :			
On Insurance accepted		9,00,000	66,000
On Insurance Ceded			84,000

Other Expenses and Income :

Salaries ₹ 15,60,000 ; Rent, Rates and Taxes ₹ 1,08,000 ; Printing and Stationary ₹ 1,20,000 ; Postage ₹ 18,000 ; Income Tax paid ₹ 14,40,000 ; Interest, Dividend and Rent Receivable (net) ₹ 6,80,000 ; Income Tax Deducted at Source ₹ 1,47,000 ; Legal Expenses (including ₹ 60,000 for settlement of claims) ₹ 2,40,000 ; Bad Debts ₹ 33,000 ; Income Tax Refund ₹ 62,000.

Balance of Fund as on 1st April, 2022 was ₹ 1,59,39,000 including Additional Reserve of ₹ 13,50,000. Additional Reserve is to be maintained at 10% of the net premium of the year.

Ans. [Operating Profit ₹ 1,759 thousands].

10. Following information has been extracted from the books of A.A.K.P. Insurance Co., Ltd. in respect of their marine business for 2023 :

Particulars	*(in lakhs ₹)*		*(in lakhs ₹)*
Direct premium received	100.00	Income tax deducted from dividend	6.00
Reserve for unexpired risk as on 1-1-2023	120.00	Profit and Loss A/c as on 1-1-2023 (Cr.)	20.00
Claim outstanding as on 1-1-2023 (net)	40.00	Other Expenses	2.50
Bad debts	20.00	Re-insurance premium received	10.00
Income from investment and dividend		Direct claims paid (gross)	50.00
(gross)	20.00	Re-insurance claims paid	8.00
Commission paid on direct business	10.00	Rent received	10.00
Expenses of management	10.00		

Prepare a **Revenue Account, Profit & Loss Account and Profit & Loss Appropriation** Account for the year after taking into account the following further information :

(*i*) All direct risks are re-insured for 20% of the risk. (*ii*) Claim a commission of 25% on re-insurance ceded. (*iii*) Provide 25% commission on re-insurance accepted. (*iv*) Provide 65% for income tax. (*v*) Outstanding claim on 31-12-2023 60.00

Ans. [Operating Profits ₹ 42 Lakhs; N.P. ₹ 14.7 Lakhs; Surplus carried to B/S ₹ 34.7 Lakhs]

11. Following balances relate to the S. Insurance :

	Year ending 31st March, 2022	*Year ending 31st March, 2023*
Premiums	5,00,000	6,00,000
Commission on Direct Business	22,500	30,000
Commission on Reinsurance Accepted	17,500	25,000
Commission on Reinsurance Ceded	32,000	24,000
Claims under Policies (paid during the year)	76,250	1,42,250
Depreciation on Furniture, Car etc.	12,750	15,750
Profit on Sale of Motor Car	6,000	Nil
Loss on Sale of Old Furniture		2,000
Double Income Tax Refund	14,000	7,000
Audit Fees	10,000	10,000
Salaries to Staff	1,25,000	1,35,000
Printing, Postage & Stationery	46,500	57,500
Legal Expenses (not relating to claims)	5,000	4,000

Miscellaneous Expenses	15,500	22,500
Bad Debts	750	22,200
Reinsurance Premiums	50,000	1,00,000

Total amounts of estimated liability in respect of outstanding claims as at 31-3-2021, 31-3-2022 and 31-3-2023 were ₹ 34,250, ₹ 44,750 and ₹ 55,550 respectively.

Reserve for unexpired risks as at 31-3-2021 was ₹ 3,20,000 and the Additional Reserve was ₹ 32,000. Reserve for unexpired risks was to be provided for at 100% and Additional Reserve at 10% of the net Premium income for the year ending 31-3-2022 and 31-3-2023.

Prepare **Marine Revenue Accounts** of S. Insurance Co. for the years ending 31-3-2022 and 31-3-2023 in the prescribed form. **All figures given in the problem are in thousands rupees.**

Ans. [2021-22—Profit (₹ '000) 16,750 ; 2022-23—Loss (₹ '000) 1,000].

Skill Development Activities

1. List any six companies which have exercised buyback of shares.

Ans.

	Record Date	Issue Size Amount in crores
(*i*) Jagran Prakashan Ltd.	Jan. 6, 2023	345
(*ii*) Triveni Engineering and Industries Ltd.	Dec. 23, 2022	800
(*iii*) eClerx Services Ltd.	Dec. 30, 2022	300
(*iv*) Technocraft Industries (India) Ltd.	Dec. 30, 2022	150
(*v*) Larsen & Toubro Ltd.	Sept. 12, 2023	10,000
(*vi*) FDC Ltd.	Aug. 25, 2023	155
(*vii*) K.R.B.	Aug. 25, 2023	325
(*viii*) FDC	Aug. 25, 2023	155
Quick-heal Technologies	March 8, 2022	*Price/Share* ₹
Tata Consultancy Services Ltd.		4,150
Sinclairs Hotels Ltd.	Sept. 29, 2023	200
Siyaram Silk Mills Ltd.	Sept. 18, 2023	720
B.S.E. Ltd.	Sept. 14, 2023	1,080

2. Prepare an Investment Account with imaginary figures

Ans. Please see Illustration 10 of Module II (Investment Account)

3. Prepare a table of Rebate on Bills Discounted with imaginary figures.

Ans. Please see Illustration 13 of Module III (Financial Statements of Banking Companies of the text book).

4. Prepare a schedule of premiums with imaginary figures in respect of life insurance companies.

Ans. Please see Illustration 3 of Module IV of the Text Book for Schedule of Premium.

5. Prepare a statement of claims with imaginary of General Insurance Company.

Ans. Please see Schedule 2—Claims Incurred (Net) of Illustration 5 Module V of the Text Book